Women and Animation

a compendium

Edited and designed by Jayne Pilling

BRITISH FILM INSTITUTE

bfi

Exhibition & Distribution Division

First published in Great Britain in 1992 by
the British Film Institute
21 Stephen Street
London W1P 1PL

This publication has been produced by
the Exhibition & Distribution Division of the British Film
Institute to coincide with the three-volume BFI/Connoisseur
Video compilation of animation films made by women,
Wayward Girls and Wicked Women.

ISBN 0 85170 377 1

Cover design: Leonard Chinnery & Jayne Pilling.
Back cover still: adapted from Vera Neubauer's *Animation for Live Action*.

Printed by St Edmundsbury Press Ltd, Bury St Edmunds, Suffolk.

Table of Contents

All uncredited articles by the editor.

Introduction

by Jayne Pilling

Animation is area in which women as artists and filmmakers have made a real impact over the last two decades, far greater, proportionately, than in live-action feature films.

I have no intention of running through the old arguments about whether animation is for art or for laughs, for adults or for children, whether it is to be considered a deviant branch of 'real' cinema or an extension of the artist's palette. It can be and has been all those things, and more: a reflection of animation's unlimited potential as a medium for communication.

It is the exciting achievements of a large number of women, or rather, the films they have made in the medium which prompted this publication.

Women have always comprised a large part of the animation industry's workforce - as paint'n'tracers, or ink'n'painters, in-betweeners, colourists or designers. In the field of animation films for children they have had a more creative and authoritative role. Women have also often been in demand for voicing cartoon characters - particularly if the characters are children, as adult women are seen to be more experienced, and reliable, than child actors. And of course there is June Foray, who voiced and gave indelible personality to many of America's most cherished wacky cartoon characters.

What has changed over the last twenty years for women in animation has been the developing opportunities to make their own films. The number of films made as well as the range of subjects and diversity of styles has increased dramatically. The variety, vitality and interest of so many of these films deserves some celebration and documentation.

If you go through any standard history book on animation - or in fact through most of what has been published on the subject - women are, to coin a cliché, notable largely by their absence. Of course, there are exceptions. Amongst these, the best known would include Germany's Lotte Reiniger, who in the 20s pioneered an exquisitely delicate form of silhouette animation drama; Mary Ellen Bute, an American artist who made several experimental abstract films in the 30s; through the 40s and 50s and 60s women working in partnership with their husbands such as Claire Parker (with Alexander Alexieff), and Faith Hubley (with John Hubley) and Britain's Joy Batchelor (with John Halas), though it is still common to see films made through the creative partnership of Evelyn Lambart and Norman McLaren credited to the latter alone. Caroline Leaf in Canada and Alison de Vere in Britain were names to emerge in the early 70s.

The late 70s and the 80s have been interesting not only for the emergence of a far greater number of women animators, particularly in the UK and the North American continent, but also for the development of a range of work that specifically addresses women's issues. Some of this work has been quite explicitly feminist in intent, from the agit-prop impulse of Leeds Animation Workshop to films concerned with redressing cartoons' tradition of sexist imagery. Vera Neubauer's more experimental work has moved away from 70s feminism to explore, most productively, some of its contradictions and problematics. A younger generation has felt free to explore a range of subjective experiences, in a sense taking feminism for granted. Some reject an explicitly feminist stance, preferring to address women's experiences through humour and aim for the widest possible audience.

Clearly, the development of women in animation has a lot to do with the impact of feminism on funding policies in arts institutions and television, i.e. there's been a concern to redress the 'traditonal gender imbalance', to increase both women's access to the media and the range of representations of women within it. In the US, the rise of independent and alternative filmmaking was a contributory factor. In the UK women in animation have benefitted from Channel Four's remit to innovate, though developments in art education have also played a significant role. Since the mid-70s the growth in the number of courses offering animation in art colleges and polytechnics, and the diversity of approach across these institutions, have fostered a richly creative environment of emerging talent. This has been particularly useful to women, since before the development of more inter-disciplinary approaches to teaching, animation was usually seen as an adjunct to the larely male-dominated areas of graphic and commercial design.

The most interesting aspect of all this is that animation as a form offers such potential to explore women's issues in a way that simply isn't possible in live-action filmmaking. At the most basic level is the production process itself. Although traditional cel-animation tends to be expensive because it is labour-intensive, it doesn't necessarily have to be, simply because it's possible to make an animation film by oneself, even at home, and with virtually any material as well s the traditional tools of drawing and painting. The technical skills required are far more varied and less specific than in live-action, therefore less crucial in the sense that a good animation film doesn't necessarily demand expert drawing skills - for example, using collage, cutouts, object animation. Because the choice of form in animation is so wide, it can be less inhibiting i.e. there's no set standard to adhere to, no set length or conventional structures. And perhaps most important of all, it isn't bound to conventions of photographic or dramatic realism that dominate most live-action filmmaking. (Of course, all these elements still impose a degree of discipline in order to realise a film successfully.)

As novelist Jeannette Winterson has commented, 'For women with a talent for art and an interest in film, animation offers both a challenge and a safe place.' A challenge because of the unlimited potential for expression (and self-expression), and a safe place because it can offer a private space in which to experiment. The filmmakers featured in this book have a range of very different concerns and approaches to their work, and a comparable diversity in their attitudes to what being a woman has to do with animation, (in some cases, nothing at all) a recurrent theme is the issue of control. Whether its informed by a distaste for the hierarchical nature of male dominated live-action films or commercial animation studios, by personal or socially inculcated lack of confidence, for many the attraction of animation has been, initially at least, that it can be done by oneself. And yet the result can be shared by many.

Lesley Keen's *Taking a Line for a Walk*, one of the earliest films C4 commissioned from a woman animator, explored artist Paul Klee's famous dictum on the potential of art. To paraphase, in this instance, animation is uniquely capable of taking an idea, an emotion, a set of observations - anything at all, for a walk to see what emerges - and take the audience along with it.

Ideas, feelings, issues can be presented not as linear arguments - to be accepted or rejected by the viewer - but imaginatively embodied, enacted, literally played around with for the viewer to experience and interpret for themselves. Serious issues such as incestuous sexual abuse or women and the law can be explored in ways unthinkable in feature or documentary film, and often far more imaginatively and accessibly. It is noticeable that women have been making some of the most innovative films in animation in recent years.

Animation can also give voice to the intensely personal - in content as well as in terms of production: unhampered by the constraints of naturalism or the organisational complexities of live action feature filmmaking. The animated short film can provide, quite literally, a blank page on which to draw forth an imaginative vision which can communicate, and can do so also without words. Transcending the boundaries of language can also give voice to that which is hard to articulate, because so bound up with unconscious feelings, e.g. to desire and fantasy. Sex - as in sexuality as well as stereotyping is also approached with an audacity, and authenticity, rarely found in animation made by men.

About this book.

The aim is primarily to document women in animation whose work tends to the use of the medium as an art-form and/or personal expresssion. The subtitle, 'a compendium' is intended quite literally. A range of different voices, experiences, approaches.

Perhaps it is worth mentioning what isn't covered here. There is no attempt to provide a comprehensive history of women in animation. This would have to include their role in the entertainment industry, both in Hollywood and elsewhere. Research is only just beginning in this area, and it is for others to follow up. Bruno Edera, in his important article *L'Animation au Féminin*[1] mentions several women working in Holywood studios from the the 20s to the 50s, to whom could be added others.[2]

In the same article, he gives a roll call of women from the 20s onwards who were directing films rather than simply animating them.[3] Many, if not most of these were making films for children. Again, an important area crying out for research, but outside the scope of this publication, although animation filmmakers whose work is primarily independent but who have worked on children's films are included. Representation of women in animation or cartoon films is a field which has already generated some critical and analytical work.[4] However, I have preferred to concentrate on the women making films, and the films they have made. Where animators whose work has been extensively and well discussed elsewhere, in publications that are easily obtainable (e.g. Lotte Reiniger, or Mary Ellen Bute in Cecile Starr and Robert Russett's ground-breaking *Experimental Animation*),[5] it has seemed more useful to include material not so easily available, that might stimulate interest.

There is no overriding thesis about the specificity of women's animation, although there are some persuasive arguments to this effect. Men and women are socialised as children in different ways, with the result that women tend to be more able to explore and share personal experience (cf Deborah Tannen's work in psycholinguistics exploring the differences in the way men and women 'hear' one another, in her book *That's Not What I Meant*). Animator Susan Young has commented interestingly in relation to this that the socialisation of boys encourages hierarchical play and a tendency to act out as a possible explanation why men tend to dominate character animation. She feels this is also a reason women have been more active in developing new styles and forms of animation.

There is very little critical or analytical writing about animation generally, in contrast to live-action or even experimental filmmaking. In addition to material written specially for this book, it seemed useful to reprint a number of articles which are not easily accessible, or known, to the general reader (unlikely as that person might seem in the area of animation) or to many students, either because of limited library holdings or simply because bibliographies for animation are thin on the ground. These include a variety of approaches: feminist theoretical, how-it-was-made, straighforward interview and comment, more or less detailed analyses of individual films, general surveys of production in particular countries, personal statements by filmmakers. Above all, I have wished to suggest the enormous range of different voices, styles and concerns of women working in animation.

The emphasis tends towards American and British films, simply because there are a lot more of them, they are more widely distributed, and they are likely to be more familiar. However, I have attempted to cover as many women whose work is known to me, as possible. It is clear that opportunities vary enormously between countries. Canada's National Film Board of Canada has done perhaps more, historically, than any other institution to support the development of animation as an art form, and have provided opportunities for many women filmmakers. There is a need for a detailed study of its role - and the results- in this area. Latin America is a big gap. Although the odd film has emerged, there is little tradition of art animation that is known about. In Scandinavia nearly all animation production is for children or educational/public service films. In Eastern Europe and what was the Soviet Union women have been largely confined to making films for children, and it is only in the 80s that some interesting adult animation films have started to be made. I have worked with a fairly wide definition of animation, to include experimental filmmakers who have used animation techniques, as the cross-over can often be very interesting.

There is also, inevitably, an element of personal preference in the choice of filmmakers covered.

The contents and structure of this publication are fairly straightforward. Many filmmakers who are mentioned briefly in, for example, survey introductions to individual countries, are discussed in more detail in the A - Z section. Whilst this is an attempt at an international biographical filmography, it follows the same 'compendium' principle, explained in the introduction to that section.

Women animators are not a race apart, confining themselves to women's issues or subjective points of view. I hope the diversity of work covered makes this quite obvious. Several filmmakers I spoke to resent being categorised or 'ghettoised' as women rather than simply as animation filmmakers. Ultimately, what matters most is that the quality of the work is recognised, and hopefully more widely seen.

A final anecdote. Some years ago I had a Polish visitor who was keen to check out what was of interest in current British films. I mentioned a couple of films, including Karen Watson's *Daddy's Little Bit of Dresden China*, which deals with the experience of child sexual abuse. 'No, no,' he said, apologising for his poor English, since I had not understood him, 'it's animation I'm interested in, not documentary.' 'It is animation', I replied, and tried to describe the film. He gave up. It was clear he simply couldn't see how animation could deal with such a subject. Which perhaps says something about women's contribution to animation.

As time and resources were extremely limited, this compendium can only hope to be an introduction, and a stimulus for further work. To keep costs down, it has been produced by myself, a relative novice in desktop publishing. As a result, there are some inconsistencies, and probably errors. I would be grateful for any additional information, corrections or views, in the hope that a revised and expanded edition might be possible in the future. - Jayne Pilling

References
1. Bruno Edera, *L'Animation au Féminin*, La Revue du Cinéma, December 1983. Women such as Nadine Simpson, Carmen Maxwell, Ethel Kulsar at Disneys in the late 20s, and in the late 30s Phyllis Bonds, Retta Scott; Edith Vernick, Lillian Friedman at the Fleischer Brothers studio; La Verne Harding at Walter Lantz, then at Hanna Barbera, Filmation, and De Patie Freleng.
2. Tissa David, or Mary Blair, for example, have worked in classic cartoon studio system.
3. See Introduction to A -Z.
4. Sybil Delgaudio, *Seduced and Reduced: Female Animal Characters in Some Warners' Cartoons*, in The American Animated Cartoon: a critical anthology, ed. Gerald and Danny Peary, E.P. Dutton, New York, 1980.
5. Robert Rusell and Cecile Starr, Experimental Animation, (New York: Da Capo, 1988).

Acknowledgements

I would like to thank all the contributors and filmmakers for their part in this publication. Thanks are also due to the Australian Film Commission: Shane McConnochie in Sydney; Conchita Pina and her colleagues AFC in London (for sterling efforts at very short notice); also in Australia, Roger Palmer at Latrobe University, Victoria; John Eyley and Keith Bradbury at Queensland College of Art; Jane Taylor at the National Film Board of Canada's London office; Hélène Tanguey, National Film Board of Canada in Quebec; Hubert Sielecki of Asifa Austria; Pat Webb of ASIFA UK; William Sloan at MOMA, New York; Matthew Yokobosky at the Whitney Museum, New York; Gunnar Strom, ASIFA Norway; Maureen Furniss at the University of Southern California; Anatoly Prochorov and colleagues at Pilot Studio, Moscow; Margaret Deriaz, Goethe-Institut, London.

I am grateful to Sally Dowden and John Smoker in BFI Publishing; my colleagues in Exhibition & Distribution Division for their help and moral support: Barry Edson, Paul Taylor, Alan Gregory; along with Heather Stewart and Karen Alexander, especially for their editorial comments and getting me through the final stages; my assistant, Linda Carruthers-Watt, for her ever-cheerful patience, eye for detail, and, in the rush to meet deadlines, performance above and beyond...; Elaine Burrows (National Film Archive) has given much appreciated advice and support.

Marjorie Brown of Evergreen State College, Washington, provided early encouragement and information; Cecile Starr kindly shared her knowledge in the area of experimental film. Bruno Edera's extraordinary generosity in sharing his data mountain must also be recorded.

Others to whom I am indebted for donating their time include Ruth Lingford, Lesley Sharman, Jill McGreal. Roger Noake has been especially generous.

On the production side, I would like to thank Ron Inglis for his advice, input and tolerance (frantic phone calls out of hours); Jim Hickey at Edinburgh Filmhouse. Special thanks are due to Matthew Hoffman and Steve Conaway at the *Independent* and all in the *Independent*'s Computer Room, without whom this publication would not have been possible: Barry Allen, Matt-with-no-name; Anthony Phasouliotis, and Leonard Chinnery, who deserves special mention for his invaluable skill and knowledge, patience and generosity.

And finally, thank you Peter Ridley.

Stills: Courtesy of the filmmakers, BFI E&D, National Film Archive, and for the following titles, Channel Four Television: *Black Dog; Blind Justice: Some Protection;: Feet of Song; First Night; Girls' Night Out; The Mill, The Stain.*

This book is dedicated to the memory of Andrijana Hewitt

Lotte Reiniger

an interview with Alfio Bastiancich

Charlotte Reiniger was born in Berlin 1899. As an only child, she was indulged in her artistic leanings, although her parents would have preferred her to have had a safe office job. Although she moved in avant-garde circles in the heady period of the 20s her work has, fundamentally, little in common with that of experimental filmmakers like Walter Ruttman, Eggeling, Hans Richter or German Expressionism, although stylistically there are some influences. Most of her films were inspired by fables or music, and are notable for their extreme delicacy, ironic humour and fantasy. She also achieved a degree of expressivity in her characters remarkable given the limitations of silhouettes in this respect. At the age of 23, she began work on one of the first feature length animation films, The Adventures of Prince Achmed, *more than a decade before Disney's* Snow White and the Seven Dwarves. *Although* Prince Achmed *is a narrative film, there are semi-abstract sequences in which she experimented with wax and sand on backlit glass. Her technical invention also extended to the design of an early form of the multiplane camera (which separates foregrounds and backgrounds into layers to give a three dimensional effect), again, several years before Disney had built his admittedly more complex camera.*

The following is edited from a long interview with her by Italian animation critic Alfio Bastiancich, a year before her death in 1981 - Ed.

When I was at school, all the children used to do paper cut outs, silhouettes, and I loved it. Later, I got the theatre bug and used to put on shows. When other children were out playing, I was 'animating' my silhouettes. I'd make them perform 'Snow White', for example. When I was older, my parents were so pleased to see me sitting at home cutting out silhouettes as it was a peaceful hobby, and it didn't take up much room. I built my own shadow puppet theatre.

Were there any Chinese shadow theatres in Berlin?
No. There were puppets in the museums, which I didn't actually see until much later. It's not really true that I was influenced by Chinese shadow theatre. There's a lot of difference between my way of animating characters and that of Chinese shadows: they move the characters in a kind of wavey ripple whilst I used a flat background and moved the characters through articulated joints. I also varied the lighting: theirs is frontal, mine was lit from above.
When cinema appeared, I was bowled over. What I remember being most excited by were the fantasy films of Georges Méliès.

How did you move from the miniature theatre and your dolls and puppets to work for the cinema?
I was lucky. In 1915 I went to a lecture given by Paul Wegener, who'd made *The Golem*. He was talking about the technical side, and special effects, which I found fascinating. I was fifteen. I said to myself: this is a man I must meet. I enrolled at the Reinhardt Theatre School but it was simply a ruse to get to meet Wegener. My parents were desperate. As I was an only child, they pretty much indulged me. So I went, and to attract the actors' attention, I made silhouettes of them in character: they must have been good because a book was made out of them. I was 17 by then. Most of the silhouettes were of Wegener...he was interested in the visual arts, and was very kind to me, he invited me to his house, which was a meeting place at the time for many people in theatre and cinema. I pestered him so much that he ended up giving me small parts in his films. He also had me working on decorative intertitles.
In 1918 Wegener introduced me to a group of young people who had just started a studio for scientific and experimental films, and he suggested they take me on. The people involved were Professor Hanslik, Hans Curlis, Karl Witte and Carl Koch.

The studio was the Institut für Kulturforschung. The first film you made there was Das Ornament des verliebten Herzens (The Ornament with a Love-sick Heart). *What kind of film was it?*
It was a balletic duet: a man and a woman moved around a wreath, which was made up of figures expressing their feelings. At first the man and the woman are very sweet and gentle, then they quarrel, and the wreath quivers. The woman leaves and the man is very sad, and weeps, but she returns and the ornament is reconstituted in the shape of a heart.

Was it a film made with silhouettes?
Yes, and it went down very well. It was only five minutes long, and was shown in cinemas. It was sold almost immediately, in the US, for quite a high price, but I believe it is now lost.

What kind of work was done by the Institut?
They made geographical, anthropological, and often political films. Bartosch and Hanslik, for example, made *Hände weg von Obershlesin (Hands off Upper Silesia)*. Carl Koch made films on the museums' artistic heritage. In one, on Meissen porcelain, the objects rotated slowly in the light. This was quite new at the time even though it's now common to see sculpture presented that way.

Between 1920 - 1925 did you make any commercials?
I made some short publicity films during the making of *Der Fliegende Koffer* (one for a brand of ink, another for Hattman's chocolate company, another for talcumn powder). They were for Julius Pinschewer who invented the publicity film: he contracted with cinemas and his initiatives were very interesting. Walter Ruttman was also making films for him; everyone loved working for Pinschewer because it paid so well.

Did Pinschewer have a studio or did you work somewhere else?
He had a cinema studio with two or three animation tables.

Were they all made with silhouettes?
Yes. The one for talc was done with white silhouettes. We illuminated the characters from above, against a black background.

Was Berthold Bartosch also part of the Institut?
Yes. We became very very good friends. He lived with us for about fifteen years. Carl was interested in geographical films and together they did all the ethnographic work.

Berlin was a very lively cultural centre at that time: did you go to the cinema, theatre, exhibitions?
Oh yes, there was everything. It was a wonderful time, we loved going to all the exhibitions. Once Chagall came to see our films, I was very proud that he liked *Cinderella (Aschenputtel, 1922)* a lot .

In 1921 you also made The Star of Bethlehem?
Yes, it was a film I made in the modern style, very Expressionist.

No relation to the Star of Bethlehem *film you made for Primrose in 1956?*
No, that was something else entirely.

How did you come to meet Fritz Lang?
Lang wanted to meet me to discuss my making Kriemhild's dream sequence for *Die Nibelungen*. I went to the great UFA studios, where they showed me an animation stand. They were all quite crazy there. Lang wanted all the actors to stay in costume and make-up in case he suddenly wanted to shoot a scene that hadn't been planned for. His wife wrote the scripts and would sit next to him at work, doing her knitting, and at the same time working out a populist version of the Nibelungen.

Lang asked you to make the Dream Falcon for the film?
Yes. Lang wanted the falcon to be white, I wanted it to be transparent, but he wasn't keen. I started to get fed up and tired, I just couldn't get it white. I thought that Ruttman would be really happy doing it, so I said to Lang that Ruttman would be good. So I managed to get out of it, and in any case I was due to start *Achmed*.

Did Ruttman work at the Institut?
No, he was never part of the Institut. He worked with us later on, for *Achmed*. He showed his films in Berlin in 1921, and we were all very enthusiastic about them. We became friends. We admired him enormously and he was so pleased to have people who appreciated his work.

Let's talk about Prince Achmed. *How did you meet the producer Hagen?*
Hagen came to the Institut one day with some other people. He was a banker, but was also very interested in educational films. My husband was making a film for him, about Egypt. So he then saw my films and the way I worked and suggested I make a feature film, something that had never been done before. It was an offer I couldn't turn down. That was in 1925. We rigged out a studio in his country house, in Potsdam, above the garage, but then we left as it was too difficult to work so far from Berlin. It took three years' work.
The story was inspired by *A Thousand and One Nights*. I read the whole book until I found a story that would lend itself to animation…everything I liked about Prince Achmed went into the film: the horse, the magician…I started drawing, did sketches. The film was done scene by scene. Ruttman built the background sets. It was quite rare to see such entirely different temperaments working together, since Ruttman was a lot older than I and was considered a great artist whereas I was only a novice. I

was very scared of him but he seemed quite at ease doing the movements for the backgrounds whilst I worked on the characters' movements in the foreground. The result was two negatives which we then put together.

Your husband worked as cameraman on the film?
He wasn't simply a cameraman: he had a great understanding of cinematic language, truly extraordinary. He was the brains, I was the crazy one.

Bartosch made the Aladdin's voyage sequence: what was Ruttman's contribution?
He did the sequence in which the Magician makes the flying horse appear. It was very complicated thing to do, using thin sheets of wax underneath a machine he invented. Then he did the lamps and all the effects in the final battle between the Magician and the Witch. Whereas for the sequence in which Waq Waq's devil fights the white spirits we all worked on it together.

The film was finished in May 1926. How was the preview at the Volksbühne on Bülowplatz?
Hagen was exhausted and having problems with the film, as no cinema would take it, they didn't dare. He was furious. Since we only had the cinema for a Sunday morning, we wrote postcards to everyone we knew, and all our friends, inviting them to come.

So it wasn't a screening for the press?
No. There were press there, for which we had to thank Bert [Brecht] who knew who to invite…he was very astute.

And how was the film received?
We were all very anxious since it was a Sunday morning in May and nobody went to the cinema in Spring, and it wasn't easy to get to, you had to take the underground. But in fact there were a lot of people, the cinema was bursting at the seams. I was in the lighting box and saw all these people waiting for my film, Fritz Lang among them. A professor from the Institut was there to say a few words beforehand, he was very famous in the field of Asian studies. He was simply supposed to present the film, we didn't want him to talk for long, but there he was, talking and talking, mon Dieu!… I was so nervous and people were getting restless. Then he suddenly stopped in mid speech and disappeared. What had happened was that the projector had broken down, and my husband had gone to try and find a spare part, but it being a Sunday..well, he broke into a shop to get it. Then he came back and told the professor he could stop

The Adventures of Prince Achmed

talking, which was a great relief. What a story!

And did the audience like the film?
I've never seen anything like it. They clapped at every effect, after every scene.

Was the orchestra conducted by Wolfgang Zeller?
He composed the music and that morning had brought his orchestra, for no payment at all. He became famous because of the film, one of the most famous cinema composers. He was also invited to the Paris and London screenings .

Is it true you stuck photogrammes on the score so the musicians could follow?
Yes: that way they could follow the tempo and knew where they were in the story.

The music for the current version isn't the same?
No. It's a shame because the music was wonderful, always in synchrony and there were some very interesting effects.

But since Zeller's score still exists…why wasn't it used for the reissue by Primrose Films?
Because it was scored for a large orchestra and they didn't have that kind of money: the new music needs only a few musicians.

Was the first version of the film in colour?
Yes, all of it. We shot it in black and white and on the negative indicated the colours we wanted for each scene: it was very time consuming. We tried with Technicolor but the colours were too dense and corroded the silhouettes. At Filmagie on the other hand they did the backgrounds in colour and projected the silhouettes in

Cinderella

black. We were very pleased with it. That way, I found, the colours didn't over impose, indeed, shooting the film in black and white with a range of greys, the colours lose a lot of their liveliness and that gives the film a greater sense of movement.

The original negative was destroyed in the war. But the British Film Institute had had a negative made. When I went to London for the first time I met the person who'd been working on the film. It was the son of that banker from Potsdam who'd financed the film. As a child he used to sit and watch us working in the make-shift studio above the garage. He saw it as a kind of family affair, and had worked like mad to reconstitute the colours and tinting in the film.

In July of that same year the film was shown in Paris at the Comédie theatre on the Champs Elysées.
Yes, the Comédie theatre was adapted for the occasion. At first they didn't want to say it was a German film, since although the war had been over for quite a while there was still anti-German sentiment. There was a ballet before the screening.

Was it on that occasion that you met Jean Renoir?
Yes, my husband got talking to him, he invited us to his home and we became friends.

Then, for the company Comenius, you made the Doctor Doolittle *series (1928). For* Ten Minutes of Mozart, *you changed production companies?*
We had let the relationship with Hagen lapse because of disagreements over synchronisation methods on the film *Die Jagd nach dem Glück (The Pursuit of Happiness)*. It was a total failure from every point of view. We shot it in France, in Antibes, and Renoir worked on it too, which created a lot of problems since he was too much the 'director'.

Up until 1933 you made films for various production companies, then Lotte Reiniger Film was created.
Yes, by myself and my husband, and the first film we made was *Carmen*.

Music is a recurrent motif in your films.
Yes, but I always gave my own interpretation to the music. In *Carmen*, for example, I felt the bull was the real protagonist, so I made him the film's central character. I also wanted to do 'Lohengrin' but it wasn't possible as it was on the Führer's proscribed list.

You made a lot of films during this period. Did you always start from scratch with the characters, for each film?
The main characters would be cut out afresh every time, whilst secondary characters would get a change of costume. Then for the main characters I'd have to do new cut outs for the close-ups; these had to be quite large since otherwise you don't get any expressivity. Animals were so difficult to do that once I'd found a way to do one I'd use it over and over.

You relied on hand movements for expressivity...they're always quite important in your films?
With silhouettes the hands are one of the few ways which can convey the characters' feelings.

For the backgrounds you used tissue paper?
Yes, I use multi-layered tissue paper, but I've also worked with glass and sand.

In those first films I've been struck by the modern interpretation of the stories, the freshness of the characters, their impetuosity, their sensuality. In your films, Achmed, Harlequin, Carmen, *for example, there's an element of sensuality that's quite marked...*
That's the way I am.

Between 1934 and 1935 you produced six films altogether: that must have been an enormous amount of work!
Yes, Carl went to Paris to work with Renoir and I joined him there, but the situation was too difficult to stay, so we went back to Berlin and started to work like crazy to demonstrate what we could do. So I made *Papageno* and the other films.

Were you happy with your version of Papageno?
I like it a lot because the music is so good.

Galathea *is a case apart: how did you come to make it?*
Ah, at that time I was going to England a lot, I had a friend there who made me listen to him play on the piano, a composition he'd done as a boy. It amused me a lot and I decided to make a film inspired by this piece of music.

The story was your own?
Yes, I made it up, it's the story of a Pygmalion who falls in love with the statue of Venus and prays to make her alive. The Gods bring her to life but on condition she's sterile.

Then you went to England for an exhibition of your work.
The exhibition was very successful. It was in 1935, my husband was in France with Renoir, and I stayed in London to work with John Grierson at the GPO film unit.

How did you meet Grierson?
Through the Film Society, which had screened several of my films. Fortunately, since if they hadn't made negatives of many of my films they wouldn't exist today.

What did Grierson ask you to do for the GPO?
They asked me to do a *Post Early for Christmas* ad with silhouettes, which I could do since I had all the material I'd brought for the exhibition and so I could set up an animation stand. As well as that film I made some other little films which I don't recall.

HPO

The GPO Film Unit was at its most creative at that time, a real hotbed of documentary filmmakers. Who did you know there?
Cavalcanti, I worked mainly for him.

And the young Norman McLaren?
No, I only met him many years later, in Canada.

During this period until the outbreak of war you were going to and fro between Paris and London, where you made The King's Breakfast *and* The Tocher.
Yes, *The Tocher* was a film which was based on a Scottish custom: parents gave a dowry to their newly wed children. In my film it doesn't work that way: it's a romantic ballet in which a young man is chased away by

The Tocher

the fiancée's father, becomes desperate, but then goblins appear to him and give him a casket, telling him to go and interrupt the marriage of his beloved with another. The young man jumps on a horse, and after a long journey finally arrives as everyone is going into the church, gives the casket to the bride's father who is delighted when he opens it to discover a Post Office Savings Book.

Was Benjamin Britten's music taken from a pre-existing recording?
Yes, they had various pieces of music and told me to choose amongst them. I chose that one because it was based upon a piece by Donizetti which Britten had reworked in the modern manner, and I liked it a lot.

During your trips to Paris, you made a little shadow theatre for Renoir's La Marseillaise?
Yes, but it was only a little thing. I went to Paris because I liked to be there when they were making films.

You also designed costumes for the London theatre?
Yes, but I'd also been doing costume design in Berlin, before I made *Achmed*.

When war broke out, you joined your husband who was working on Tosca *with Renoir in Rome..*
Yes, although joining him was very difficult. The people at La Scalera were very nice; the director was an opera fan and he suggested I did a version of Donizetti's opera *L'Elisir d'amore*. So whilst they worked on the *Tosca* script I worked on my film. Then Renoir left, having only filmed a couple of scenes, so they asked my husband to finish the film. From then on I worked as his assistant.

So you had to stop work on L'Elisir?

Yes, we had even synchronised the soundtrack, but the editing was never finished.

It was fascist Italy then: what kind of people did you socialise with?
Mainly Visconti. Then de Sanctis, and that whole group. They used to come round in the evening, listen to Carl.

Since Carl was a Socialist and Rome was the anti-fascist movement's base, your house was an outpost of socialism?
Yes. We were also visited by the Nazis, but they thought we were French because of the association with Renoir.

When did you leave Italy?
Christmas, the last year of the war.

And you went back to Berlin? [They returned despite the situation there, as her mother was still in Berlin.]
Yes, in Berlin I started working on *L'Oca d'ora* (*The Golden Goose*) for the Reichsanstalt für Film und Bild. It was a big organisation with magnificent studios, so I could get on with my work, and they gave us food vouchers. My husband worked on script development from literary subjects.

But she was not able to finish the film…
We worked in hiding for a whole year. We wanted to be there for the end of the war. For we knew Germany was going to be defeated. We had no way of communicating with the outside. I'd leave some of my silhouettes in bookshop windows, and the odd poster, so that anyone who knew me could get in touch. There were rumours that Carl and I had committed suicide.

In 1949 you moved to London for good?
Yes, my husband was very ill, and needed an operation. In Berlin we had nothing to eat, the doctor said I should take him to England, where we could at least get milk and vegetables. So I wrote to my friends in England, who put us up and Carl was soon much better.

When and how did you meet Luis Hagen, the founder of Primrose Films?
Back in 1935; he was the son of the man who had produced *Achmed*. The one who used to play near me as a child in the studio at Potsdam. He had a small production company in London and we signed a contract with him. That's how we were able to stay in London and continue working.

With Primrose Achmed *was reissued and you started*

making films for television: the BBC, and American TV.
Yes, I made a whole series of shadow games for the BBC, then a film like *Achmed, The Magic Horse*.

The number of films you made in 1954 alone is awesome…
Yes, we were working like madmen. Just me and my husband.

You give the impression it's not a period you like to recall.
To be honest, no. We were under too much pressure, it's not possible to make films at such a rapid rate.

So, from 1953 to 1963 you never left London?
No, we were always working.

You didn't make any films for a long time after the death of your husband?
I made some puppets for the theatre, things like that. Carl's death was a terrible thing: there was no other collaborator like him the world. He was a great technician, and a real expert in cinema.

Reiniger demonstrating her technique.

A few years later you started travelling, giving workshops, lectures. Did this help you get over the crisis?
Yes. I met the Canadians, McLaren, Co Hoedeman, Jacques Drouin; they gave me a lot of encouragement. I also made another film *Aucassin and Nicolette*.

What do you think of Disney?
His films are technically perfect: too perfect.

Torino, 24 April 1980.

Reprinted by kind permission of the author, see ß. Translation by Ed.

The Education of Mary Ellen Bute

by Lillian Schiff

During a conversation in July 1983, Mary Ellen Bute, painter, animator, feature film director in a career of more than fifty years, spoke appreciatively of influential people and events in her life, adding a great deal about her experiences and work. She also spoke of hopes and plans for the future, especially those concerned with funding for post-production needs of her current film on Walt Whitman.

It was immediately apparent that the body of work couldn't be separated from the comfortable upbringing, the endless seeking for knowledge, and sharp perception and intelligence, the humour and tenacity. This very small, thin youthful person with honey-coloured hair and a Houston accent, this lady with most considerate manners, was one of the first Americans and probably the first woman to make abstract animated films, the first in the world to use electronically generated images in film, and the first to make a film based on a James Joyce novel...

She seriously observed, she'd always been a joyous person. It's credible. Anyone in this generation who is lucky enough to see the lively, happiness-making first film, *Rhythm in Light*, and others that followed in the 30s, 40s and 50s, will understand that an upbeat person had transferred her feelings to the dancing ping pong balls, crumpled cellophane, sparklers, and patches of light, all rhythmically moving against a painted background. Recent viewers at a retrospective of her work mentioned 'excitement', 'delightful sensation of involvement in the film,' 'pleasurable feeling washing over one.' Theatres kept that film and others such as *Color Rhapsodie*, *Parabola*, and *Polka Graph,* on for weeks - in one case for two years - with long running feature films. Viewers wrote and telephoned their delight and asked for information about the director.

Her original distribution technique was unorthodox, and her subsequent placement of her animation shorts, serendipitous. Imagine an attractive young woman convincing a Radio City Music Hall manager to show a black and white film along with *Becky Sharp*, the first feature to introduce improved, full colour Technicolor to the screen. 'They only knew the fees Disney asked, and they paid me the same. They recommended my work to other theatres, and I did quite well for a while.'

To go back a little: as a young art student, Bute had also been enthusiastic about music and drama and curious about their scientific bases and aspects. 'After studying at the Pennsylvania Academy of Fine Arts, I went to New York and learned stage lighting at the Intertheatre Arts School in Greenwich Village. There were always Texas connections and others who introduced me to the next step in my quest. When I created a stage set for dancer, Jacques Cartier, the Shuberts bought it for *The First Little Show*. That meant I had theatre credentials necessary for acceptance in George Pierce Baker's drama workshop at Yale in 1925. I was one of ten women in a very large class.

At the end of the first year at Yale, Bute applied for a position in the drama department of the first floating university - it originated at New York University - which would start its trip around the world on September 18, 1926. 'The ship was the *Ryndam* with 450 young men and 50 young women and a staff of 60. The director told me a Columbia University professor already had the job I wanted. I didn't 'hear' him. My father got me a secretary and I began working on drama pages for the *Ryndam*. Every few days I mailed some pages to the director, including plans for a collapsible stage set based on lead pipes. Six weeks before the sailing date, the man originally hired, cancelled, and I got the job.'

It was clearly a major experience in her life with stored impressions and ideas for a future career. As the ship went through the Panama Canal, students presented a pageant about the original inhabitants of North and South America. Eight months later, the group - some of them with diplomas earned en route - arrived at Hoboken. They had visited 33 countries, studied traditional academic subjects, prepared dramatic entertainments for foreign guests, hosted foreign students and lecturers and explored museums and galleries, theatres and countryside from Tokyo to London.

'How did I become a filmmaker? Well, for a long time I thought film was too commercial, but something was probably pushing me in that direction. I eventually arrived at a particular kind of abstract film with music, which was called 'seeing sound.' What I saw in my mind, as I listened to music, became sketches, then designs for animation.' She did no cel animation, she said, and all the work was in 35mm. Early influence came from Kandinsky, himself an observer of relationships between colour and music, whose paintings made her think of frozen music. She wanted to 'undo' the parts and make them move.

Other ideas and impressions derived from the work of Oskar Fischinger, whose 'absolute' films using simple shapes such as squares, circles and triangles, were closely related to music in their rhythms and emphases. For a time Bute worked with Thomas Wilfrid, perfecter of the Clavilux - Museum of Modern Art habitués will remember its long running performances in a little downstairs room - a light organ which could be played to create amorphous, moving colours on a screen, but the instrument could not give her the kind of control she was seeking.

At one time Bute worked with Leon Theremin, inventor of an electronic musical instrument, later used by avant garde composers Edgard Varese and Henry Cowell, among others. Theremin had come to America from Russia at the invitation of the Wurlitzer organ company to demonstrate the Theremin which could be played by moving hands or a baton in the air over a keyboard. The title of Theremin's thesis, *The Perimeters of Light and Sound and their Possible Synchronization* - Bute assisted at its presentation - indicates the kind of thinking that led to her electronically generated films of the 50s.

She still found it hard to think of filmmaking as a way to earn a living, but by the early 30s she had become an animator of her own abstract art. She charmingly told how fate - 'or something' - dealt with her mistake in thinking that Melville F. Weber, co-director of *Fall of the House of Usher*, who worked with her on *Rhythm in*

Light would be a cameraman. She inquired at a lab where two young fellows flipped a coin to see who would become her cinematographer. Ted Nemeth, later her husband and frequent, valuable collaborator, won. Mr Nemeth, gifted photographer of commercials and documentaries and of Jim Henson's well-known and beloved *Time Piece*, recently reminisced that he rushed her out of the lab before the other fellow could get to know her.

Rhythm in Light took two years to make. After learning how to use the 35mm Mitchell camera, other cameras and the optical printer from Ted Nemeth and his five brothers (brother Ernest got special credit for being a talented teacher), and observing studio activity, she became quite independent as a cameraperson as well as image designer and a painter. She recalled beginning this phase of her career with *Escape*, a tale in colour of a triangle imprisoned behind a grid of horizontal and vertical lines, and struggling to be free. The elements of this film, abstract as they are, and illustrative of Bute's wish to make her visuals like music - rhythmic, mathematical, moving forward in time - also reveal poetic and humorous qualities which she probably could

not avoid in view of her own effervescent personality and wide interests in literature and theatre. In his 1948 essay, *Experimental Cinema in America*, Lewis Jacobs notes the 'strangely pictorial effects' of Bute's films, and their 'comedy, suspense, pathos and drama.'

By 1950 Bute had made nine short abstract films; one, *Spook Sport*, animated by Norman McLaren. As choreographer/director of her films, almost all of them reminiscent of dancing, she often planned the movement of her abstract forms according to a personal mathematical system she had learned from Joseph Schillinger.

He had formulated a system of music theory useful in teaching American composers, especially those who wrote commercial music. George Gershwin, for example, had been his pupil in studios run by musician Gerald Warburg, where Bute and Theremin had experimented with painting and music.

In Bute's black and white film, *Parabola*, it is possible to see parabolas as sculpture. Small models on a slowly revolving turntable reveal their various aspects. To Darius Milhaud's *Création du Monde*, light plays on the parabolic sculpture which resembles gothic arches, art déco architecture and conches, but which is actually solids or bent rods weaving to the right and left. *Color Rhapsodie* is splashes of paint on glass, and a treasury of green, teal, yellow, red large solids and exploding blobs, fireworks and pinwheels, illustrating how Bute 'saw' Liszt's *Hungarian Rhapsody No.2*.

In *Abstronics*, an article for *Films in Review* (June-July 1954), Bute described the origin of her work in electronic generation of animated forms. 'For years I tried to find a method of controlling a source of light to produce visual compositions in time continuity...' Dr. Ralph Potter of the Bell Telephone Laboratories agreed with her that the oscilloscope, an instrument which converts electronic impulses into visual patterns in motion, would serve her purpose. Adapting that instrument, Dr. Potter designed and constructed equipment which allowed the filmmaker to create a repertoire of light forms.

In *Abstronics*, her first film to use the new medium, probably the first ever to include video technique, light forms dance against painted backdrops to the western music of Aaron Copland's *Hoe Down* and Don Gillis' *Ranch House Party*. This is how it was done: At the controls of her instrument Bute created light forms: wheels within wheels, lively ghosts, combinations of curves, lariats, ovals, disks, parabolas. She moved the forms electronically in a series of whirlings, twirlings, vortexings, zoomings, pinwheelings, splittings, somersaultings, all in counterpoint to backgrounds of endless roadways, a sunset, a diamond. As she directed the light forms onto the fluorescent screen of the technique, *Mood Contrasts*, Bute added new light forms and movements for a lush, oriental ambiance suggested by Rimsky-Korsakov's *Hymn to the Sun* and *Dance of the Jugglers*. These works appeared 15 years before Nam June Paik, world famous video artist, wrote in an unpublished essay: 'I have treated a cathode ray tube (TV screen) as a canvas and proved that it can be superior canvas. From now on, I will treat the cathode ray as a paper and pen.'

By 1965 Mary Ellen Bute, always a courageous experimenter, was astonishing and delighting many viewers with her officially invited feature, *Passages from James Joyce's Finnegans Wake* at the Critics' Section of the Cannes Film Festival. She called her film a 'reaction' to a novel for which several writers had previously attempted scenarios and found the effort very difficult.

Shown commercially after an excellent reception at Cannes, *Finnegans Wake* has in recent years drawn responsive viewers to screenings in museums, schools, libraries, and meetings of teachers and artists...

Sensitively and dramatically photographed by Ted Nemeth, and completed seven years after Bute had conceived the idea, *Passages* is a trove of superimpositions, flashbacks, varied angles, slow motion, intercutting, rapid motion, stop action, negative images, documentary footage, and finally subtitles added after the Cannes showing. It brings in television, the H-bomb, the twist, interplanetary rockets. Bute believed that Joyce would have accepted the modern elements in a film based on his 1939 novel, and she even quoted a line from Joyce's *Finnegans Wake* that mentions television...

This inventive, strongly independent filmmaker had a long career, an early period of commercial success and then only intermittent recognition by serious film critics. Few film students have heard of her work or seen it in their classes. Film historians have given her little or no attention. Neglect has been righted somewhat and the perpetuation of wrong titles and dates and incorrect facts corrected in an excellent, informative essay on Bute as animator by Cecile Starr (in *Experimental Animation*, edited by Russett and Starr)... Response at Bute programmes engendered a sense of 'we've just met a real, curious, stubborn, optimistic, courageous, talented person who has been an important part of twentieth century film and video history, and we've seen proof of her research and accomplishment.'

On the day of the meeting mentioned in the first of these paragraphs, Mary Ellen Bute was very much in charge, very much the gracious host in tiny Gramercy Park where she clearly and steadily spoke 'under' the infelicitous racket of horns and radios that was trying to push through the shrubbery. She was obviously practising being strong and well after a recent illness. She believed that God had propelled her to achieve exceptional experiences.

She had a long list of what she still wanted to talk about: her devotion to the American Pioneer Women Film Directors Project, her gratitude to Cecile Starr, some special things about Ted Nemeth and her two sons, etc., etc. So we planned to meet soon again. But that was not to be. Mary Ellen Bute died on October 17, 1983. The world had lost one of its pioneer women filmmakers.

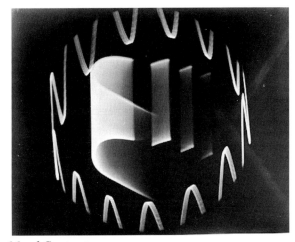

Mood Contrasts

This is an abridged version of an article first published in *Film Quarterly*, reprinted by kind permission of the author. See ß.

Faith Hubley

an interview with Pat McGilligan

John and Faith Hubley broke away from Hollywood in the mid 1950s to form their own independent, small-scale studio in New York City, making animated films in an anti-Disney visual style that was closer in form and spirit to European surrealism and impressionism. They pioneered the use of name performers and of their own children with improvised dialogue. They sponsored marvellous jazz and new-music sound tracks. Their (mostly short) films were not about talking animals, but about adult and philosophical themes: the absurdity of war, the nuclear threat, environmental concerns, over-population, lover marriage, childhood development, spirituality, and feminism.

The highly original and straight-from-the-heart films that resulted from their collaboration have been fêted worldwide - with three Oscars (out of seven nominations to date), film festival citations from Jerusalem to Zagreb, and museum anointings. Their films were never block-booked into theatres and their household ledger did not always balance, but the Hubley's became exemplars for an entire up-and-coming generation of non-traditional animated film-makers. The thirty odd Hubley short films and two short features are not only beloved by film enthusiasts, but by generations of schoolchildren, and nowadays they have a healthy 'second life' on Disney and Pyramid video.

John Hubley was the senior artist. A noted background painter for Walt Disney on Snow White and the Seven Dwarfs, Pinocchio, Fantasia, Dumbo *and* Bambi, *he left Disney after the bitter strike of 1941 and was among the founders of the alternative United Productions of America, source of Mr. Magoo and of a strong 'flat' graphic style featuring parody, serious subject matter, and abstract forms.*

John Hubley was a staunch unionist and cultural progressive whose moonlighting included production design for the 1947 staging of Bertolt Brecht's Galileo *and collaboration with director Joseph Losey in Losey's early films. When the anti-communist blacklist descended on Hollywood, Hubley suddenly found himself 'unemployable', and at a turning point in his career. The blacklist precipitated his move into animated commercials and circuitously, into marriage and partnership with Faith Hubley. Their mutual pact to produce at least one film per year according to their own artistic standards, and to sit down for the evening meal with their children, lasted until his untimely death in 1977.*

Since then Faith Hubley has upheld the legacy, with a little help from her children. Sons Ray and Mark chip in, and Emily and Georgia, apart from working behind-the-

scenes on their mother's innumerable projects, have themselves produced a bumper crop of Hubley animation.

An optimist to the core, Faith Hubley has survived much: a Hell's Kitchen childhood; Hollywood and the name-naming; her husband's death; and her own ten year brush with supposedly terminal disease. In 1986 she produced her first solo feature, The Cosmic Eye, *in which three be-bop visitors from outer space postulate on the history and future of human species. She four-walled it herself in New York City and Los Angeles, to ecstatic reviews ('enchanting, affecting and exhilarating' wrote Judith Crist; 'an ingenious work' reported Michael Wilmington of the Los Angeles Times, 'seraphically childlike and delightful'.*

Your official biography says that you were born in New York City and studied theatre before coming to Hollywood.

I worked as a stage manager and I studied with the New Theatre League at the New School. I studied the Stanislavski Method for years - acting and directing - under Brett Warren and Lem Ward (in New York), and later with Lee J Cobb, J Edward Bromberg, Morris Canovsky and Phoebe Brand in Los Angeles. These were the old Group Theatre people - which brought me full circle, because seeing the Group Theatre, while I was still in high school, is how I became interested in theatre.

Did either of your parents paint or draw?
No. My father was a dentist and my mother played the stock market, and in fact the reason I didn't go on to school was because they wanted me to be a dentist.
There was this hilarious pressure for me to become a dentist. For example, I had to pass 'Hygiene' in high school but in order to pass you had to have a piece of paper signed by your parents saying your teeth had been cleaned. My father, who was a Russian-Polish immigrant Jew, was my dentist and he wouldn't sign the piece of paper unless I agreed to become a dentist. So I left home and started doing theatre at 15.
I got married to a radio announcer. He knew all about music and theatre. That's how I got involved in the theatre. For example, I booked talent for the New Theatre League.

Who did you book them for?
Mostly unions and organisations. I met people like Mr Blitzstein and Earl Robinson, all the people of that time who were so wonderfully talented. I booked Woody Guthrie - Woody was always so vague - he was very grateful to have a teenage girl who could tell him where to go and how much to charge. It was very exciting. I learned a lot from booking. I really got to talk to these people and to ask all sorts of questions about their work and that wonderful period of ferment in the theatre.

How did your radical politics and life-style spring out of your upbringing?
Through my father - in a negative way. I had joined the American Student Union, as practically anybody with half a brain did, in high school. I was very anti-fascist. My father had all of these tactics in order to get me to be a dentist and at one point he came to the school and told school officials that I was a Communist and a prostitute and I had a bad heart and I never brushed my teeth. It was part of this effort to turn me into a dentist.
I think my parents perceived me as their meal ticket. If only I would become a dentist, I could take over my father's practice and support them in their old age. So they kept turning me into the FBI. Those kinds of experiences really had a lot to do with my becoming political.

You were very together, politically, for a teenager. Was it partly the era, partly New York City .... ?

I was a very fortunate child. I had gone to one of the great public schools in Hell's Kitchen and had wonderful teachers there, who really taught us to think. We were told to read everything and anything we could. We could really weigh everything. It was just a wonderful school. English was a minority language - mostly French, Italian and Greek were spoken; there were Orientals and Blacks; everybody was very poor. I remember that one student was a prostitute. Our teacher said, and I'll remember this until the day I die, 'None of you make fun of her. None of you be cruel to her. She had no choice. Her father's an alcoholic, her mother's an alcoholic'... I used to walk with her, I was proud to walk with her, and I guess my father saw me doing that and thought I was a prostitute because I was showing solidarity with her. That's how we were raised at PS 17.

How did your marriage come about?
I decided I had to get married to obtain some legal rights, only I had never had a date in my whole life, and I had barely talked to boys. They had a musical quiz on the air at WNYC where if you knew all the answers or could identify the pieces of music you won a free concert ticket. My prospective husband was the host of the show. Because I was shy, and because I had such a passion for music, I gave the answers to my girlfriend and she was picked out of the audience. He invited her to the ballet and later, when he found out it was me who knew the answers, he took me to the ballet.
If things were normal, we would never have gotten married. Marriage kept him out of the army and it kept me out of jail.
Obviously such a marriage couldn't work because we were too young. I left him and stayed with some friends in the New Theatre movement until my father came to get me with the police.

What did you do?
I went back to my parents. My parents, at least, were a familiar torture and it was just a matter of waiting it out until I was 18. I went to business school, earned money in an office, and worked in the theatre at night. My father wanted me to get a divorce and take alimony. I was proud, I had a good brain and a good heart, thanks to PS17, and I said, 'I won't take alimony. It's immoral. I won't.' So when I was 18, I went to Reno for a divorce.

After you went to Reno, and got your divorce, you kept going?
To Los Angeles. I wanted to be as far away from home as possible. This was 1943. I was so ashamed of this

failed marriage that I just wanted to serve. My plan was to work in a defence plant till the war was over. I was going to go to school at night. I got fired for being too fast. 'Slow down, and don't be so serious' they said. I said, 'There's a war against fascism and it is serious. I'm not going to slow down ....' They gave me three chances and then they fired me. I was considered a disturbance on the assembly line. Without wishing to make trouble I was a troublemaker.

So I decided to go into the movie business. One could do training films and learn a craft. I got a job as a waitress across the street from Columbia and applied for a job as a messenger.

It was during the war and the boys were all being drafted, so it was just a matter of time before one could get picked for something else and then could move up. It took about five minutes for any smart girl to figure out what jobs were available. The studio was wide open. You could learn budget and organisation.

I picked Columbia because of Lawson. I knew his book on the theory of the technique of playwriting, and I felt any studio that would hire him would have to be the best studio. There must be people there who could read and write and think.

Being a messenger at Columbia was like going to film school because you could go any place and you were sort of encouraged to ask questions and move up.

I would say I had a very good experience at Columbia, except that I wanted to be a music editor and the only department, in editing, that would not consider women, oddly enough, was the music department.

Were you aware of being discriminated against as a female?
Oh sure. You couldn't be a cameraman or a sound person. They just said, 'You're a girl.' (laughs)

Even the progressives?
They were a little more subtle, but same thing. A friend Dede Allen and I were trying to get hired in editing and they would say, 'No, you can't because you're a girl.' We'd say, 'Well, why not?' They'd say, 'Well, you're not strong enough...' Then we would gain a lot of weight and show them we could lift heavy boxes, and then they would say, 'We're not relaxed with you. You don't swear...' then we would practice saying 'fuck' and 'shit' and then they would say, 'That's no way for a girl to talk'...

I made a commitment to myself to work in the studios for four or five years and learn a craft, because I knew that it would take twice or three times as long to do that in New York at that time. I wanted to have a real strong hands-on background. I wanted to be never afraid of machines. I didn't want to be afraid of anybody. In a funny way I wanted to understand the economics, the budget and management of the studios, so that I would never be seduced by Hollywood.

When I came to a dead end (at Columbia) I went to Goldwyn, then to Republic and a couple of other studios, then I came back to Columbia. When I worked at Republic as a music cutter, because they hired women there, I was assigned to work on *Spectre of the Rose*, which was directed by Ben Hecht.

I loved George Antheil, a brilliant composer, who wrote all the scores for Hecht's movies. George let me cut stock music to make up the score for the film, then he took what I cut and wrote the score. Through him and his wife I met most of the refugees from the European community in Hollywood - Isherwood, Auden, Stravinsky, and so on.

How long did your progression up through the ranks at Columbia last?
A couple of years. I got real pissed when I found out I couldn't be a music cutter. Because I could read and write music, and most of their music cutters were musically illiterate.

During all this time in Hollywood, were you doing any painting?
Yes. I took a number of courses at the People's Educational Centre. I also took screen writing from Edward Dmytryk, directing from Vincent Sherman, and a class with John Howard Lawson on the history of the American democratic tradition.

My painting teacher persuaded me to take six months off, in 1945, and receive unemployment while freelancing, and to use the rest of the time to paint and write and grow. That was my education. I was a young person and I didn't need that much money. I was making a lot of money anyway, most of which I gave away, and not necessarily to the movement. To anybody who needed it.

Besides showing modern art, Clara Grossman's gallery also had a dandy film society in Hollywood, the only film society which showed the classic films. The greats would come!

Carl and Dede and I took over Clara's film society and we did a Russian series, a French series, and an American series. For the American series Irving Lerner was our mentor, so we found all the old docs of the 1930s, the independent films of Frontier Films. And we showed some Hollywood classics, like *Our Daily Bread*.

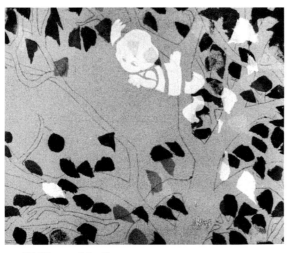

Children of the Sun

Cockaboody

Windy Day

Starlore

Step by Step

Moonbird

How and when did you meet John?
I met John in Hollywood during this period, when he was in the Army. People used to say that we had the same smile and that we were apt to make the same jokes in different places.

We were friends for a long, long time before we were married. We stayed in touch and were involved in projects together. For a while we were trying to do some documentary together, with Ben Maddow, about lynching and civil rights, but we never made it. That was typical of Hollywood, even with the good folk. Endless dreams!

Were you beginning to think about animation?
I had seen Johnny's stuff at UPA and I thought in my heart of hearts, while never articulating it, since I knew I was meant to be a painter and I loved the cinema, how lucky he was to be in this art form that was eclectic. I thought, 'Wouldn't it be wonderful to make something out of that art form, something more than meets the eye?'

Did you have a model for your thinking, at all?
No. But in our film society we showed the work of Georges Méliès, which I don't really like, but I like the idea of it because it is fantastical. I loved the avant-garde in France. I always loved surrealism and the experimental film-makers. There was a film we showed called *Menilmontant*. I loved this film. I can't tell you why. It was a surreal film, a lot of action, full of canals and steps, by Dimitri Kirsanov, a Russian emigré director. It was pretty close to a personal vision (laughs). I just knew that someday I would direct films and it didn't matter to me whether they were drawn or photographed. I still don't like that division.

I just knew I was looking for a medium that would express what I was feeling inside. Don't we all? I knew it would be in film, it wouldn't be at the studios because they were not set up for art, and I knew I'd have to be patient and work at it, and eventually it would happen.

At the end of this period, in 1947, the House Un-American Activities Committee (HUAC) descended, and I gather that you and Johnny were both blacklisted. What was your situation?
I was freelancing. I had two goals: I wanted to edit one picture before I left California and I got to edit Irving's picture. And I wanted to be a script clerk on one really expensive Hollywood movie with a lot of people and a lot of management. So through the union I got this job on this film called *Heaven Only Knows*, a two-million-dollar picture.

It was a Western with special effects, Brian Donlevy, Robert Cummings and a cast of thousands. When I finished that, it was time for me to do something else in life. I was still booking the next film series, which was the most important part of my life other than painting. But I hadn't clearly decided to leave Hollywood. I went back East for a vacation, and then I decided not to go back to Los Angeles because I just didn't feel like it. I was given to quixotic whims. I just wanted to work in New York. And mostly I wanted to go to Europe. I also wanted to work on a serious, heavy documentary and I became Leo Hurwitz's assistant on *Strange Victory*. It's an interesting film, about how the War victory wasn't really a victory.

Did you finally go to Europe?
After I finished *Strange Victory* I went to Paris and then to this International Conference of Working Youth in Poland. This conference was amazing. I will never forget it. It changed my life. Grew me up.

At this conference we got to meet working youth from all over the whole wide world. We learned that was such a place as Vietnam! There were children who were working in the mines whom we could talk to about their working conditions.

Then I had made this promise to myself way back in the messenger room of Columbia that, because I was a lucky girl who grew up in Hollywood, I owed the world something. I had pledged to work on a reconstruction brigade one day. And at the end of this conference, they asked, 'Does anybody want to work on a railroad in Czechoslovakia?' and I raised my hand.

We dug trenches and we laid railroad ties - for three weeks. Then I went to Prague. Later, when I was running out of money, I went to Rome, contracted meningitis and nearly died, spent four months in a clinic and nearly lost my vision. Afterwards I bopped around Italy with a friend of mine. Wrote a screenplay about the Mafia with Basilio Franchina, a director. I met a lot of people. I had the best time.

My mother cabled me that I had a job waiting for me back in New York on a feature that was going to be shot. The director, Bernard Vorhaus, was blacklisted. So I came home and worked on Bernie's picture about delinquent girls, *So Young, So Bad*. I script-clerked it, in short order I became an assistant cutter, and before long I was editing a feature called *Go, Man, Go*, about the Harlem Globetrotters, directed by Jimmy Wong Howe.

Where was Johnny all this time?
In Hollywood. What he did as a solution to the blacklist

was set up a commercial company, Storyboard, and he started making a lot of money doing commercials. He had a front man, but he was making it big. The front was getting the business and signing the contracts. But everybody in town knew it was Johnny doing the commercials.

Then Johnny was hired by Yip Harburg to do *Finian's Rainbow* as an animated feature. But Johnny was a fella who was famous for never being on budget, and certainly never being on schedule. So Yip, whom I knew from my youth in Hollywood, asked me if I would be Johnny's assistant in Los Angeles.

I said I had to think about it and asked if he had to talked to Johnny. He said, 'No, but everybody knows Johnny loves you and you love Johnny'. I said, 'That's different, that's friendship. You have to ask him'. So Johnny was in New York doing something on *Finian's* and we met. He said he wasn't sure I should come to Los Angeles because we both knew that we had controlled our friendship for ten years and after all he was a married man with three kids. But we decided I would take the job and so I went to Los Angeles again.

Then the picture blew up. All the preparations were done, the storyboarding was done, the score was recorded, the animation was in progress; we went out to lunch one day and came back and there was a padlock on the door. That was it. The official work was the blacklist. They said it was because of Johnny. But I think it had something to do with some power struggle among the backers of *Finian's...*

Then we went off to Europe on a trial marriage. We thought we should travel together first. And we fought and fought and fought, but we did find out there is such a thing as a middle road, so we decided we were going to get married. Johnny went off to get his divorce, which was hard, but he did. This was 1955. Johnny opened up a New York office of Storyboard and soon after sold the Los Angeles one.

How did you envision your partnership at the outset?
When Johnny and I got married, and we wrote our wedding vows, the agreement stated that we would make one short film a year, and eat with our children oce a day.

How did you finance your early avant-garde animation?
To begin with, Johnny had a commission from the Guggenheim, to make *Adventures of an Asterisk*, a film about a child's vision. We had just had a new baby and we tried hard to capture all that intensity in this film. The film turned out to be a visual experience about the vision of a little child, which is so pure and so wonderful, about

how what is perceived by those eyes for the first time is tactile and felt, and about how that pure vision, as the child slowly grows in society, is made to follow certain rules.

Were there other grants and commissions over the years?
Johnny and I never got a grant in our whole married life. Not one. *Moonbird*, for example, we financed ourselves and it took about 25 years to pay off and only now is it making a little bit of money. There were some commissions certainly, but they would not be vast sums of money, not like in advertising, but it was money. And if UNICEF commissions one to make a film about how hunger affects the world's children, that's like performing your social obligation, and getting paid for it.

I gather you have always done a little moonlighting.
In the beginning, I continued to work in live action for financial reasons, working on *Twelve Angry Men* and other movies, and also to give Johnny a little breathing space. Johnny kept up his commercial activity in New York and I hated advertising and I still do with such a passion. I would have thrown those people out of my office.

Then along came *Markie Maypo*, which was different. (laughs). This was an amazing advertising phenomenon. Maypo was a cereal made by a little company in Vermont which was bought by a liquor company, Heublein, to offset their profits. The company wanted to do a commercial that was a non-commercial. So we did a commercial about this little boy wearing a cowboy hat who hates the cereal and goes 'Yuck!' and his father has to force-feed him - 'Here comes the aeroplane!' We named him Markie, after our son, who did the voice. It was a little one-minute documentary on feeding a child. And it took off, though it wasn't supposed to. It was supposed to NOT sell the product.

We got paid a lot of money, and were able to finance at least half of *Moonbird*. We lived from film to film like that for a very long time, until we began work on a feature (*Of Stars and Men*) on which we ended up owing an awful lot of money.

It seems to me that when you and John were working together, ironically, you had more of an upper hand when it came to actually choosing the subject matter. In the sense that, given his background as a more traditional and commercial animator, the films you began to work on seemed to spring more out of your sensibility. Privately, it seems, you were very, if not dominant, at least very assertive in terms of what you were doing together, and that's one of the things that kept John on track.

I think I have a natural ability to enthuse. It's genuine, I have to believe in what I'm doing, and when I have that enthusiasm, it's irresistible. So I think that's what happened, although being flexible, we couldn't work around a theme until we found that part of the theme that Johnny felt good about, and that's what made the collaboration very strong.

Why were you, and are you, so opposed to a narrative form?

For my taste, I think the obligation of animation is to deal with material that live action can't, and to look for that form and content which is beyond an actor, which is beyond the adaptation of even a very fine book.

How did your collaboration work, in terms of the initial writing?

It just evolved very naturally. We would discuss the structure, then we would each do a draft. The rule of the game was that if there was anything that either of us were violently opposed to it, it was just out the window. After a while there would be something like three or four pieces of tape on a roll with John's name or my name, pieces that we had given up that we really hadn't given up in our hearts of hearts, hoping that when the whole thing was put together, maybe the other person would change their mind.

How much of what we see in the joint Hubley films are your own drawings?

Hard to say. Less than half. We would get the visual expression together, then Johnny would usually do the amalgam. Especially in the films that deal with children or were about being a mother - I knew how certain things should look - but Johnny knew animation. Having had all the Stanislavski training, I also had really strong feeling for how the characters should act, in some cases. Because it was not just drawing, it was character analysis, writing with the characters.

The story and the storyboard, how the picture looked, were joint. It was a two-people vision. Even though Johnny was a better artist and certainly had all this experience, I was like a primitive working with somebody who was very trained.

There wasn't anything in the picture we didn't discuss together, but there was a conflict between the public and private image. The private image was fine. Working together was no problem; we could argue yet have a healthy, strong collaboration. Whereas the public image was more Johnny. Johnny would do the public end, the handling out of the work to other people, till we got back to the editing at the end. That coincided with my training in live action because I had worked with a lot of directors. The meeting with the animator, and the hand-out of the animation, is very crucial, because even though you have all the drawings, you need to communicate the timings, and the animator has to understand the spirit of the film. That is what the director explains. That was always private between Johnny and the animator, with the exception of Bill Littlejohn, because sometimes, especially on *Carousel*, I wanted to act out some of the characters.

I gather Johnny was always doctoring your scenes.

Yes, which made me feel very inferior. He was the senior artist and he was ten years older. The turning point for me was *Carousel* because I was sick by then and there were certain passages that I painted, really in my own hand, and which (for the first time) Johnny didn't change. Or didn't doctor.

The big question was sharing the directing credit which happened for the first time on *Cockaboody*, in 1973. It was the first time I ever got a co-credit, a co-directing credit, which was very upsetting to him. It was difficult for Johnny to share as much as he had to.

Later on, Johnny began to change of his own accord.

Is there a way you can generalise for me the Hubley technique and approach, in animation, as opposed to the more traditional ways and means?

This is a good chance to say something that has to be said: Johnny was not an animator. Johnny was a designer-director. For years, we were scrupulous about saying, 'No, we don't animate.' An animator draws meticulously, and makes this magic of things moving and turning and taking shape. Bill Littlejohn animates, or Shamus Culhane animates. We design and are film-makers.

You should explain the difference to me.

There isn't a word for an animated film-maker, but they're really two things. There's animation, the craft, and there's animation, making the whole film. In the Disney studios the craft people were the animators. Disney knew exactly what he was doing when he emphasised the craft separation so that nobody would have the film-making power; that's not only a political observation, it's an artistic one.

For the uninitiate, what is layout as opposed to back-

ground?

Layout is like staging a scene, designing how the scene is going to move, the action. But the layout person would probably have nothing to do with the sound, for example, he would just take the drawings from the storyboard artist and say, 'How does this scene work?' It's like being a second-unit director. It's not conceptual.

How would you generalise about the differences between the Disney style of animation and the technology and the technique that you pioneered on a small scale?

The big change was that we figured out how to make films in a very small space. It's as simple as that. Personal films that required half a dozen people.

From a technical point of view, since John didn't have to deal with the studio, he didn't have to use conventional ways, so we could do anything we wanted to do. Anything! We explored reticulation and paper as a medium, and it was the beginning of eliminating the hard-cel and the hard-line that I've always felt was ugly.

And cel-animation is, was, inhibiting. One would have to have certain kind of skill to do it as handmade mass production. I'm not a specialist in it; I just know I hate it - I hate the way it looks and I don't like the feel of it. I hate the hard edge and I don't see why anyone should learn to be tidy. I am a bit of a slob and I like a free-flowing line and texture. That was our contribution - aside from content and the amazing changes in sound using children, using jazz and wonderful composers, using improvisation - to liberate animation from itself, and to go to watercolors and to paint pastels. It was a big, big liberation and resisted by the industry.

Your sources for films - from Harlow Shapley to Erik H Erikson - are so, for want of a better word, esoteric. Is there any way you can generalise for me where you sought and derived your intellectual inspiration?

Remember, we had this ten year friendship, followed by a very brief and intense courtship. The floodgates opened during the courtship and we discovered we both always had this feeling about science. You know, for example, that Johnny always wanted to do the story about Galileo's life. He did the stage design for the Los Angeles production, directed by Losey, and helped block the scenes.

It was like being kids again and we started asking each other what we really wanted to do in life. A lot of what we really wanted to do revolved around taking the ideas that we knew, the emerging visions of the planet, which were being presented to the public in very technical jargon, almost in another language, a high-priest form,

and to break down the gulf between insiders and outsiders. It was a shared obsession. We wanted to be that bridge.

One of the things that strikes me about your films is their relationship to jazz. They are very sensory and you can let them wash over you and really enjoy them, and sometimes feel more than know something about what they are trying to tell you.

They're physical, almost like a good massage.

And of course some of them have such fabulous jazz sound tracks. I want to ask you about jazz people - like Benny Carter and Dizzy Gillespie. When and where did you meet them? You've had such a long collaboration with both of them.

Benny I met independently of Johnny the first year I was in Hollywood. We were trying to raise money for an inter-racial hospital, and this classical pianist named Lucille asked me if I would go backstage with her to ask Benny Carter for some money. I said, 'Of course!' because growing up in Hell's Kitchen, where there was a lot of jazz in the street, there was nothing more beautiful to me than a horn player. When Johnny and I did our first film, *Adventures of an * (Asterisk)*, there was no question that Benny would do the score.

At one point, when we first got married and had these explosions of feelings, we did a film called *Date with Dizzy*, which is a live action film, a satire on advertising. That was one of the first times we worked with Dizzy. It had live action and some animation. We shot it in one day and we had so much fun. An advertising agency paid for it. I'll never know why.

I gather you and Johnny were both profoundly influenced by the leading art of your generation, that is, by the surrealists and modernists, the leading French painters.

Picasso, very strongly, for Johnny. For me, more Paul Klee and Mirò. For me, I was influenced by the side of them which is primitive and childlike and by how they allowed that to stay a part of their sophisticated vision. I like the directness and the passion of a child's vision.

What was difficult, because there were difficulties, was in making a film like *Stars and Men* (in 1961), which I still think is a beautiful film, finishing it and putting everything we had in the whole wide world into it, borrowing the money to finish it, having critical acclaim from Bosley Crowther of The New York Times, and then no distributor. Then, Johnny would say, 'I don't want to be an educator. I want to be seen'.

Why did you feel the need to take the financial and creative risk of a feature?

Johnny always wanted to handle a longer length. And we wanted to do something that related to the marriage of science and art. Then we read this book by Harlow Shapley, 'Of Stars and Men', which was an overview of evolution. Dr Shapley thought the next stage of evolution was psychic and that we had to start preparing for it. The first thing we had to do was stop destroying the planet and get rid of weapons, then we really had to work on a new development, and he went through a kind of history of western science to make the statement.

Of Stars and Men was a wonderful film. It played for all of a week in New York and then totally disappeared. We ended up owing all this money which we eventually paid off, but it left Johnny with a sense of incompletion, because I think he really wanted it to succeed.

That haunted him. As time went by there were more debts and there were more children. There was a middle period of work, including *Tijuana Brass*, which won the Academy Award, which is not our best work. It was commissioned by Herb Alpert and his partners, and they're lovely people. But the film represented, artistically, the compromise of those years.

Was Johnny giving voice to this compromise? Was it a struggle between you, behind the scenes, or was it inarticulate?

It was half and half. I know it was something we used to talk about. It coincided with a period where we had a policy not to do commercials, and we were doing a lot of stuff for Children's Television Workshop, Electric Company and Sesame Street, which was like a refined form of one-minute commercials, selling education to children. But it's not work from the heart and I think if you do a lot of it, it corrodes the eyes.

There were some nice films during this period, like *Eggs*, but generally there was a lot of effort to launch features.

You told me that, previous to Watership Down*, there was a final period of working together which ended with an artistic flourish.*

It started with *Eggs*, when Johnny's spirit was returning, and for my taste it continued with *Voyage to Next*, the last short film we made together. By then I was sick and there was the major work, *Everybody Rides a Carousel*, in 1976. It was commissioned by CBS during a period when they must have been under some pressure to do something decent for families and especially for children and it is based on Eric Erikson's life cycle and 'Childhood in Society'.

I can remember when we finished it and we took it to Cape Cod, where Erik and John Erikson lived, for a showing at a lovely little theatre. The last stage of the film is about the old age of wisdom, and we ended the film with the metaphor of a merry-go-round, this carousel, with the last horse going off into the fields to die. I had practised learning death, or befriending death, and I remember sitting next to Johnny and starting to cry at the end because it was like I was saying goodbye to everybody. It was so ironic, in a way, that Johnny died, and I was supposed to die, and didn't.

You and John had actually started work on The Cosmic Eye*, am I right?*

We had started a project with Carl Sagan which turned into *The Cosmic Eye*. If we had gotten the money for *The Cosmic Concert*, as we were calling it then, we would not have done *The Doonesbury Special*. *Doonesbury* was the backup if *Cosmic Concert* didn't get financed. But if we had done *Cosmic Concert*, John was going to let me do one, maybe two sequences of my own as part of what he called my 'witch act' - because he didn't go along with all this mythology.

And spirituality and metaphysicality.

He thought it was interesting and privately he would say to Bill Littlejohn that she has something none of us know about, and we should let her go with it. So Johnny and I signed the contract for *Doonesbury*. We did the storyboard, Garry Trudeau wrote the script, we recorded the tracks and then we took a vacation. After which, Johnny went into the hospital for this so-called simple by-pass, and never came out. He haemorrhaged and died on the table.

Can I ask you about your own illness? I understand you were diagnosed with terminal cancer over ten years ago.

In 1974 the first lumps were found. I was teaching the storyboard class with Johnny at Yale, preparing *Voyage to Next*. I'm not going to say cancer is fun, it isn't. But it has been an opportunity for growth. On occasion, I would have my sessions with students in the chemotherapist's waiting room, which in a way was wonderful for them because, especially in the 70s, cancer wasn't talked about. The students would practice telling their storyboards to the other patients so that in a sense they were practising performing and getting other people's input. I could almost see the room change from a funeral parlour to a place with a real life force.

I had a mastectomy and the initial assumption was everything was going to be fine. Then after the operation my doctor said, 'I think you should have radiation.' Then after I had radiation I went in for a check-up and he said, 'I don't like your lymph count. It's terrible. Take a deep breath, because I think you have to start preparing to die. I would give you, if I were being generous, a year, and if I wasn't being generous, six months.'

So for a while I was just living six months at a time. A lump was found in the remaining breast and my doctor's partner told me he was going to book me a hospital room to have my other breast taken off. And I said no. I felt it was just stress-connected and that I was too mixed up about everything in life and that what I really needed was a rest. So I rented a cabin in Maine and went away for a month in the summertime, leaving Johnny with the children. When I came back, the lump was gone. I changed my eating habits a lot, I had this very strong Italian chemotherapy programme, and I kept growing more lumps, which I kept making go away or they would turn out to be benign.

Up until Johnny's death I was still in and out of the hospital, with these lumps coming and going. The last time I was in the hospital was 1977. After that I just went back every six months for check-ups. After about ten years I took myself off the list of the doomed. I'm just now beginning to think I'll live. It's only in the last year that I have decided to plan for old age.

How did John's death and being diagnosed with terminal cancer influence what you began to do as a film-maker, individually, without John?
There's something about accepting mortality that gives one courage. It certainly stood me up straight.

Finishing *Doonesbury* without John was honestly the hardest thing I've ever had to do in my whole life. I had to deliver one sequence at a time to NBC and go through censors and committees, and all the time suffering from cancer. They were trying to fire me because I was a mere woman. Garry (Trudeau) was very supportive. It was just a horrendous period.

But to be serious, I felt I had no choice. I could not afford not to be unafraid. I could not threaten to commit suicide, because I was already dying. Every neurotic behaviour pattern was just cut off.

How did facing death affect your subsequent choice of material?
I always felt that every film had to make a statement, but now I felt I could waste no time. I felt very guilty about not finishing *Cosmic Concert* after Johnny died. But I didn't want to give up the idea entirely because I still wanted to do a long piece that was a continuation of *Of*

Stars and Men about how creatures from another planet must view us.

In time I finished *Whither Weather*, a film about the effects of weather on our planet. Then the Year of the Child inspired *Step by Step*, which dealt with the history of child abuse, the condition of the earth's children and what their yet-to-be-gained rights are. After *The Big Bang and Other Creation Myths* and *Sky Dance* I began to see how I could shape these elements into a feature film. I planned *Hello* as a short which would work as the climax and in this roundabout fashion, after eight years, I completed *The Cosmic Eye*.

Has it been a problem, distributing as well as financing your films?
Most of the time. It has been up and down, down and up, up and down.

Isn't that discouraging?
No, I swear I don't care.

Isn't that a paradox? To make movies that are about things which people should become of aware of, or think about, or become concerned about, but the films do not reach them.
It's a paradox. But, how much can you do? I know a lot of film-makers, and Johnny used to be one of them, who would go to waste worrying about that paradox. You can't really lose your life's blood agonising over the state of money or distribution. Either it will get better or it will get worse; it's out of our control. All we can do is do our best work.

But it sounds like it always got bad or worse - never really better.
But something would always come along. Nowadays I run into second-generation people who say, 'You know, that film changed my whole life!' So maybe it was shown through churches or in schools or a lot of Sunday schools, I really don't know. But the quality of the viewing was so serious that it could really touch a fellow human being. And the quality of an audience is much more important than the numbers.

That's not a very Populist viewpoint.
Well, I'm not very Populist person.

That sounds elitist.
I don't think so. What I mean is, it's not the quantity of the audience, it's the quality of the contact with the audience. But I think all good ideas, and this applies to

science, religion, philosophy, or politics, are shared first, intensely, and then it is exponential dissipation, or communication. I think that we're very misled by the electromagnetic force into thinking that we have to be on a screen simultaneously everywhere at once.

I believe my situation is changing, maybe because of the availability of home-video cassettes. In any case, maybe because I'm older and wiser, I don't lose energy agonising over why there aren't more audiences in the United States. One has to have a personal adjustment and a social adjustment. My social adjustment is one of rage, and my personal adjustment is one that enables me to work.

For example, I've just begun work on a new short titled *Amazonia*, inspired by two South American myths and a shaman's warning that we must save the vanishing rain forest. I have shared the experience of developing the storyboard with my 18 students at Yale this semester, who have designed their own visual pleas on behalf on the rain forest. If I stopped working to think about the problems of distribution or where I will find the rest of the budget of *Amazonia*, I would be paralysed.

One of the things that I'm grateful to Johnny about is that he was really brave and walked out on the mainstream. His insistence that the medium could handle - handle is the wrong word - but express much more has, I think, taken animation down a different road than the main one, in other directions. I am continuing down that road. It's a long way from growing up in Hollywood and what we thought then or what we perceived.

My choice as a working artist is not to play to the marketplace. It's not because I don't know how. I've chosen another path. As hard as my life is, and it is hard without Johnny, I wake up every morning and I can't wait to get to work.

Patrick McGilligan's complete 'Interview with Faith Hubley' appeared in *Film Quarterly*, Winter 1988-89, published by the University of California Press. This is an authorized excerpt.

Evelyn Lambart

an interview with Joan Churchill

The contribution of Evelyn Lambart to the films of Norman McLaren has often been neglected, although McLaren himself was always keen to acknowledge it. She had what might be termed a technical imagination, a particular gift for rising imaginatively and inventively to a technical challenge which in turn stimulated her creatively. She was largely responsible for the extraordinary range of textures in Begone Dull Care, and she was as inventive in relation to sound techniques as she was visually. Her own films are rich in human observation and detail. -Ed.

On a sunny day in September, Co Hoedeman and I drove to Sutton, a quaint and cosy town nestled in the mountains. We arrived at the beautifully landscaped home of veteran filmmaker extraordinaire - Evelyn Lambart. The following are some of the things she had to tell us.

I've always been concerned with what I see, and the world of nature has always been wildly exciting to me. I've almost always been deaf and so my interests were focused on the visual world. From my early youth I had paintboxes put before me and I was encouraged to draw, paint and read, and also to study botany. I bless my mother especially for that encouragement, as these interests serve me very well.

My father was quite a photographer and we had cameras throughout our childhood. When I was about six years old I was given a simple camera, and when he saw that I could manipulate that one, he took it away and gave me another. He looked at everything I did. He was interested in efficiency and wanted me to learn to do things well. He showed me his system and bought me a little black book, where I was expected to write down everything I did. We also did our own darkroom work. So I was terribly interested in photography and art, and these subjects occupied my mind a great deal.

Evelyn studied commercial art, then after college worked for a year and a half on illuminations for the Book Of Remembrance [*a commemoration of the Canadian war dead*].

It was valuable experience for me as it was very delicate work that required a fine hand and a good sense of colour. This was the beginning of a kind of refinement in my work. After that job I had more confidence in myself, and I thought, wouldn't it be marvellous to work at the National Film Board, so I went to Ottawa. They said to come back on Monday, which I was very glad to do. That was in 1942.

I started out as a letterer, but that didn't last long. I was good at it, but too slow, so soon they had me doing maps. One day Norman came by. He was working on a film, a film which doesn't exist anymore, but anyway, he was using heraldic devices and he asked me if I could do the job. I was able to do a very good job. From then on Norman found other jobs for me and so it was then that we began working together.

It was also at that time that Norman started the animation department with people such as René Jodoin. George Dunning, Grant Munro, Jean-Paul Ladouceur, Stuart Legge, Jim MacKay, Laurence Hyde and Art Price. Norman took a personal hand in the training of these people and whatever project was chosen, Norman directed.

I worked for a couple of years on the prestigious project, *World In Action,* a monthly twenty minute current affairs programme which was a political commentary on Canada and the world..I created maps and all kinds of very fancy diagrams. I loved doing those diagrams...giving a visual representation to an idea and making it work still fascinates me.

After *World In Action*, I began work on my first film, *The Impossible Map.* As a concept, it was an absolute natural for me because I had really worked projections to the limit with all the maps I'd been doing. Those maps were drawn on flat pieces of paper, in perspective and lit in such a way as to make them appear round, and any action that took place over the map had to be calculated so that you really thought you were looking at a globe.

I was always thinking about the relationship between the round surface and the flat surface, so I decided to use grapefruits. We didn't have any globes at the time, or the money to buy one. So, I painted maps onto the grapefruits. At one point in the film I take a rolling pin and smash one of those grapefruits to show that if you take a round surface and simply push it flat, you end up with a very irregular thing. Maps are a calculated distortion and anybody looking at a flat map should realize that. That was really the point I wanted to make in the film.

That film was made with seven cameramen. We were using an old Cinéspecial which used to break down all the time. It couldn't stand up to single frame animation. It was a movie camera and using it for single frame work gave us a lot of trouble and a great deal of despair. We also did our own lighting and the only equipment we had were these big old floodlights. We had nothing to measure the colour temperature and there wasn't any voltage control either. Eventually we were given two cameras and when one broke down it was taken to camera repairs. They didn't like us down there.

We always, all our lives, pushed the equipment beyond its limits and damaged it, and then we would have to invent something new. The business of doing mixes and fades with that old Cinéspecial was also pretty tricky. We made little cardboard devices and the results were very poor mixes and fades... This was still in the days before opticals, and it was just the beginning days of colour film. I was very pleased when it was agreed that we would use colour for the film.

I must say that in those early days everybody was always highly co-operative. There was never any question of discrimination. I didn't feel any differences displayed between the men and women. This was partly due to my own background. My father had taught us that certain behaviour was expected of women and certain behaviour of men, but that we all had the same intellectual capacity. When it came to earning a salary, of course Norman earned more than I did, but then I earned more than some of the other men. Everybody was on a full time contract, but there were no holidays and no one was permanent. Grierson believed that this would lead to stagnation, so everyone was reviewed every three months and in this way the deadwood went out the door pretty fast. There were no politics like there are now. Things were developing, everyone was breaking new ground and the people were all terrific. It was a big team and everyone was struggling to get by. The work was exploratory and originality was valued tremendously. Derivative work was absolutely hated. We didn't do any cel work at all, in fact we were highly contemptuous of Disney...

We were all so excited and pleased to be doing something despite the terrible equipment and the poor surroundings. Grierson wouldn't have a clock in the place. He didn't want us to be conscious of the time. You were expected to work until you dropped and that's pretty much what we did. Grierson was always pushing for content over technical excellence. Don't forget the war was still on and there was no money. Grierson used to say 'Do not pursue the comfort of technical excellence'. He was such a dynamic person and he felt very strongly about the message being important and vital.

It's true that at that time I was very proud of the films coming in and out of the Film Board, even if the mixes and fades did jiggle. Because of the war there was a tremendous need for films and public information. So we were all very involved in the war effort. It was a frightening time and it was vital to our culture, our society and to our lives that we not succumb to Nazi Germany.

We admired the work of John Hubley, and the European connection was close to our hearts. There were many original people at work there. We loved anyone who was inventive and who loved to work, and we hated the fat cats. I love the work of Trnka; in fact we loved the Czechs... they were way ahead of us. They had a tremendous tradition of puppet animation, and we were just starting out.

Every Friday night at the Board there were staff screenings of films from Hollywood and abroad, as well as many first run features not yet released. It was during those screenings that we found our inspiration and our education. We saw the most exciting things and everybody attended.

Begone Dull Care was a highly inventive film and one of our favourites. We had two moviolas set up so that the film ran from the first machine about twenty feet and then ran through the next one until it came back to the start where it was wound up. We would put wet acrylic paint on the film, starting at the moviola one. Then we would run along and jump on the floor at different places so that the dust would come up. The dust was sort of oily and when it landed on the film the paint would withdraw from it, creating a very interesting pattern. We did this in a way that we had of rhythm going. Another time we shook the film out of the window to pick up some of the dirt from Sparks Street...all these shots are in the film.

Norman was a moving spirit in the invention of animation techniques. There was always something new brewing in his mind. Always something that he was going to need help with and I was always so interested and keen about what we were doing and what we would do next. Sometimes I think I'm really a piece of Norman. You can't work that closely with a person for so long and not feel that. We co-ordinated so well together. Occasionally there would be a disagreement and he would say, 'Let's do it both ways then'. He was so bright and mostly he would be able to convince me, but there were times when I would say, 'No, I don't think that's the best way', and so we would do it both ways. So my things often got on the screen too.

Mainly there was agreement between us. We were compatible. Our feeling for time and colour was the same. It all became integrated because every tiny detail was discussed back and forth until we came to an agreement on what was acceptable. Except for one thing, I like red and Norman didn't. I always went for brighter colours than he did and I learned to accept the kind of groan that would come, when I did use red. There was a certain way too that he would put his head to the side if there was something that bothered him.

Norman worked in the old tradition and I think I probably do too. We didn't have video in those days and so you had to cover yourself when you shot in case something didn't work, so that there were always alternatives. But Norman would shoot ten alternatives. I was able to visualize better than Norman. I was good at sitting there, thinking, now what will we do? I would ask myself how the thing was going to cut together, and I think as a result I would shoot quite efficiently. Norman would shoot ten alternatives and the horrible thing was that he would want to see all the alternatives cut together. Once he'd seen it all, well then, he'd throw out what didn't work, but he was enough of a purist never to discard anything without really cutting it in and looking at it.

Norman had great prestige. I feel that all my life Norman's mantle has fallen a bit on me and I think people respect me mainly because I was working with him. Norman was a big figure. Everything that we created was so good and we won many prizes, but working beside someone of his stature had certain disadvantages. I often felt very insignificant beside him, but he respected me very much.

The NFB moved from Ottawa to Montreal in 1957. It was quite a change, but one that we were excited about. At least the thought of a new building and new equipment was enticing.

It was in the early 60s that I started thinking about the idea of doing my own films. Norman was beginning to take an interest in ballet films, which didn't hold any interest for me. As long as there was artwork, technique or animation to be done I was interested, but ballet films weren't my department at all. Until then, the relationship had been so comfortable and so successful that there'd never been any reason to think otherwise. I felt very lost at that time; I had always worked with Norman and I found it difficult to have to make my own decisions. I had to force myself.

In 1975, I retired from the Film Board and decided to have a house built in the country. It was quite a change moving out here and it took nearly six years before I felt really comfortable. But, country life is better than I anticipated. For one, I hadn't expected to find the interesting people roundabout. There are many retired folks out here. People who have had very interesting lives and who continue to do interesting, challenging things. People in their fifties are at their peak I think, both intellectually and physically. As you get into your sixties you're less active, but your judgement is better. You don't have to run around in circles as much as before. When you're younger your job fills your mind completely, but as you get older you need other interests and activities. *(Evelyn is now 74).*

I often think of films that I'd like to make out here, but then I wonder about all the time it takes...The last film that I made was here in Sutton, *The Town Mouse and the Country Mouse*. I identified so much with the country mouse. The town mouse was overfed, sloppy and very unrealistic.

I'm really very content living out here becoming a country kid...and I'm always busy...but every so often I think of an idea that I could do here with the material available and with the knowledge that I've acquired. The beauty of the flowers is terrific. The way the whole thing develops and the way the seed pods evolve, it's just incredible. You know, human beings think they're so wonderful. We're surrounded by things just as wonderful, but we don't seem to be aware of it, or we take it for granted. I'd like to do a time lapse thing with this environment. A beautiful film could be made about the flowers and plants changing through the seasons. I remember a film from France that was made years ago called *La Ferme...The Farm*. I don't know how they did it, but it was fantastic. There were mixes as you watched the whole year go by. How they kept the exposure constant? I don't know.

Life is a very rich thing. There's so much in it. There's a lot more than just making films. Mind you, making films is pretty good, but there's more than you know. Don't think that if you ever stop making films, that's the end of everything... *September 24, 1987.*

Reprinted with kind permission from *Asifa Canada's Special Issue on Evelyn Lambart*, January 1988.

Sayoko Kinoshita

First impressions of Sayoko Kinoshita are somewhat deceptive. She's almost stereotypically the Japanese female: diminutive, self-effacing ('My husband is more creative than I am'), her conversation interspersed with high-pitched giggles. Yet her achievements bespeak a steely determination, and unflagging sense of energy and purpose.

The creative partnership with husband Renzo clearly works on two levels. She produces the animation films he directs, works on their conceptualisation and design, writes the scripts, and also animates. But, just as important to her is the work of raising consciousness about the potential of animation as an adult art form, as opposed to the mainstream of commercial cartoon production in Japan. 'My talent is not so brilliant as an animator…my talent is to make things happen…and to work to enable animation in Japan to develop as an art industry'. As distributor, and as lobbyist for, then director of the Hiroshima Animation Festival, she has worked tirelessly to achieve this aim - which would have been simply impossible, she says, without her husband's constant support. He has taken on many of the functions normally quite strictly defined as the province of the Japanese housewife: 'I am very lucky, since I am away from home so much, he will cheerfully look after the house, wash the dishes, sort out my travel arrangements, pack for me.'

So how did she get involved in animation? After graduating in industrial design, she was looking for more creative work, and read about an animation company looking to recruit. Taken on as administrator, it was there she met Renzo, a cartoonist. They soon established themselves in TV cartoons and via a TV variety show for which they produced animation inserts aimed at an adult audience. Though the latter was very successful, they were frustrated with conventional 'cartooning'.

Seeing Paul Grimault's *Le Voleur de paratonnerres*, they were inspired by 'animation's potential as art', to set up the independent Lotus Studio, to finance their own films from commercial work. Their second film, *Made in Japan* (1972), a satirical and densely packed analysis of the West's impact on Japanese self-consciousness, won first prize at a New York festival. Yet this boost to their confidence did not improve funding opportunities back home.

It was then that she realised they had to do more than simply make films, if animation in Japan was ever to change. And so began a twelve year campaign to create an international animation festival.

In August 1972 they travelled to Hiroshima - as do thousands of Japanese every year to commemorate the victims of the nuclear bomb. They already had in mind an idea for a commemorative film, *Pica Don*, and approached Hiroshima's City Council - who were horrified at the prospect of such a serious subject being turned into a vulgar cartoon. So the Kinoshitas went home to Tokyo and made the film, once again with their own money. When *Pica Don* was finished, in 1978, they sent it to Hiroshima where it languished on a shelf for several months before a chance projection of another film prompted a screening. The Kinoshitas, abroad at the time, came home to a barrage of media interest, and the film was shown all over the country and went on to win international acclaim.

Sayoka was asked by a friend in Hiroshima what she would like in recognition, and replied: 'An animation festival'. Given a tiny staff of three, she lobbied for sponsorship for seven years and in 1985 the first Animation Festival in Hiroshima was held, with great success. The generous prize money awards and hospitality offered to animators made it one of the most important festivals world-wide. Unfortunately, disagreements over artistic control led to Sayoka's resignation, yet undeterred, she started a small festival in a Tokyo suburb, financed, as usual, by Lotus' commercial work. And her distribution activities continued, resulting in three permanent screening spaces for animation in Japan. They also have helped many young animators by making available their studio equipment. In 1990, she re-assumed directorship at Hiroshima - on her own terms.

She regrets the ten year gap in filmmaking (outside commercial work) due to the time and energy spent promoting animation, and feels that when she and Renzo did get back to making their own films, quality suffered somewhat.

Over twenty years after they set up Lotus, they have received their first commission from the Peace Museum in Hiroshima: finance and creative carte blanche for a thirty minute film. *Saitama* should be finished in 1994.

Made in Japan

Candy Kugel & Vincent Cafarelli

Candy Kugel was studying at Rhode Island School of Design when she heard Jack Zander talk about animation, and asked him about work opportunities.

'He gave me a list of animation studios, and I managed to land a summer job at Perpetual Motion Pictures to run errands, keep out of the way and to stay for the whole summer for $25 a week (I know it was 20 years ago, but it was a pittance then too). But I was grateful and it was a terrific way to learn the craft. Since I was still a full-time student the other employees found me kind of 'quirky'. Traditionally, Ink and Paint was staffed by women and Animation (assisting and in-betweening) were men. Since I was interested in and encouraged by my bosses to do animation, the others found it odd.

'Most of the animators (and assistants) were men who wanted to do comic strips and books and sort of fell into animation. Generally, they hadn't gone to art school, but were terrific artists and draughtsmen nonetheless. They saw me as a hippie and found it weird that this was what I wanted to do – they assumed I would marry and be out of the busines soon enough. I got kidded by the guys a lot and told I was 'getting so good that soon they'd have to break my fingers'. The inkers and painters told me often I wasn't part of the 'girls' (I&P) but one of the 'guys' (Animation). At one point, in 1973, I went to Disney to see if I could learn 'classical' animation. Not too subtly, I was told that women didn't animate – but if I were interested in backgrounds…

'In 1974, after graduating, Perpetual hired me again. This time to do a 2 minute sales film. It would last all summer, they would give me in-betweener wages and I could join the Union. I was thrilled! It was a cheap film (which is why I was hired) that I designed and layed out. When it came to the time to start animation, Vincent Cafarelli (who had recently joined Perpetual on staff since his studio had folded) was happy to help me. He was the first animator I had met who was happy to share his secrets and guided me through the project.

'Fortunately, Perpetual got a contract with NFBC to produce 2 one minute animated cartoons a month for the newsshow *Weekend*. Vinny and I found ourselves part of a full-time staff producing the spots and commercials for the next five years. Sometimes we worked on the same pieces, sometimes not. Sometimes I designed and layed out, sometimes I animated, sometimes I assisted him. In 1979 Perpetual got contracts to do five *Berenstein Bears* specials and *Strawberry Shortcake in Big Apple City*. We both worked as animators on them and co-directors on two.

'In 1982, Buzz Potamkin (Perpetual's president) broke from his partners to form Buzzco Productions. He took Vinny and me as his creative team, and there we co-directed *Deck the Halls with Wacky Walls*. Buzz always wanted to do long format programming and he found that it was difficult getting the networks to take a New York City studio seriously. In 1985 he moved to Los Angeles, and Vinny and I took over the company, changing the name to Buzzco Associates.

'Between 1976 and when we formed our own company, I made several independent film in my own time, outside of work (see A–Z). Vinny always encouraged me in these projects and shamed me into finishing them!

'Since then we have worked together on the projects we've gotten. Although we've tried separating our rooms – it has worked out that there's about six feet between our desks with a potted plant in the middle as a room divider. I often do the storyboard and layout work and Vinny does the animation – but we have developed a shorthand that allows us both to contribute to both processes– and we both have opinions on what the other has done! It was funny when we were working on *A Warm Reception in L.A.*, although we had been working together for over ten years, it was the first time there was no final client, boss, arbiter to decide whose solution he liked best. So we had to work it out together – it made us very uncomfortable until we figured out how to resolve it. And that basically became the better idea won. Since then we've done two other films, *Snowie and the Seven Dorps A Passive/Aggressive Fable for the 90's* (1990) and *Fast Food Matador* (1991) and we're currently working on a fourth: *We Love It!*

'I'm not sure how we've figured out how we work together. In interviews, Vincent, who is very shy, lets me do all the talking—but I'm thrilled when he's comfortable enough to enlighten the questioner. Vinny's always been very supportive of me –in front of interviewers, etc, so I don't feel like a Claire Parker, Joy Batchelor or even Faith Hubley. And I am supportive of his talents too, so I don't think either of us ever feels slighted, but I guess you should check with him!'

Snowie and the Seven Dorps puts a new slant on an old fairy tale –updating it to explain such new age pop-psych phenomena as passive/aggressive behaviour, co-dependency, compulsiveness and enabling. It even brings a new insight into the Prince's immediate passion for the sleeping Princess. The energy and debunking spirit recalls earlier classic spoofs such as the Fleischers' *Snow White* and Clampett's *Coal Black and de Sebben Dwarves,* and relocates Snowie to Hollywood to satirise the movie business. The script crackles with sharp wit, and the graphic style has the effect of bright neon colours on black.

Leeds Animation

Experience of womens' discussion groups, the sharing of personal experience, observation, research and analysis, the desire to put such experience to productive use were hallmarks of the growth and development of 70s feminism. It's instructive to consider how this process has worked in relation to women and animation in two quite different cases, which in some ways reflect the changes within feminism over the last two decades.

Of all the independent film workshops established in the early 80s, driven by radical politics and aesthetics, few had as much impact at grass roots level as Leeds Animation Workshop, a womens' collective.

The group of women who made Blind Justice *a quartet of films on women and the law were all products of 70s feminism, but their approach, and the films produced, were very different.*

Leeds Animation, a feminist cooperative was founded in 1976 by Gillian Lacey who got women together to make a campaigning cartoon film about the need for nursery education, made from the point of view of children – hence the title *Who Needs Nurseries? –We Do!* Most of their films use cel animation, in a populist and accessible cartoon style, although more recent films have employed cut-out, collage and live-action. In 1984, they became the only animation group to become a 'franchised workshop' after extensive negotiations between independent filmmakers, funding bodies, the union ACTT, and Channel Four. This gives union dispensation for different rates of pay from those in the mainstream industry for independent and grant-aided filmmakers and provides continuity of employment to production-based, non-profit-distributing workshops employing a minimum of four full-time workers, and which are also involved in distribution, education and exhibition. Trades unions and local authorities also gave support. Leeds has

maintained a non-hierarchical division of labour, unlike the practice of commercial animation studios.

They aim to produce films which explore issues and stimulate discussion in an entertaining, often witty and accessible way, and also advocate positive action. Their cartoon style, with its nod to the tradition of newspaper 'funnies', meant they often succeeded in reaching audiences that wouldn't normally see themselves 'relating' to the issues involved. Rather like watching an animated version of Andy Capp, in which long-suffering spouse Flo wises up and finds alternative employment, demonstrating a common-sense approach to issues such as health and safety in the workplace, local government, unionisation and sexual harassment.

Their films, available also on video, are accompanied by resource packs for users, who include arts and community groups, education, trade unions, and special interest groups.

Risky Business looks at issues around health and safety in the workplace, with a factory worker gradually realising she can make a difference and play a positive role for herself and colleagues. *Council Matters* demystifies the workings of local government, and invites active participation; *Pretend You'll Survive*, an anti-nuclear film, has been widely used in peace campaigns. One of their strongest - and most controversial- films, *Give us a Smile* expresses the reactions of women to the violence, both physical and ideological, with which they are confronted everyday. 'A strong cocktail of live-action, montage of advertising issues and handdrawn animation'.

Out to Lunch graphically demonstrates ways in which men dominate language, monopolise space, and structure women into a subservient role.

The changed political climate of 80s Britain has, inevitably, impacted on sources of funding. However, Leeds Animation are managing to survive: a new film, *All Stressed Out*, on women at work, is due in 1993.

Gillian Lacey reflects…

I worked for many years in commercial animation before moving north and starting the Leeds Animation Workshop. I had made a couple of my own films by then but could no longer find meaning in the world of TV series and adverts. Living in Leeds, it slowly dawned on me that I could use my animation skills in a more political way. The result was a community based group working on a film about the need for more nurseries. The other women involved came from a variety of backgrounds and the film was successfully used in campaign meetings around the country. Encouraged by this we carried on in the same vein.

Our way of working was the product of its time. Job creation trainees came and went. The working class members, who were few, dropped away. One or two men worked with us until the group decided to remain women only. None of the other members had backgrounds in film or animation but we were united by political commitment. The whole thing was a great high. Other workshops were springing up and we were all part of an upsurge in independent filmmaking, energised by our sense of breaking new ground. We believed passionately in the ideals - the opportunities for women, a flat rate wage, no individual credits on the films, a collective work process. I stayed for eight or nine years, working in the back-to-back house that came to be the workshop's studio. It was right in the heart of working class Leeds although the composition of the group never reflected that. Did I sell out? Have my beliefs changed? What went wrong for me with that collective process among women?

As the years went by I wanted to change. I wanted to develop new skills myself, to explore live action film in parallel to animation. I wanted to get away from the community politics belief that we could, and should, do everything ourselves. This belief seemed to have become enshrined in the workshop's unwritten rules. Enabling people creatively is an important activity but it needs to happen at all levels. I was beginning to feel dis-abled, restricted, bound to a formula. I was feeling increasingly that radical ideas deserved radical means to convey them and that for too long we had been smug about our grassroots style. I wanted to see something more imaginative, more original. I did not feel we were able to supply that without widening our experience. My vision of the workshop was to expand the group, to have visiting animators from whom we could learn new skills, to have movement within it, working on individual projects, taking on placements, expanding into live action. The others felt they were not ready for that. They felt that all the necessary skills were there within the group and that animation should remain the focus. So I left.

The group has remained very stable. The work continues to be committed to issues and still embodies the original aims of the workshop - use of a style that is accessible to a wide audience combined with the creation of cartoon women who do not have huge tits and eyelashes. But times have changed.

When the Leeds workshop started there was very little challenging animation being done and as a result there was always an excited audience waiting to see what the next films would be. This is no longer the case. As more animators have taken on issues and the making of meaning in innovative ways the Leeds work has unfortunately been marginalised. Form, when accompanied by content, can now take a more prominent place in the debate again and it is perhaps time to make a critique of the socialist/ feminist imagery used in both animated and live action work in the last few years. A politicised audience is prepared to work hard at a film and a younger or less aware audience is used to reading the complex images of TV ads. Audiences can feel patronised by films that fail to acknowledge their ability to 'read' meaning.

Into our fourth term of Conservative government I am convinced that we need new approaches to old problems. Although there is still an audience for 'propaganda' animation in what has become the Leeds workshop's house style, I think that in opposition we need to keep up, not only with the issues but with the means of conveying them.

The workshop has now changed some of its work processes; but too late for me. My experience with Leeds Animation taught me many things. It was an invigorating time. I miss the support and stimulation that being in a group often provides. I also learnt many things I didn't want to know: that collectives can reduce everything to the lowest common denominator, unacknowledged hierarchies may emerge, equality is difficult to achieve and commonly held political beliefs do not necessarily make for good working partnerships. This critique of collectives is not new and Leeds is not exceptional. My experience simply mirrors that of other people in other places.

Since leaving Leeds Animation I've worked on my own and in other partnerships, with women and with men. Some partnerships are successful, others less so. I am still searching for ways to answer all the questions that I raise myself. I choose to work in less rigid structures with a variety of people. A recent ray of light comes from my work with animation students who, despite limited resources, produce films which explore meaning in ways that are inspiring and original. Maybe the future lies with them.

Blind Justice is a four part series on women and the law, consisting of four individual animated films, each exploring a particular aspect of how the law affects women's lives. *All Men are Created Equal,* (illustrated above) made by Monique Renault, serves as introduction, tracing the origins of western law back to classical Greece, and how misogyny has survived intact through the centuries. *Someone Must be Trusted*, by Gillian Lacey and Christine Roche, is constructed as an opera in three tragic acts, concentrating on the inherent bias of the tribunals and courts of law. Lacey's *Murders Most Foul* relates a real case, in the form of a Victorian melodrama, in which all the dramatic rules are twisted to expose a villain who gets away with it, a murdered wife who gets her own back and a judge who has to eat his words. Marjut Rimminen's *Some Protection* is an exciting new form of creative 'documentary', based on the true story of persistent offender Josie O'Dwyer, with her own voice as commentary. The film shows the devastating effect that detention and imprisonment have on young girls who are sent in 'for their own protection'.

Innovative in its approach to the subject, it was also an exciting new form of collaborative filmmaking between five women.

Gillian Lacey, although somewhat disillusioned by her experiences at Leeds Animation, was keen to find other ways in which women could work together, and extend her own development by working with more experienced animators and women more established in other fields. She contacted Monique Renault, a French born but Holland based animator whose feminist films she had long admired. She had met French Canadian feminist cartoonist Christine Roche, who lives in London, through teaching, and also liked her work.

Roche had recently collaborated with Marjut Rimminen, a Finnish animator based in London with a highly successful commercials studio, on an animated short film version of her cartoon collection *I'm not a Feminist but...* Roche and Rimminen had experienced problems in the film's making, due to the inevitable changes of meaning and emphasis in animating, and literally giving voice to a selection of single cartoon drawings from a structured collection, but they were both keen to explore collaborative processes further.

After Lacey had raised development money from C4, she approached documentary producer Orly Yadin (previously known as Orly Bat Carmel), whose credits include *Power to the Imagination*, and the epic series *The March of Time*, to join the group as producer. Yadin formed Smoothcloud Productions. Apart from dealing with budgets, contracts and liaison with C4, Yadin had to ensure a conceptual overview, and see there was no overlap between films. She was also more directly involved in the production of Renault's film, in Holland, which involved live action shooting for rotoscoping, and the voice over.

The group met several times to discuss general ideas, research findings, and decide who was doing what. They then worked on their films individually, coming back to the group with storyboards which would then be open to criticism and suggestions. Yet the actual creative work was left to each individual, something which prevented 'death by democratic discussion' and the need for absolute consensus which for many dispirited women came to represent the experience of women's discussion groups. As Roche has commented, 'the creative process needs sometimes to proceed by intuition'.

Orly comments on the differences between the 70s and the 80s as that of 'a group of women trying to maintain our ideals, a political intent in terms of cooperation but now we were also trying to ensure people got paid the proper rate for their work; and making films for television means a much more tightly controlled production process.' There were a lot of difficulties...but at the end of the day the artists involved are still friends, and still talking.

Although Smoothcloud was established with the intention of keeping the original group together, Lacey's retirement from direct animation making (partly due to RSI), and others wishing to pursue different directions made this impossible. However, Yadin has continued working on various live action projects with Lacey, and they both hope to produce young, emerging talents in the animation field. She also produced *The Stain*, a further experiment in collaboration between Roche and Rimminen (discussed further below).

Since Roche was not an experienced animator, she and Lacey co-directed on *Someone Must be Trusted*,

The Stain

with Christine doing storyboard, character and background design and some key drawings, and Lacey animating. Although part of the process was facilitated by their living a couple of streets apart, Lacey left for some time to go to Australia where she made most of her film: 'In retrospect, I feel we could have collaborated more closely. I could have been more open, and more supportive.'

Christine comments on the differences in approach between herself, as graphic artist and illustrator, and that of animators. 'For me, background and character design is quick - often animators find it more difficult. For a cartoonist, line in character is very important; for an animator, it's the movement.'

Marjut Rimminen came across her subject through her researches into women and criminology, in which she was assisted by animator Gail Pierce. When she met Josie, she felt they got on immediately. 'As an animator, I function best in my room, in a kind of solitary confinement. When Josie says the only escape from horrible reality was to go inside her head, I understood that very well.' After meeting Josie several times, she worked for over a year, listening to hours of taped conversations. 'It was like I needed a period of solitary confinement with this voice of hers, which touched me deeply. Although I had to select and cut down for the voice-over, it seemed she had everything so concisely expressed already, in the sentences she spoke'. The idea of visualising prison as home, and the outside world as a fairground to which Josie makes excursions, with a corresponding distinction in colour and technique (full cel and brilliant colour for the latter, monochromatic and paper for the former) was established fairly early on, the commentary was reworked during the production process.

Some Protection

As is the case with Suzan Pitt's *Asparagus*, it's rare to meet someone who's seen *The Stain* who hasn't been, quite simply, knocked out by it. Like *Asparagus*, it is also equally difficult to describe. This is precisely because its use of animation to convey complex ideas through visual images and movement makes any synopsis somewhat misleading. It's worth stressing the roller-coaster energy and tight construction, brilliant editing, unusual camera angles and exhilarating musical score which all drive the narrative along.

The film was 'inspired' by a news report of octagenarian twins who shot themselves after a violent family feud over a tiny gravy stain on a tablecloth. However, this was merely the starting point for a dark fantasia on the family, and the invention of a family drama behind the suicide.

The original treatment stated the form would 'embrace fairytale and fantasy, gothic, comedy and thriller and whatever other genre' found 'suitable for the chosen tale.' Lesley Sharman, reviewing the film, points out that 'Fairy tales frequently explore the horrors inside the domestic cupboard, often crammed full of evil mothers, traitorous fathers, and twisted siblings. In the old days, the apparatus of magical settings and props helped distance the reader from seeing how close the stories were to everyday life, as did later glosses which scape-goated step-parents and step-siblings.'

'Once upon a time…a beautiful lady and a rich gentleman lived by the sea', a slightly ironic female voice intones as we see a castle perched atop a small island, surrounded by sea. We are told of games the husband taught her over fluid, drawn animation scenes of pursuit, along corridors in the labyrinthine house, of capture, of clothing being scattered. 'It was such a happy family they didn't need anyone else.' A baby girl is born, followed by twin boys. The three of them play games of pursuit too. A new baby girl arrives. 'What the mother got best at was hiding,' we hear… The parents disappear - literally, in the mother's case, through a wall in a room. Father? 'Well', as the voice-over says archly 'we won't go into that.' As for the baby, over scenes of her delight at the house full of games, 'sometimes the sister wondered if she wasn't too lovely for this world.' The baby teeters in her high chair at the top of the stairs, tumbles down.

'Once upon a time…' opens the second part, over a model set of a dining room in a house on an island, whose puppet inhabitants are identified as 'big sister, twin brothers and a baby who lived in a house by the sea.' The baby is in fact a crabby teenage girl, wheelchair bound, who 'retreats into fantasy which is expressed as drawn animation. The older sister obsessively cleans the house, always vainly striving to wash out a stain made by the 'baby' which will never come out, a 'stain' whose full meaning is elucidated only at the end. Meanwhile, the twins work in the City and indulge their secret perversions on the sly... As the musical soundtrack swells to an operatic crescendo [Verdi] everyone finally snaps and someone 'gives the game away', revealing the incestuous secret secret which has crippled all their lives.' (LS)

The puppet animation is intercut with drawn sequences, and pixillated live action and stills in a brilliant and rapid montage, each of which carries narrative hints, but also builds up an extended interrogation of the family. Sibling rivalry, and the fantasy of the self-contained family unit, able to provide its members with all they need, the romance of sexual exclusivity, are all conjugated to powerful effect with notions of male omnipotence, whether through the legacy of Victorian patriarchal attitudes, the male world of work or abuse of power, sexual or military. The price to be paid, of course, is repression, whether expressed through the literal retreat by the mother, the twins' fetishism, or the sister's obsessive displacement activity.

Yet all of this is achieved visually, and the arguments made are through imaginative connections. It's instructive to discover, via Roche's notebook for the film, how these ideas were developed, through sketches and word associations as well as notes. They reveal ideas taking shape, changing, rather than being pre-determined and then rigidly applied to a narrative.

On repeated viewings, the structural parallels between the two sections become clear, and the almost subliminal effect of some of the montages richly rewards close analysis. As the treatment argued, 'With animation one can give presence and meaning to concepts like: conscious/unconscious; id/ego/superego; reality/phantasy; what is the relationship between the inside and the outside; as well as express feelings, and illustrate the dynamics of relationships. We can see the baby in the family remain the baby, even though he/she might be 60 years old.

Animation provides this film with a unique tool to work on the transformations of one scenario into another, according to who tells the tale and where in time the tale is told. We want to push the limits of animated filmmaking further.'

'Like Greek tragedy, even though the outcome is known from the newspaper clipping which is shown at the start of the film, nothing prepares the audience for the inevitable climax which ensues, the sense of terror augmented by the sudden jump cuts between the drawn and the three-dimensional, which the score underpins beautifully.' (LS)

Christine Roche and Marjut Rimminen had wanted for some time to make a film about the family as an institution. They spent many hours in conversation working through various ideas, and their own personal histories. Almost simultaneously they came across a news item that sparked their imaginations. Orly Yadin agreed to produce, as she likes to alternate multi-part archivally-based documentaries with short animation films, which are much more intensive and proportionally more time consuming as productions. She pinpoints the differences between her documentary work and animation production: 'So much happens inside the animators' heads, which can only be articulated in drawings'. She has learned when she is needed, when not, and sees her primary role as ensuring her work is largely invisible and that the filmmakers' ambitions are fulfilled. Although the production period was very extended, the relationship with C4 was smooth. 'Their money people know what they're talking about, which makes things easier. Once they've seen and approved the storyboard and music (which they're given on cassette) they ask for monthly cost and progress reports, then see it at roughcut. At that point they can make suggestions, but they were quite happy with what they saw. The film actually came in under budget, and has had some overseas sales as well as enormous demand on the festival circuit.

Once C4 had provided some development money, Roche and Rimminen began to work through their ideas for the film. They used advisors in the research period, in particular a psychotherapist who specialised in the study of twins - and was also mother to twins herself. The first question she asked was 'Why does this story interest you so much?' She also gave them useful reading lists.

Christine Roche had illustrated *Women's History of Sex* by novelist and literary critic Harriet Gilbert, and she was asked to write a script to their storyboard. This was then edited, and when it came to recording, Gilbert came into the studio to work with the actress, who she had suggested and kept in mind whilst writing, on the reading.

'Originally we intended to use the fact that Christine and I had had such different drawing styles to explore the characters' different subjectivities' says Rimminen, 'but because Christine was designing all the characters, I found myself blocked.' The idea of using 3-D (model and puppet animation) for the 'reality' sequences, with drawings as the subjective or fantasies of individual characters was intriguing and although she had never worked with 3-D, with characteristic daring and determination that's what she did. In the course of the film, the distinctions became less absolute, but the combination is quite stunning.

Roche: 'I pushed for us to use more techniques, I was interested in the challenge and the potential of a collage effect. As a visual artist that gives you more leeway, to add extra things, emphasise certain objects. We wanted it to be quite theatrical, and structured it around the three sittings at table…a t the shooting stage we decided to make it morning, noon and evening, so there could be more play with the lighting.

'As a cartoonist, I'm in a sense more used to the jumpy single frame effect, whilst Marjut, as the animator has to keep continuity in mind.'

Of course, as Roche remarks, collaboration means working through compromise. Rimminen, as an animator, is used to 'total control. And to give it to somebody else, of course, it's difficult. But it's possible…if you can do it, through trust, understanding, friendship. You can make more of yourself.'

A curious change in their perceptions of how they related to the characters came about as the film was made. Roche: 'Because of the way Marjut felt towards the younger sister and the way she animated her being,

she started having a persona which I didn't think of as the way Marjut saw her. So I started resenting this child as being totally manipulative, awful and then I started identifying with the older sister who originally I didn't like very much. Then I thought, hang on, there's something behind this woman who goes round hating the cleaning and things she's doing. And she ends up alone in the house, totally mad. I felt warmer towards her, and that was a surprise'. For Marjut, 'it's not so much a case of manipulation as of survival. It was survival in my mind. The only way for her.'

They each have quite different temperaments as artists, and this reflects on the way they relate to their work.

Marjut: 'When I was a little girl I loved to dance and skate. I thought I was like a fairy, and could skate like a snowflake, but of course in reality I was not very nimble… one of the horrible moments in life was when I was dismissed from skating school because I was bad at skating. As an animator, it is such joy to make my drawings dance like I want them to.'

She likes to maintain a balance between commercial work and her own films, citing not only standard of life for herself and her family, the opportunity to develop her techniques, but also the time and total involvement a film demands. 'For that fifteen months of production I had total tunnel vision.' She recalls one scene she had spent all day working on, which was working out beautifully, and the joy and absorption she felt. She continued late into the evening. 'I had completely forgotten it was my birthday and that my husband and son had arranged a celebration.'

As a visual artist normally working in cartoons or illustration, Roche has a different take on the animation process. 'I don't like animation that is laboured, in the sense that it takes a long time. I like a new challenge, try another technique, another way. Animation is so boring… you design a character then half way through, which is about a year later, you want to change it..but you can't, as by now the in-betweeners are at work'. I think animation should be like a gestured drawing, should be saying something absurd or anarchic, be economic.I think now I would only make an animation if it was 30 seconds..at the most five minutes.

I've often been asked to do a regular comic strip, with recurring characters, but I don't like the idea of being held down. But then I'm never pleased with what I do. Never. I just want on to the next thing. If I work with someone else I can be very demanding because of that, as I'm so critical. I'm the type who doesn't want to crack open the champagne when everyone else is celebrating (laughs). On my own, I don't have that problem.

Talking with Caroline Leaf

by Talia Schenkel at Ottowa '76

Since Caroline Leaf's first film, Sand or Peter and the Wolf, *made at Harvard University's Carpenter Center in 1968 when she was twenty-two, her films have consistently been acclaimed wherever they have been shown. Her films have the conviction and apparent simplicity of great art. Using the simplest of materials - sometimes only a handful of beach sand - she manages to make us feel deeply for her evanescent creatures. With her uncanny sense of movement and timing and her refreshing unexpected transitions, she never fails to astonish her audience. But perhaps more than anything, her compassionate sensitivity to the lyricism and a humanity which one finds all too rarely in animation today. Her talent for infusing her roughly drawn characters with warmth is extraordinary. While the history of the animated film has largely been a history of either comic or tragic films, Leaf's films are among the rare exceptions. They succeed in combining humour and pathos. And she does so in a way that can be appreciated by five-year olds as well as by those far beyond fifty, because her films touch the heart.*

Lamb to Leaf:

I recall how sceptical of animation you were at first. You seemed to hover around the edges of the class, uncertain of this strange and unfamiliar medium. You would say in frustration 'Oh but I'm hopeless! I really can't draw at all!' Then, one day, I'd set an assignment. The class was asked to bring in objects or materials that could be animated on a light-box as silhouette images. Everyone found interesting things, but you brought in something quite special: a bag filled with beach sand. As you poured sand into out onto the glass and began shaping characters with it, there was born a new and original animation technique. From the first few motion tests it was obvious that you'd found your medium.

Do you remember the day when Norman McLaren visited the class? He figuratively jumped out of his socks... He stood there for the longest time, letting the sand run between his fingers, shaping forms with it and saying over and over: 'Oh Caroline, this is wonderful! In all my years of animation, I've never thought of this! He was like a kid in a sandbox. In your first film, *Peter and the Wolf*, the motion of the sand gave the film and the film's characters a flowing, metamorphic quality that was both narrative and dreamlike. You had invented the medium to suit yourself and from that time on you've kept on making films, discovering new techniques and delighting us all. (From Asifa Canada Bulletin, January 1992)

Did you always know that you wanted to do something related to film or art?
No, I didn't know what I would be. I was just an undergraduate at Radcliffe, and I just happened into animation. I think there were two film courses offered; one was documentary and the other was animation, and I just fell into animation.

Had you drawn before?
No. I thought that I didn't know how to draw, and Derek Lamb's class in animation was good for me, because movement was important and not the drawing. His idea was that anyone could animate by making things move. So we were moving key-chains and shaving cream and pencils and quarters and sand - a lot of sand. And because it's a silhouette image that sand makes, it didn't seem like drawing to me, so I thought I could do it. Also because the drawings disappear, because it's done under the camera, so nothing is left as a record of what you've drawn, that was also very reassuring to me. And it lasted for only a twelfth or a twenty-fourth of a second. It felt OK to me. I worked on a little 16mm army surplus Kodak camera with cassettes, and I made *Sand or Peter and the Wolf* there during my last year in 1968; it took me six months to make.

Did you think you were the first to animate sand?
I thought so, but last year, I met Ernest Ansorge in Switzerland. He has been using sand for years. I saw a film of his and I didn't know it was sand. I thought it was just ink until he told me; it didn't look like my stuff.

What did you do after Sand or Peter and the Wolf?
I didn't know what to do with myself after I graduated, and I went off to Italy and lived in Rome for a year. I was learning to draw and learning Italian. Then I got a fellowship at Harvard and came back and made a film called *Orfeo*. It was done on glass, the same sort of thing as in *The Street* actually, but it's somewhat embarrassingly badly drawn. It just doesn't look like the same sort of thing at all, and it was just black and white. Then I had my 'creative freelancing'. I worked in my apartment in Cambridge and made a film for a company in St Louis called *How Beaver Stole Fire*. It was based on an Indian legend and done with sand, but the company wanted colour added to it, and I had a big hassle with them, because they changed the picture after I sent them the negative. They did their own things to it, and I just didn't want anything more to do with it.

That was until 1972; I was getting a little lonely working in my apartment, so that's when I contacted the Canadian

National Film Board, and it took a while but eventually I ended up there. In the spring of 1972, I came up to the Board. I worked for the French Animation Department first, because they had a series of six Eskimo legends to make and they thought my sand technique would fit into that, and I agreed to work on it. That was really nice to work on because I got to go to the Arctic: the idea was to have the Eskimos involved as much as possible with the making of the film. Later the Film Board set up a workshop in the Arctic to actually have the Eskimos make films, but in those days that didn't exist.

What was the actual working relationship like? How did you decide whom to work with?
I had looked at a lot of Eskimo art to choose which artist I would like to work with, and I really liked the designs of Nanogak, of Holman Island in the western Arctic. But I was looking at work that she had a done a couple of years before, and when I got up there, she was making figures with lots of little bubbly lines and all the feathers clearly drawn. She had gotten much more designy and was doing things I could not really animate, so I manipulated her a little bit to get things I could animate. I explained sand to her and told her to try and make things as simple as possible. And she made creatures that I would have made myself. She didn't speak English, and I stayed at a French-Catholic mission; the missionary was the interpreter. It was really interesting. Nanogak, who was about 45, had a tape recorder, and I'd go to see her each morning and afternoon, and we'd discuss what she had done. But she couldn't take notes, so she would talk into the tape recorder to to tell herself what she might do. It was like skipping the whole literate stage of civilization and going right into tape recorders…

The Owl Who Married The Goose

How long did the film take to make?
It took me a long time to make that - maybe a year and a half. I had a lot of problems. I didn't know who the audience was and I thought if the audience is to be Eskimos, and I'm not an Eskimo, you know – some of their reactions were so strange to me. I knew I couldn't handle the animals the way they would, because I tend to make them into people. And that's why the ending seems sad, because you have some emotional feeling for the animals. On the other hand, the Eskimos don't put emotion like that into the animals at all; I think that's why they think the owl is funny, not sad…

Did you work on The Street *next?*
Yes. There was money in an educational fund to make films connected with Canadian literature, and it was rather nice that the Film Board used the money to let

Owl Who Married a Goose, 1974.
An owl falls in love with a goose, violating the natural code of species separation. The owl has problems adapting to his parental role - not knowing how to raise goslings, needing to learn how to swim and forage for food. When the owl tries to accompany his family on the migratory flight south, his exhaustion and lack of experience result in death.
Though most viewers find the story tragic in its conclusions, Eskimo audiences, who do not anthropomorphise wildlife, find the result of the owl's fatal slip in judgement very humorous -after all, owls should know better. MOMA.

Caroline Leaf

many young animators come and make short films.

What made you choose Mordecai Richler's story to animate?
I liked many stories that I just couldn't imagine animating. Somehow Richler's characters had a kind of energy that seemed to work and I wanted to do it.

Did you consider doing it in sand first?
No. I knew I wanted to do something different. I wanted to do things with colour, to develop characters, to have line drawings - all things I hadn't done before. Most of all, I wanted to animate people. I did a lot of experimenting and ended up using waterbase tempera colours on milk glass with some oil added, to keep the paint from drying. It was like finger painting. And I worked quite small also, so that every little bit of paint moving has more energy when it's blown up on a large screen. And there's less paint to push around, so it goes faster. You push it around with your fingers - no brushes. Fingers are good tools. I wanted something that would be waterbased, so that it would be easy to wipe up with cloth.

How long did you work on The Street?
The same amount of time as on *The Owl Who Married The Goose* – a year and a half.

How did you do the sound track?
The story is much, much longer than those ten minutes. In spoken time it might have been thirty minutes or something; there were a a lot of details in the text that I took out. I went around with a tape recorder to theatres in Montreal and got names through other people and asked people about kids. I had the story and, in the early days, I thought I had to follow the story very closely, so they were given lines, but I didn't know how to animate all of the scenes before I started the film, but as I'd go along, I'd get ideas.

Your transitions between scenes are incredible.
Well, I like doing those, but I think it's important to do them with some purpose, so that it's not just wild turning for the sake of turning. The purpose would be to get to the next thing. Maybe I was just enjoying myself making those turns, but also you could think maybe it was what people would actually see if they were out there. I could have made cuts, but I don't make very many cuts.

How did you get the timing on the sound track?
That came as I was animating out of my feeling of what should be the timing. I made the pauses. I recorded all the

The Street

A poignant film adaptation of Mordecai Richler's book. In an unusual technique involving the use of soft, simple washes of watercolour and ink, she paints directly on the glass stage of the animation camera. Leaf interprets the reactions of a young boy in a poor Jewish family to a dying grandmother, capturing his feelings and distilling them into a harsh but honest reality. *The Street* is an imaginative and direct statement about how families respond to aging and death. It is also a virtuoso achievement in the development of a distinctive animation style.

voices and then I put them together with my own sense of timing. I realized that the film gets better when the visuals are used without the words, as much as possible. So there were more and more pauses as I deleted things I thought I didn't need. I tried very, very hard to get lip sync; I broke down my track frame by frame and then made the lips go up and down. But it looked so absurd to see my sloppy characters with this absolutely energetic lip movement, so instead, I just made them sort of open and close their mouths, and I think that works better.

Do you find that most of your ideas occur to you as you are working, under the camera?

Well, I have an overall idea. I mean I can almost see it in my head as I go along, what a sequence is that I'm working on. But little things can happen all the time, which is what keeps it interesting, I guess. On my first film I started somewhere in the middle and built out from that in either direction. And what had already happened sort of dictated what was going to come. By the end of working on a film I'm always feeling very restricted, because there's no leeway; it's all decided what the timing should be throughout. The last slug I put in sort of feels very tight, and I get very irritated and cross that I just have to mechanically turn it out to get it over with. The decisions are all made already.

How do you decide about your timing?

People ask me that, and I don't know how to answer, because I don't think about it too much. I sit at my animation table, and I'm acting; I look in the mirror and see what something looks like. Or... I imagine, for instance, how it would look if someone's puzzled and how long it is going to take. I don't know how to make things walk very easily... So what I would do is to walk back and forth in my room and see what it felt like. It's more what it feels like than what it looks like.

Do you use any other tools to work with the sand, besides your fingers and the pipe-cleaner?

Well, I'm just finishing another sand film, based on Kafka's *Metamorphosis* and I started playing with textures. I used a stamp to get textures, and combs and forks and things - and my fingers in different sorts of ways. Mostly my fingers. Fingers are good tools...

What do you want to do in the future?

I want to make more films. It's my life. And I want always to do different kinds of films. I'd like to collaborate with people, which will help me, because I've always worked by myself...

There are thirteen or fourteen women animators at the Film Board. What do you think are the reasons that none of them is working on cels?

I've been talking with Derek Lamb about this, and I basically agree with his ideas which are that women aren't usually very interested in newspaper-type cartoons. And that's sort of how animation came out – out of a lot of that kind of material. That's sort of a man's world... There were some films at the International Animation Festival that are very much like comic strips to me. And it's because there's often an idea thing and not a feeling thing, like a joke maybe. But I think that all the women who are now working in animation are all about my age, and most of them come out of universities. If women come out of that kind of place, that's how they get into animation, and that's why they're using different techniques, because people don't go to college to get into production lines - into cel animation workshop situations. When I was a student, I would never have wanted to be anybody's inker or painter. Somehow, I took an animation class, and I wanted to do my own animation. Probably a lot of the young men animators also are not working with cels now.

Talking with Caroline Leaf was first published in *Film Library Quarterly*, 1977; these extracts are reprinted in shortened form by kind permission of the author (formerly known as Thelma Schenkel). See ß.

The Metamorphosis of Mr. Samsa

Leaf's adaptation of Franz Kafka's short story about a man who wakes one morning to discover he has become a giant insect. Begun with a grant from the American Film Institute and finished at the NFB. Animated sand on glass, black and white. Uncomplicated and unadorned movements describe and define the characters: the skilful, effortless transitions, the flowing from scene to scene and angle to angle are superbly enhanced by a haunting, frugal use of sound. 'Far from being a horror film, rather a screen vision of the story on modern man's existential anxiety.' Gianalberto Bendazzi.

All about Leaf

From a meditation by leading American independent animator George Griffin.

The Film Board might be her tree/provider but of course it wouldn't survive without her photosynthetic properties which are at the very heart of our craft, the manipulation of light and shadow to create artificial time and space. Caroline's universe is of shapes, not lines, formed directly by her hand, then in the next frame destroyed. The camera records a journey of continuously transforming material which always seems to remain constant: the technique is astounding, yet transparent. At the end of her procession she, and we, are left with memories and dreams, but no stack of thousands of cels to stuff in archives. One could speak here of economy of means but I would rather link it to the more elemental sensibilities of potters, weavers, farmers and cooks.

The anti-nature of smudges, streaks, and smears is as provisional and transitory as the 'real' nature of our waking life. It is as if she took McLaren literally, letting us experience those moments between frames, when minute shifts and strokes coax inert masses into their next inexorable position. Getting from A to B, simple as that. But only a Leaf can show us how beautiful, astonishing, awkward this choreography can be: a pooped owl caught up in a migratory charade, a beetle creeping, peering out from under a bed, a street scene depicted as a young boy's subjective blurred stream of images.

And don't forget the thread. While many of us sought refuge in the nuts and bolts of animation for its own sake, Caroline never lost faith in the healing qualities of story-telling. Her tales have a mythic timelessness, like the seasons, and dare to present characters ennobled by their very ordinariness. This is a tall order for cartooning, which has so often and successfuly relied on the reductivist pursuits of comedy. Leaf uses the grotesque glance, the clumsy gait, the blobby countenance to draw us into her circle of riddles where animals and outcasts lead lives of devastating poignance.

Then again, leaves do fall, provide mulch, and nourish further growth, only to be reborn in the spring. She's always spooking me with how she's going to chuck it all and only do live-action documentaries, work with a big crew and collaborate, go off and paint for a year. (Animation is a lonely pursuit and one never knows who is honestly responding and if it really matters.) And yet these tangents have all seemed to fortify her primary voice, given it more depth, if that were possible. Yes, the paintings are very cinematic and contain exciting potential

A drawing by Caroline on a winter Sunday morning: Grant Heisler, Bob Pot and Roger Liboiron.

for simultaneity, a kind of temporal cubism. But my fervent hope is that while they stand alone they might also become studies for future film work. Composting has its limits.

Two Sisters strikes me, after one viewing, as a real breakthrough, combining as it does a virtuosity of experimental technique with the inner voice of an artist digging frightfully deep to question the very validity of her own art. It teaches us again how to draw in time.

The Interview

In this film, made in 1979, Caroline Leaf and another National Film Board animator, Veronika Soul interview one another and relate the resulting perceptions through their respective animation techniques. This fresh, original and introspective approach exposes the essential isolation of the artist in both professional and personal life.

'I had begun to feel that I'd exhausted myself. I'd always thought I could work just from myself, from what I had inside me, make things move by myself. But finally I got rather fed up with my interior world' said Leaf to Jacqueline Levitin, who describes the film as 'a first step outside the enclosed world of animation… Caroline's autocritique… gives us an image of herself sitting at her animation table, surrounded by animals drawn from her imagination, absorbed in her work as though unconscious of their presence. This picture seduces us by its ironic humour and its fantasy. But, for Caroline, it's a statement of her isolation. Some people felt embarassed by Caroline's very lack of embarassment in her self-exposure in the film, but it was her way of taking stock of herself and going beyond the character delivered to the screen.'

from *Femmes et cinéma québecois*, see ß.

The following is excerpted from an interview with the filmmakers by Grant Munro, see ß.

VS: We were trying to do a new form of documentary in which the technique would indicate the personality. Everything we did, any kind of altered motion, the colours of the person, whatever we showed on the screen would tell something about the person you'd never know if you followed them with a live-action camera.

It was Caroline's idea - she was on her way to the airport, leaving Montreal for an indefinite period of time and we were saying goodbye on the phone. She got this wonderful idea to make a movie together.

We couldn't think of what structure it would have because my films don't have any structure and Caroline's films are very structured. It wouldn't work if we started out very confused which is how I normally work.

CL: We recorded hours of ourselves talking and then condensed it down.

VS: The first tapes we did when we found out we didn't know very much about one another. We talked for about thirteen hours and made a list of questions back and forth to try to get why we felt the way we did or why we were who we were. It was very revealing for me. Caroline was such a different person compared to what I thought.

It's very funny, the film was only in the word-stage for many months. We just talked and wrote on cards. As we got into it more we realized that the words didn't mean the same things at all to us. We had visualized things so differently and after long, long sessions on one card, it became clear how completely opposite we were. Even now I think as we visualize, it's always going to be different for each of us.

On the various techniques used, which included xeroxes and still photographs… It's a lot of stuff that neither of us have ever done before. We were very interested in using blurs in stills. Caroline is represented by a lot of 35mm stills that are all blurred in motion, so while there's a single image held on the screen in which nothing is moving, the blurs are incredibly frantic. There's much more tension and anxiety and motion in that still than there would be if we shot her live action because Caroline appears very calm and focused.

VS: We're exact opposites all through the film and we're trying to do that not just on the track but also visually.

CL: We've had criticism from the few people we've shown it to because we don't seem to connect with anybody else.

VS: I think that's true. Both of us are used to working under very isolated circumstances and if there is any interaction it's just going to be between us as a result of the film but people feel it's such an exclusive friendship. Everybody said it's going to look like a women's film not only because we look like lesbians but because there are no people, no people in our lives. It's just us and we don't appear to even want anybody or need anybody or miss anybody. There are many days like that where it's just us and for months all we did was just be together. Very strange.

Two Sisters

Caroline Leaf talks about the making of the film…

It had been ten years since I had done animation. I knew that I wanted to work in different techniques and not be tied to a camera. Film is a long strip and the work looks all organised unlike paper which is here, there and everywhere. Scratching on film kept things clear for me. It seemed like the minimum of material that kept me close to the film itself was ideal. Working under the camera was pretty close to that. Scratching on film would be really the pure idea if it could be directly projected the way Pierre Hebert's works are. But, because of the rather complicated psychological and dramatic story that I was telling in *Two Sisters*, I couldn't work with such small frames like Pierre does because I needed to make more complicated images. That is why I thought of 70mm.

Before I started to scratch, I did a very detailed storyboard as a way of getting used to the graphic style I would be working with, but also to try to visualise the story. And then I got into quite an uncomfortable situation because it was okay to tell the story on the board, but it didn't mean that once it was all animated it would work on the editing bench as a film.

Because I could control the pencil on the paper very well I was lost when I started scratching on the film for I couldn't get as much detail. It took me a while to find out that scratching on film is not the same as drawing on paper. On the Steenbeck, the animated scenes didn't work very well. I had followed the drawings quite carefully, because I thought I would save time in a way and in fact I had to rewrite the story and change the ending, which in turn changed the beginning. So I would do little drawings to familiarise myself with a scene, but I didn't pay much attention to them as I scratched because you could only hit on the final result once if you are trying to duplicate something. You have to look back and forth and you can't concentrate on what you are doing.

I spent a year and a half scratching the equivalent of 13 to 14 minutes of film. At 12 drawings per second, it gives approximately 7,200 drawings. As for the colours, if I scratch a strip of colour film and scratch just a little bit, the red emulsion comes off and you get the green, and if I scratch more I get to yellow and when I scratch all the way down, it is white, As for the blue, I used blue film.

When I decided to do an animation film again, I took a couple of themes from an unfinished feature length script that were interesting to me. One was the idea of a very enclosed little world that gets thrown out of balance when someone from outside enters. Another was the idea of power and manipulation. A couple of people helped

Two Sisters

A man swims across the sea, and a caption announces 'There are islands in the wide blue sea where people hide away.' Inside a house, the sounds of two women, Marie and Viola Gé, humming and sighing. Viola is working at a typewriter; Marie brings coffee, unlocks a drawer and brings out a mirror. The sisters deliberate but Viola's condition is pronounced to be no better. The man comes ashore and bursts into the darkened house; he tells Viola he has read everything she has written and asks her to inscribe one of her books.

Marie is furious about the effect of Viola's books on their lives, and pushes Viola roughly into the light, revealing her facial disfigurement. While Marie continues to remonstrate, Viola goes outside and sighs with rapture at the new sensations of sun, space and air: she writes in the man's book 'To a stranger who sees me in sunlight.' The man leaves and Viola finds Marie has locked her out. When they face each other again, they realise everything has changed; amid mutual declarations of love, Viola returns to her typewriter.

The opening sequence is in dazzling colour, but over the gentle outdoor scenes a note of melancholy is introduced by a recurring musical theme, which heralds the closeted shadowy world of Marie and Viola Gé. The relationship between the two women is complex: Marie is both her sister's jailer and protector, the feelings betwen them a mixture of anger and defiance, pain and fear, admiration and tenderness.

Leaf's vision is impossibly romantic - that the good vbright world outside can illuminate and cure our inner darkness - but it is persuasively understated. Within eleven minutes *Two Sisters* conveys more emotional depth than many full-length feature films. From a review by Jill McGreal in *Sight & Sound*

me with the script at different stages when I found it difficult.

The idea of a repelling individual who has a very sensitive soul had already attracted me to do *The Metamorphosis of Mr. Samsa*. I think that everyone goes by how people look much of the time when there is a lot more inside. I feel it is a tragedy if someone is really deformed because that is not how they are inside, but it is hard to approach someone who repels you.

From an interview with Denyse Therrien, *Perforations*, April 1991, ß.

American Independents

By the mid 70s there was a flourishing independent animation scene in the US, in comparison to Britain, which began to make an impact at international film festivals. It was also notable for the emergence of a number of women animators with an impressive rate of output and range of different voices.

The impact of the women's movement clearly had something to do with this, in creating an encouraging climate and influencing, to some degree at least, the availability of funding at national and state level, as well as creating an audience for the films themselves. Animation, with its ability to play around the parameters of fine art on the one hand, and accessible 'cartoons' on the other, seemed to present new opportunities for exploring issues (particularly gender stereotyping and sexist imagery) as well as offering a potentially unlimited field for self-expression. The effect of the 'sexual revolution' of the 60s also could be seen in the way women were able, in animation far more than in live-action, to deal with sexuality, and its representation, from a female point of view, e.g. some of the films by Suzan Pitt, Mary Beams, Lisa Crafts.

Suzan Pitt, Kathy Rose, Sally Cruikshank, Jane Aaron, and Mary Beams are discussed in the following section. Other animators who have made an impact in the last decade include Christine Panushka, Joanna Priestley, Amy Kravitz, Stephanie Maxwell, Deanna Morse, Maureen Selwood, Emily Hubley. African American animators have also started to emerge - such as Eloise Philpot-Brown, and Chenzira Ayoka and Saundra Sharpe, who both work mainly in live-action, but have made animation films. all of whom, as well as those mentioned below, are featured in more detail in the A - Z section.

Maureen Selwood's Odalisque

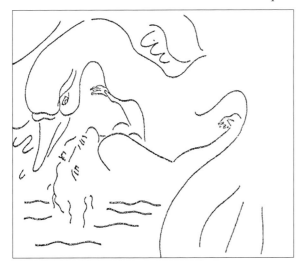

To state the obvious, the United States is a vast country, and therefore opportunities, in terms of production and distribution (i.e. getting films seen), are that much greater. Calculating the proportional difference in relation to other countries seems a pointless task. There are, however, some aspects of the American scene which are quite different, to that in the UK.

The level of film criticism, and indeed of film reviewing, is simply far higher in the US. And there is far more of it, in both academic and newspaper and magazine publishing. In the UK, it is extremely difficult to get weekly film reviewers to watch animation, never mind write about it. But in the US, animation films and animators have been written about in fim journals such as *Film Library Quarterly*, *Wide Angle*, *Sightlines*, *American Film*, *Film Comment*, to name just a few. Not all of these magazines have lasted, but others have sprung up, including *Animation* and *Animato*. *L.A. Weekly,* and New York's *Village Voice* in particular, have fairly consistently covered independent animation.

Although animation is very much the poor relation of academic film studies on both sides of the Atlantic, over the last decade there has been far more serious study of animation in the US, and a Society for Animation Studies, though international in membership, was created three years ago through American initiative, although its concerns are, not unnaturally, largely around American animation and its history.

Although in both countries there are a range of opportunities to study animation, it's striking how many American universities, as well as art colleges, offer courses. Equally striking is how many practising animators are also teaching at academic institutions - unlike the situation in Britain, where animators tend to teach part-time, and where art colleges are rarely seen as having the prestige of the university network (although this has begun to change recently). And, as is well known, teaching is far better paid in the US.

Cal Arts, as the California Institute for the Arts is known, has built a reputation for its teaching, under Jules Engel's inspired, and inspiring, direction. Rhode Island School of Art and Design, the School of the Art Institute of Chicago, and, more recently, Rochester Institute of Technology, are also institutions whose names recur when talking to American animators, as centres of good teaching and encouraging of animation as an art form.

Suzan Pitt has just finished a five year stint as Associate Professor at Harvard's Carpenter Center for the Visual Arts (where Caroline Leaf, as a student, discovered her gift for animation), in order to finish the film she has been working on for the last two years. Yvonne

Andersen, for over twenty years a major force in promoting access to animation for children, can point to several ex-students who have gone on to become teachers as well as filmmakers. One notable example is Amy Kravitz, who started animating when she was eleven years old, at Andersen's Massatchusetts Yellow Ball Workshop, and is now Associate Professor of Film/Video at Rhode Island School of Design. Her work there has prompted praise for its innovative approach - and the course at Rhode Island is quite unusual in that it insists students actually produce finished films to complete their degree. For many animators, teaching isn't simply a secure living that allows them to make their own films, but a process that feeds back into their own work. Deanna Morse, for example, after making a series of films that were visual explorations, followed by films for children, then 'explored regional themes and memory (e.g. *Charleston Home Movie*), based on my life and work as a filmmaker-in-the-schools in the South…' Teaching at the South Carolina School for the Deaf and the Blind has also led her to incorporate American Sign language, as visual symbols, into her latest work-in-progress.

There also seems to be a lot more networking amongst American animators: regular newsletters from regional 'chapters' of ASIFA (the international animation organisation) contain news and views on what's going on in both the commercial and independent sectors: production opportunities, screenings, reviews of films and books. (The networking aspect seems very American - cf the Apple MacIntosh culture that has developed in the 80s). This work is done by animators and enthusiasts, who are also often active in organising screenings of work. Joanna Priestley and Stephanie Maxwell, for example, have curated film programmes that have shown across the US, and in Maxwell's case, in Europe too.

Joanna Priestley's Voices

Priestley is based in Portland, Oregon, which is often cited as having a strong and suppportive animation community. The success of Will Vinton's claymation studio there, and a well-established tradition of film and animation teaching, have been contributing factors. Cecile Starr has also pointed out that 'the South Carolina Arts Commission, Sinking Creek Film Celebration and the Alabama Film/Video Co-op have helped set an atmosphere in which independent women animators have gained some recognition in the South.'

The US has a long and rich tradition of avant-garde, or experimental filmmaking, which has sometimes incorporated animation techniques. Mary Ellen Bute was, as discussed earlier in this publication, an early pioneer of experimental animation, whilst Marie Menken and Storm de Hirsch used animation in some of their films. It is always difficult - and not necessarily productive - to make hard and fast distinctions between what is 'truly' animation, and what isn't. Economics is a factor too, since video art has also developed enormously over the last fifteen years, and for some filmmakers it has been a cheaper medium, as well as offering new formal possibilities and a more immediate way of working. It has also, because located within fine art, accrued more funding opportunities. Anita Thacher can be seen as both animator and video artist: what's important is the quality, and excitement of the work. Doris Chase was a pioneer in computer animation, and then moved into making dance films and video art. More recently she has been making a series of live-action narrative fiction films, often with feminist themes. The work of Sandy More is more often programmed in art galleries than in film programmes - partly because she has been making installations arising from her animation, partly because her work has seemed to be taken more seriously in art circles.

Amy Kravitz and Stephanie Maxwell are quite unusual as women animators who work largely in abstraction, although for both the physical contact with material (however unusual in relation to traditional animation) and paper and/or filmstock are important. Maxwell also has strong connections with animation and experimental filmmaking in Europe. Karen Aqua was first drawn to animation via the 70s climate of experimentation and crossing of boundaries between art forms, citing the influence of Frank and Caroline Mouris, as well as Russian animator Yuri Norstein. Her films are non-narrative, often playing with animation's potential for metamorphosis.

Working directly on film is usually associated with abstract or experimental film. Rose Bond, a Canadian who has long been based in Portland, Oregon, is an interesting example of someone who started off in abstraction in her early films, but has moved to narrative fiction, whilst developing her camera-less technique of painting and drawing onto clear film leader. Her researches into women and history have resulted in two films, *Cerridwen's Gift* and *Mallacht Macha,* intended to form part of a trilogy on the role of women in Celtic mythology.

Computer animation has been a growth area in the 80s. John Lasseter's achievements (assisted by his computer programmer wife Mary) have proved traditional cartoon values (ie well-developed characters, story and humour) still survive, in the face of the mind-numbing technical wizardry-for-its-own-sake of much computer animated work. Yet it seems to have been women who have made some of the most interesting computer animation in terms of art or personal animation. Lillian Schwartz began her pioneering work in computer-generated arts in the 60s, and has continued to inspire and enthuse many across the plastic and graphic arts, as well as in film and video. Joan Staveley's fascinating films are autobiographically inspired, whilst Chitra Shriram is keen to develop her exploration of Indian culture and mythology by experimenting with computer-generated imagery. Another Indian animator based in the US is Simi Nallaseth whose *Diabolic Wife* is a witty and effective computer piece on male chauvinism.

The conservative backlash of the 80s has affected US funding sources, in terms of the amount of money available and arts promotion generally. Most independent animators have had to finance their films with commercial work - some more willingly than others. The TV childrens' programme *Sesame Street* is a regular source of income for some filmmakers; MTV and rock videos generally provide another. Sally Cruikshank has made several animated credit sequences for Hollywood feature films, whilst Ruth Hayes has made an enterprising venture into flip-book publishing. Cutbacks in state funding, and the decline of 16mm film distribution were factors in Mary Beams' decision to abandon personal filmmaking in the 80s. But, as Amy Kravitz points out, grants rarely, in any case, include a wage in addition to material production costs. She feels financial pressures curtail the rate at which personal creative work is done, rather than necessarily leading to a decline in output. Terry Thoren's work in developing the International Tournée of Animation, (originally created by Prescott Wright) on a more commercial basis, partly enabled via his company's being a subsidiary of a chain of art/ repertory cinemas, has certainly provided new sources of income -and in some cases, production finance, for some animators; although as a commercial venture the choice of films tends towards the populist. San Francisco-based Mike and Spike also distribute animation programmes theatrically with succesful touring programmes, whilst video distribution of independent animation is developing too, albeit slowly. Laser-disc is another growth area, and a distribution format that seems particularly appropriate to animation, given the extremely high quality, and the potential for contextualising material to be included via its multi-track capacity.

The Quazy World of Sally Cruikshank

by J. Hoberman

Some of the most original populists in American cinema are situated under the nose of an industry which unwisely ignores them. I'm thinking of Bruce Conner, master of the 'found footage' compilation film; Pat O'Neil, whose handmade special effects consign most sci-fi films to the nineteenth century; and George Kuchar the low-budget confluence of Douglas Sirk, Tennessee Williams and Coco the Clown. Add to the list the name of Sally Cruikshank, who has all but single-handedly resurrected the Depression-era 'funny animal' cartoon - as authentic an American idiom as jug band music or situation comedy - and made it totally her own.

Cruikshank, as one film critic observed, 'makes children's films for adults - or rather for the child who lives on inside the adult.' Her cartoons revel in the depiction of impulse behaviour, their characteristic image is the amusement park (with its promise of fun and freedom, a suggestive metaphor for America itself). Adroitly, Cruikshank evokes a range of native fantasy vernacular styles, from fin-de-siècle Coney Island and 20s movie palaces to the futurama deco of Hollywood cabaret scenes and Miami Beach hotels to the Day-Glo gaudiness of cities' psychedelia. Her sound tracks offer a nostalgic

Quasi at the Quackadero

pastiche of 20s and 30s popular music, while her narratives suggest the input of sci-fi visionary Phillip K. Dick or protosurrealist Raymond Roussel.

Having read neither author, Cruikshank says she works out of her unconscious and gets her ideas 'off the street,' occasionally cribbing something from vintage cartoons. The last time she was in New York, she included two of these in a programme of her work. One was a reflexive representation of an animation studio; the other had two mice enjoying a candy orgy on the moon. Both were produced by the unsung Van Beuren studio, they were among the first cartoons to be sold to television, sure to

be half-remembered by any American kid who grew up with television in the early 50s. You can tell exactly what Cruikshank saw in these films, recognise exactly the things she's lifted and still marvel at how slow-footed and filled with wasted motion they are compared with her work.

An angular attractive woman, who wouldn't look out of place in *Little House on the Prairie*, Cruikshank was born in Chatham, New Jersey, and majored in art at Smith College. While classmates laboured over geometric abstractions, she compulsively drew 'wobbly, funny animals', using them in *Ducky* (1971), a primitive water-colour and paper anim–ation that she filmed with a Bolex tied to a ceiling pipe. Despite a lack of sympathy for hippie drug culture, her discovery of R. Crumb's Head Comix was a revelation: 'It was almost too good,' she says. After graduating, she left for San Francisco, then the Mecca for underground cartoonists.

She produced her second film, *Fun on Mars*, in a class taught by avant-garde animator Larry Jordan at the San Francisco Art Institute. *Mars* (where 'every night is a New Years Eve') proved a congenial landscape for Cruikshank's ducks. Gawked at by middle-aged tourists, they form Busby Berkeley chorus lines, ride their bicycles across the sky and go surfing en masse. ('Kinda my reaction to California,' she says.) Her most experimental film, employing a host of shoestring techniques, *Mars* makes the most of its limitations - this plotless exercise in chase and transformation, collaging old postcards and punctuating its score with random quacks, has a crude vitality that's as touching as it is triumphant.

Chow Fun, released in 1972, mixes paper animation

with Cruikshank's first attempt at cel animation (a technique that separates portions of the drawing onto separate layers of clear celluloid, at once dispensing with the need to redraw the entire composition for every movement and allowing for a palette of brilliant vinyl colours). Tighter than her earlier efforts, the film is a delirious meditation on the toy factory motif common to 30s cartoons (possibly because it suggests their own means of production), with a cast of bouncing jack o'lanterns, big nosed flowers, Kewpie dolls, and obsolete robots working on an asembly line to a rumba version of 'Heartaches'. That *Chow Fun* and *Fun on Mars* both won prizes at the 1973 Ann Arbor Film Festival encouraged Cruikshank to try her hand at more ambitious, full-cel animations.

Two years in the making, *Quasi at the Quackadero* (1975) was the film in which Cruikshank introduced her characters Quasi and Anita. Although she refers to them as ducks, they are actually more suggestive of cuddly reptiles. Quasi is a bratty, bright yellow twerp with thick glasses, a red beanie, and a family resemblance to Ub Iwerk's Flip the Frog. The acerbic Anita is twice his height, looking something like a feminized version of the alligator from Pogo, a Clara Bow cupid's heart at the end of her snout. Quasi speaks in a gutteral quack, Anita in a hoity-toity whine that substitutes w's for r's. (Cruikshank supplies Anita's voice herself 'but not in public'. The ducks' relationship is a curious one, compounded mainly of disastrous dates, nasty pranks, and infantile fantasies. One is never sure if Anita is supposed to be Quasi's fiancée or his baby-sitter, and neither is Cruikshank. 'I don't know' she says when asked, 'it's up to you'.

The plot of *Quasi at the Quackadero* involves a trip to a futuristic carnival whose attractions include various mind-reading, time-travel, and reincarnation machines, as well as vaudeville reenactments of 'your shining moment' or previous night's dream. Quasi unwittingly reveals his fantasy of devouring Anita, and she manages to maroon him in the Pleistoscene. But both returned (along with Snozzy, a suave rival for Anita's affections) in *Make Me Psychic*, completed in late 1978.

Against a further elaboration of Cruikshank's distinctive milieu - smiling flying saucer mobiles, tap-dancing mummies, anthropomorphic high rises - Anita attempts to 'seize control with mesmorama' purchasing some sort of hypnotic device to develop her capacity for telekinesis. Quasi escorts her to a fête that's a cross between a nightclub in an Astaire-Rogers flick and a three year old's birthday party. When he humiliates her by yanking away the chair she's about to sit in - leave it to Cruikshank to use the most primitive childhood joke

of all - the enraged Anita pulls a 'Carrie', unleashing her powers to send assorted ducks, birds, and lysergic potato heads flailing out into the cosmos. Appropriately, *Make Me Psychic* had its San Francisco première on the same bill as *The China Syndrome*.

Living modestly, with a sizable collection of old 78s, in an apartment just off the Berkeley campus, Cruikshank supports herself by doing commercials. She's the head animator of Snazelle Films, a Bay Area producer of advertising films, where she has worked since 1972. 'For the last two years, all I've done is put twinkles on products,' she says. 'They still haven't gotten over *Star Wars* .'

As with any independent filmmaker, money is a problem. *Quasi* cost $6,000, *Make Me Psychic* more than twice as much. Both were self financed. In 1979, Cruikshank received a $10,000 grant from the National Endowment for the Arts to develop a storyboard and trailer for 'an animated musical comedy extravaganza', *Quasi's Cabaret*. The trailer - an action packed parody of Hollywood coming attractions - was completed last year. Promising 'the ultimate in tropical pleasure and excitement', it ends with Anita conjuring up a vision of 'ancillary merchandise' and making a direct pitch to the audience: 'I hope you will consider producing Quasi's Cabaway.' For my money, Hollywood couldn't give a better Christmas present to America, or itself.

This article first appeared in *American Film*, December 1981 and is reproduced by kind permission of the author.

Face Like a Frog

From the CLICK move CLICK move rhythmetics emerge supernatural movie personas who move in impossibly difficult and complicated dances of expression. Move move move...and spilling forth out of darkness appear dances of expression, creatures and worlds limited only by the energy and technique of the animator. These animated creatures, phantoms of illusion, granular spirits, transport us physically by enlivening and kinetesizing a wealth of fantasy already existent within us. We respond empathetically, vicariously, unbounded by laws of weight, gravity, or time. We are released to delight and co-exist with figures who freely disengage autonomy from propriety. Like the loss of restriction in a waking dream, the animated film flies against reality, beating its alternating CLICK-frame wings against the window of our imagination.

Sally Cruikshank just sits you down in your seat and says, 'Here we go...' No seat belts for her weird and wonderful adventures where Betty Boop turns psychokinetic in the form of Anita, and Donald Duck is a quasi duck-faced self-centred hipster in an animated musical world more mad than any LSD adventure. Sally Cruikshank says about her creative process: 'I don't care about the audience...I find music I like and in it I see a real strong motion that creates this weird feeling..I can picture motions and crazy cuts..I can almost turn the music inside out so this weird picture is going with it...there's this breathless crazy

feeling I 'm trying to achieve. When I finish a film I can't remember what I was ever thinking when I started it. I think animation is such a direct process that you don't want to filter your images by being that self-conscious about them at the time...I don't want to analyse my characters because I'm *creating* them.

In another way the characters and the worlds are like grooves that were formed early in my head, created in childhood playmates and stuffed animals and lengthy dialogues with imaginary friends...and they came out again in the films as dramas enacted and reenacted.'

Sally's films are cult favourites that reflect a sensibility which loves the 'real' cartoons of the 30s but can't quite swallow the too cute, too bouncy, just too clever mentality. Her films neatly parody the cel-painted glisten and all-out studio effort to please in many cartoons of the Fleischer and Disney genre. They hype up, turn up reality with colours and motions intense enough to jive a more media-experienced audience brought up on MTV. Her cartoons are macabre, contrary, and never hesitate to dig at the human race. They typify the best of the animation avant-garde because they are unique and passionate visions forever loyal to their maker's imagination. Her films are funny and satirical but in their 'not-aim-to-please' sensibility they are not cartoons, merely, but artful works which dig and stir as well as entertain.

Excerpted from Animation and the Creative Process, *a paper presented by Suzan Pitt, at the Society for Animation Studies First Annual Conference, October 1989.*

J. Hoberman's article was written in 1981. In 1986, Sally Cruikshank was honoured as one of the first recipients of the American Film Institute's Maya Deren Award for Independent Film and Video, alongside Stan Brakhage and Nam June Paik.

Whilst working as consultant on the Joe Dante sequence in Spielberg's *Twilight Zone* (the only one that really works in the film), she met and married her present husband and subsequently moved to Los Angeles. Over the last few years she's contributed sequences to *Sesame Street*, made the delirious and densely packed musical short *Face Like a Frog*, and spent a lot of time developing two feature films, but didn't get anywhere - although she points out that *Roger Rabbit* took six years to get off the ground. She made the animated opening credit sequences for the feature films *Ruthless People* , *Mannequin*, *Lover Boy*, *Madhouse* (although some of the movies sunk wihtout trace, the credits were usually remarked upon favourably). On this last, she took the opportunity to experiment away

from her usual dayglo colour palette, and went for a more pared down style 'more of a UPA look'. It was also a chance to work with music, directing the animation rather than animate directly. 'I like the directing and I really like the ideas. I love hearing music and getting concepts and working it all out and then at that point and then it's kind of finished for me... I keep thinking if I simplified my style it would be possible to do shorts and not feel ploughed under by the workload. But my style is so compulsively filled and I don't really like simplicity.'

For those wanting a fix on the continuing adventures of Anita, one projected feature film (planned to include live action) was to have been *The Love that Makes You Crawl*: 'a love story between Anita, who's a failed stewardess and secret agent Snozzy who's trying to recover some used robots. In the process he joins a secret society and they go around the world on a sex tour on the Titanic 2. It's fairly racy by animation standards.' (quoted from Animato magazine, 1992.)

Joanna Priestley

Priestley came relatively late to animation. After studying painting and printmaking at Rhode Island School of Design and at Berkeley, and a spell printmaking in Paris, she returned to Oregon. The success of a film society she and a friend founded led to a job at the Northwest Film Study Center, where she discovered animation via a visiting animator who brought a programme. 'Coming at animation from a background as a painter and printer, I was impressed with the fact that you could make images move and express emotion.' She took a workshop in filmmaking, went out and bought some index cards, and pretty much made it up as she went along... five years later, she finished her first film, using a stock of rubber stamps left over from a failed mail-order novelty business. Though she now has her index cards custom made, she still has a fairly simple set-up. 'My drawing table has a piece of masonite cut into it. I register with a corner of the masonite. Pretty rough. And on my drawing table I have an L-shaped piece of cardboard cut out. I register against that piece of cardboard.'

She then decided to go to CalArts to do a MFA (Master in Film Arts) because of its reputation and the filmmakers who had emerged from there. She returned to Oregon and over the last decade has been teaching cinema history at the Pacific Northwest College of Art, and making her own films - on her own resources, and with some grant aid. In 1990 she, with producer Melissa Marsland and directors Joan Gratz and John Haughsie set up a commercial animation company called Animakers: recent commissions have included sequences for *Sesame Street*.

Priestley's work is characterised by the quite personal nature of her films, and a desire to work with a range of very different techniques. On the personal inspiration of her films, she points out the that for the amount of time and emotional investment it has to be 'something deeply cared about'. She has an interesting take on the self-revelatory aspects of personal films: 'I know sometimes people find that embarassing, but, you know, by the time I get a film done, I've changed and gone on to different things. So for me it's not so personal any more, because I'm a different person and can look at them with a different eye once they're out there.'

She likes to push her limits, trying different methods and techniques. 'I'm a big fan of Norman McLaren, and all of his films are completely different from each other. Ever since I became interested in movies, I had studied his films and knew that's the direction I wanted to take' - but with a much more personal emphasis. *Dancing Bulrushes*, based on a traditional Chippewa tale about Coyote, the trickster, was created under the camera,

She-Bop

animating sand on back-lit plexi-glass. *Voices* is a light-hearted, humorous exploration of the fears we share: of the dark, of monsters, of ageing, of being overweight, and of global destruction. *Jade Leaf*, an abstract moving painting, combines graphic flow with geometrical shapes, whilst *Times Square* is a collage of city shapes and sounds. *She-Bop*, a powerful, mythic poem about women and spirit, uses puppet animation. *All My Relations* satirises the pitfalls of romance, from marriage, childbirth and upward mobility to the disintegration of a relationship, accompanied by vicious attacks by a household pet. With a soundtrack by two improvisational comedians, metamorphosing forms represent ever changing feelings. This comedy of errors is framed by a series of assemblages which reinforce the message implied in its archetypal characters whose lives, loves and dilemmas are familiar to many who have bought into the American Dream.. *After the Fall* is a pictographic expression of the alienation and isolation of the individual in post modern society and how individuals must plant the seeds of their heart's desires to find answers. *Hand Held*, her most recent film, combines real hands with animated drawings in a fable about creation, oppression, and recreation. An oppressive, grey hand and tiny stick figures representing the world's races collide in a classic David and Goliath confrontation, with a hilarious soundtrack by a group of improvisational comedians.

This will to experiment is encouraged by the community of animators and artists working in Portland: help, advice, and opportunities for collaboration, and a close realtionship with labs. 'Portland is a fabulous town to be a filmmaker in'.

Priestley also curates animation programmes for local and touring exhibition and is involved in commmunity work.

Jane Aaron

by John Canemaker

In Jane Aaron's colourful, exhilarating animated films, real landscapes, rooms, objects, and live performers serve as backdrops for paper cutout characters and designs. Her 1977 short film *In Plain Sight*, for example, featured drawings of chickens strutting and pecking among pixillated poultry; in another scene, cloud drawings mounted on a placard posed against a blue sky billow and alter shape in tandem with their airy, real counterparts.

Traditional cel animation techniques were disappointing to Aaron, because 'only a small part of the environment was represented. For me, there had been so much more - my coffee cup, the window, the day changing, the seasons changing. So, I moved the camera back and started to reveal what was around the drawings.' Basically, Aaron's technique is a variation on the earliest made at the turn of the century: selective camera recording and frame-by-frame manipulation of objects before the camera. Aaron places her camera in a real setting, often indooors, sometimes out, as in the 1983 short *Remains to be Seen*. On comfy couches and lawn chairs, she places cutout figures, and clicks a frame or two of the film. Then, the figures are replaced by a series of drawn figures, each slightly changed sequentially and shot frame-by-frame,

The resultant imagery is startling, often funny and touching at the same time - a magical contemplation of what is real, what is not, and how an artist sees and transforms reality.

Traveling Light

Patterns of Movement

Aaron sometimes uses abstractions to represent textures and patterns of movement. In *Traveling Light*, 1985, a shaft of sunlight passes through a house over the course of a day. In this case, the 'light' was in fact hundreds of tiny pieces of paper shifted slightly frame-by-frame across walls, over furniture and through rooms. The smooth, naturalistic movement of the light disguises the fact that it is paper, the colour changes as the light passes over particular objects. For example, it is pastel blue when on a dark blue tabletop, or milky green when moving over an artichoke.

In keeping with another old animation signature, Aaron often feels compelled to destroy the illusion and announce her presence. (The anti-illusionist 'hand of the artist' iconography goes back to the earliest animated films.) In *Traveling Light* the silky beam of light crosses over a chair, then literally falls to pieces on the floor. Filmmaker Aaron, seen from the waist down, enters the scene and sweeps up the paper scraps into a dustpan.

Applying Techniques

Aaron's work has been celebrated at the New York Film Festival and the Museum of Modern Art. The fresh charm and vitality of her technique has also been noticed in the commercial world. New York's *Village Voice* recognised that Aaron's films 'should be brought to the attention of the record company executives' for use in music videos: *Set in Motion*, 1986, is visually outrageous, and it has a beat. You could dance to it. In fact Aaron produced and directed the music video for Donald Fagen's 'Century's End', shown on MTV.

In 1987, Aaron won a Chicago Emmy for *Image Union*, an animated opening for a local TV show on films and tapes by independents. In 1983, Aaron's special techniques were applied to an informational film about child abuse, *No More Secrets*.

The cheerful whimsicality of Aaron's films, often described as 'playful' and 'lighthearted', belies a precise technique and a rigorous concentration and discipline. The two-minute *Traveling Light* , for example, required a year of labour and planning, with certain scenes taking one hour to set up just to shoot two frames.

'After *Traveling Light* I wanted to do something more spontaneous.' A grant from the MacDowell Colony, an artist's retreat in New Hampshire, allowed Aaron time to contemplate and experiment on the film *Set in Motion*, described in detail in this article.

'I usually begin' says the filmmaker, 'with some kind of technically experimental approach. At MacDowell, I began to be interested in moving all kinds of paper around a room and have the paper define the space. I moved the paper over the surfaces of the room. The paper followed the contours of the wall, defining edges from walls to floor, or from the floor to the edges of a lamp.' Aaron feels her art is basically 'a different way of looking. One favourite reaction to my film *Set in Motion* is when people say that's what things look like when they're sitting in their living-rooms by themselves staring into the distance.

'It's the spirit of everyday objects. All my images are fairly domestic and ordinary made extraordinary. Matisse is a great inspiration for me for his use of colour and his passion for life. Other influences are painters dealing with light, like Edward Hopper, Claude Monet, and Pierre Bonnard. Bonnard's images of everyday objects, even his framing of an image, is important to me. His painting 'Red Checkered Tablecloth' looks like a set-up from *Set in Motion.*' Another inspiration is contemporary artist Judy Pfaff, who does 'extremely colourful installations.'

It is important for Aaron to 'make the filmmaking process fun. It's nerve-wracking, because the camera can't move for days at a time, and you have to be careful and remember how and where you moved everything. Another problem is hitting the right timing. Sometimes, it gets really tense on the set just from the concentration. But often, I'll look around at my crew and and I'll be amazed at what we have created. We try to have fun. What we're basically doing is concentrating very hard and being serious about moving these pieces of paper around.'

When thinking of a concept, Aaron first sketches her ideas in doodle form, usually with Prismacolour pencils on any bond paper available. She does not prepare a storyboard in advance of shooting. 'I do it backwards' she admits. 'I shoot polaroids of finished set-ups after viewing successful dailies (the film footage developed by the lab). Looking at the Polaroids in sequence helps me see how the shape of the film is developing.

'One of the primary needs of *Set in Motion* was spontaneity. We'd get footage back, sometimes only after thirty feet of film after five days of intensive shooting. We'd look at the dailies and someone would say, 'I love the way the blue goes down and under the rug.' I'd forgotten it happened, it was not planned out,' she says.

Aaron does keep a detailed log of each day's shooting. For a brief shot of ribbons of colour travelling over boxes, the filmmaker noted the time she and her crew began and that 72 frames had been shot by 2:15pm, and that they took a break. On that particular day in January in 1986, the Challenger exploded, and she notes, 'We stopped for the day.' [Challenger was the US space shuttle which on 28.1.86 exploded shortly after lift-off killing the five men and two women aboard.]

The log also records who worked on what section of a scene, on what object, and how everything moved, e.g. 'At 24 frames, the bed starts moving in. At frame 84, the bed is in, and we start to pan as purple starts in.' At this point, Aaron reluctantly fired a worker because 'he kept tripping over everything and made the whole set move.'

Aaron first tests everything in the space allocated for shooting. For *Set in Motion*, she used her loft, and, for months the area was set apart only for the filmmaking, since nothing could be disturbed. She works constantly on the abstract paper cutout she will need throughout the development of the film, since thousands of pieces of paper will eventually be used.

Shooting the Scenes

When shooting, Aaron uses a 16mm Bolex camera firmly placed on a steady tripod. The Bolex has a motor to allow a third of a second exposure of f8, which means that only a minimal light level is needed.

Once two frames of the desired image have been taken, Aaron's crew comes onto the set and moves props very specifically for the next frame. Each scene is created this way, so that the motion is eventually fluid, but actually recorded frame-by-frame with infinitesimal changes painstakingly set up.

This frame-by-frame transition is the essence of creating animation, but it is complicated by the use of real life settings, real objects, and real people as the backgrounds for Aaron's superimpositions of moving forms.

Once all of the scenes have been photographed, the next task is editing and synchronising a musical score composed on the synthesiser by Donald Fagen. Fagen had also worked on *Traveling Light*. This process was done over five 10-hour sessions with Fagen.

Aaron's future plans include more personal shorts and more commercial projects. Her fantasy...'I would love it if a great director, Fellini, Woody Allen or Francis Coppola maybe, saw my work and wanted to integrate just a few seconds of these techniques into their feature films.'

First published in How, July/August 1988, reprinted by kind permision of the author, © John Canemaker 1988. See ß.

Suzan Pitt

by John Canemaker

The loft is located on Broadway in the soon to-be-chic Tribeca area of lower Manhattan. Objets d'art, a refrigerator, shelving, boxes of drawings, furniture - a couple of antique desks, an oval walnut dinner table and chairs interrupt the oceanic space or cling timidly to the walls, as if afraid to test the water.

Suzan Pitt sits and talks and smokes yet another cigarette. She is 35 and deceptively fragile. She is small boned and has very intelligent, very blue eyes that peer coolly out of a white translucent face framed by cascading auburn hair. She gives no outward indication of the passionate forces that have given form to her nomadic life and would have ruled it were they not tempered by an iron-willed discipline and an equally passionate drive to create art. She has taken a five year lease on the loft and it is the longest commitment to one place she has ever made in her life, a life that has stretched from Kansas City, Detroit, Alabama, to Amsterdam, Boston and now New York, from where she commutes back and forth to Fountain City, Wisconsin, to visit her ten year old son, Blue, and her ex-husband, Alan Kraning.

'I've let my life get spread out sometimes and I've had to pull it back together' she says calmly. 'I haven't been a person who has made a life which is steady or had one place to live - china in the cabinet year after year in a place that I've always felt was my own. I've moved a lot, been unsatisfied with where I was at. Moved and changed, physically and emotionally as well. The film was the thing that was steadfast. It was ongoing, no matter where I moved or what I was doing. It was a constant in my life.'

The film to which Pitt refers is the extraordinary *Asparagus*, one of the most lavish and wondrous animated shorts ever made. The short enjoyed a rare dual debut at two prestigious art galleries in January 1979: the Whitney Museum of American Art (accompanied by an exhibition of 50 paintings and drawings from the film) simultaneous screening and exhibition of 'constructions' (cels) at the Holly Solomon Gallery in Soho. *Asparagus* is an overwhelming visual experience not easily described. Basically, it is a nineteen minute visual poem dealing with a woman artist's creative process and rites of passage. It is not a narrative, but rather a series of episodes full of obsessively detailed, lush, and sensual imagery. The audience becomes hypnotised, voyeurs peeping in on a private dream.

Structurally, *Asparagus* is a giant film loop. 'It could well repeat itself over and over' wrote Pitt on the Whitney Museum programme notes. Pitt's experience with looping and alternative methods of exhibiting film includes a show she organised while teaching animation at Harvard in 1976. Called *Loops*, the show was an attempt by Pitt

and her students to release animation from its obligations to singleplane illusion by combining real objects and sets with film loops to convert the illusion of discontinuous film time into 'real time'. The circularity of *Asparagus* was extended to its exhibition at the Whitney; there, audiences watched the film screened within the miniature theatre in which parts of it were created. Most of the animation was done on highly rendered cels over detailed surreal watercolour backgrounds; however, the latter part of the film takes place in a three dimensional 10-foot theatre with 200 tiny seats in which are seated as many restlessly moving clay puppets facing a procenium containing animated stage illusions. In this sequence, cels were matted into the 3-D set. 'In exhibiting the film this way I've hoped to create a situation in which people will feel a physical distance...l want the audience to always know the illusions are being made by successive drawings through time - that I'm not trying to make an illusion they can 'believe' in.'

Asparagus required four years and three grants to pull together. Judging by the formidable amount of labour and time demanded of the filmmaker (aided by a few loyal assistants), Suzan Pitt would seem to be the world's most patient person. 'What I am' she says, 'is impatiently persistent. This film was really back-breakingly hard work. Lots of times I wished it was finished but I didn't feel so impatient that I wanted to end it quickly or shortcut it in any way.' *Asparagus* is the culmination of a decade of Pitt's persistent exploration of the medium of animation as a means to realizing her painterly private visions.

She was born in Kansas City, the daughter of a local tyre company owner. The only 'artist' in the family before Suzan came along in 1943 was her grandmother, who in the late nineteen-thirties 'made beautiful hats in her own little shop'. Suzan had always drawn as a child: 'It was something I had a feeling for, felt I could do well. The thing I would do when everything seemed like it went wrong. If I felt hurt or like closing myself in, I would go upstairs and lock the door and make pictures. It was really an escape.'

Pitt elaborates on the familiar theme of the sensitive child protecting itself from a bruising reality through art: 'It's so hard to talk about. As an adult it sounds neurotic to say I'm afraid of real life. But as children we take objects and move them around. Inanimate objects seem to have life. Do you remember playing with your fingers? I did it really a lot. Played with my dolls house, toys out in the backyard. Making arrangements, making them talk and do things. Then as you grow up you're expected to take all that and make it disappear in the closet. What happens to that impulse, that drive to transfer what you see around you into playthings.'

Luckily, Suzan's drive to make visual order out of life through painting was encouraged, both at home and various schools, including Cranbrook Academy and the University of Alabama, where a teacher recognized her special talent and allowed her to have her own space at college with a key. Pitt, working in oils, created large figurative paintings 'this side of Pop art'. She made prints, created books, and painted objects; she was 'impressed' by Richard Linder, David Hockney, and Francis Bacon, 'to some extent, for 1965 was a hot period for British painters.'

She is not sure from where the impulse came, but from 1968 on she was 'making images through animation.' Her paintings, she notes, had always appeared to be shapes 'arrested in time'. She also remembers a period at school in Alabama where she made a clear choice to paint instead of becoming an actress. 'I discovered I was a ham. I have a feeling for drama and the stage, for the show.'

Somehow these factors and others led her to read books on the techniques of bringing static images to life on film. She experimented in 8mm film with almost 400 drawings for six weeks. She found that although her highly rendered individual drawings 'would take forever' to complete, full paintings could easily be moved under the camera frame-by-frame to achieve the effects she wanted.

Pitt was by this time married to Alan Kraning, an artist and filmmaker, who was teaching sculpture at the University of Minnesota. Pitt held several teaching jobs, eventually at the Minneapolis College of Art and Design, drawing/painting classes to animation classes and included the rental of a 16mm movie camera in the school budget. She now experimented in earnest and in 1969 completed *Bowl Theatre Marble Game*, an early film that displays most of the stylistic trademarks evident in her later work. There is the patient slow timing of the well-drawn cut-out graphics, the use of repetition, and images of parts of the human anatomy, and the theatre. There is also the sensuality factor: a strong sexuality that emerges through naive and explicit graphic metaphors. Even Pitt's very first film experiments in 8mm dealt with symbols of bodily functions, sex, and birth.

In *Crocus* (1971), a man with an erection that would be the envy of Priapus makes love to a woman (assumed to be his Wife). Their bodies are hidden demurely under a blanket, while 'love metaphors' of roses, butterflies, birds, a Christmas tree, cucumbers, and so on float in and out of doors and windows, until interrupted by the cries of a child in another room. The lovers then give their attention and love of another kind to the child.

There is a libidinous sensibility in all of Pitt's work, a playful feeling of 'naughty' daring and perhaps an attempt to astonish (or shock) us while hedging the titillation by using sexual symbols Pitt recalls a strict Kansas upbringing where sex was not discussed. When Suzan first showed her family *Crocus*, her mother's reaction was shocked disapproval ('How could you do something like that?'). Years later, after a sort of reconciliation had been made between the filmmaker and her mother, the entire Pitt family (except for Suzan's father who had died a few months before) turned up for the opening of *Asparagus* in New York. 'I think the excitement from the audience helped my mother to see, well, look at all these people. They're really responding to this film. They're not embarrassed. I felt a response from her. She said, 'I don't know where all these things come from inside you. I can't myself trace it, but I'm really impressed. It's great!'

In the film, the asparagus represents 'some sort of creative source' to Pitt. It is first defecated by the film's female character into a toilet and flushed away into the 'watery past'. In a thick exotic garden, the vegetable grows like erect phalli and the woman strokes it. 'She wants so much to touch it to embrace it, to make contact with it, to understand it,' wrote Pitt in the Whitney notes. Later in the film the asparagus is adored, touched or wondered at. 'But that's intellectual reasoning on my part. What I was saying was well said the way I was saying it!'

'Besides, I'm basically a heterosexual woman and that's my experience: a man with a woman and my being a woman. That's what I see. Someone with a different sexual experience would say it in a different way perhaps.

I've always felt that I was a mixture of masculine/feminine traits. A lot of artists do. Some people take on extreme masculine or feminine characteristics. I always felt I was third sex. I don't see an asparagus as purely phallic. I love the way it looks when it's coming out of the ground because it's completely formed, it stands up, looks ancient and yet fresh at the same time. But as it goes through its metamorphosis it grows up to become this beautiful, ethereal, wafting-in-the-wind fern, which is more feminine.'

It was *Crocus* that brought Suzan Pitt to the attention of the Whitney museum and its then-developing independent filmmakers programme The Whitney featured the film in a programme of shorts and commissioned Pitt to make a film commercial requesting funding for the Museum's Film Department.

In 1973, Pitt completed *Jefferson Circus Songs*, a pixillation film made with a cast of children who were her students at the Walker Art Center in Minneapolis. This mysterious, often puzzling bit of film whimsy contains elaborately costumed kids in bizarre three-dimensional settings performing Kabuki-like ceremonies. Pitt fills the screen with colour, motion, and wonderfully rich images, like a magician pulling yet another astonishment from a bottomless hat. It is a miniature Fellini extravaganza - Cocteau on an acid trip.

As Pitt's film artistry was developing and gaining strength with each new film, her personal life was about to take a sharp turn. Two weeks after finishing *Jefferson Circus Songs*, she moved to the southern part of Holland. 'I was in love with someone. I went there to live with him', she explains simply. The relationship proved to be 'a total disaster' and after three months she left the man. For 13 months Pitt remained in Holland, a woman with a four-year-old son (she had brought Blue with her from the Midwest) in a foreign country, without friends or means of support. 'It was the real low point of my life,' she says. 'It took me a long time to get over getting a divorce (in 1974) and trying to straighten out my own life. Trying to find my own way without being stooped in loneliness and depression and feeling lost. I was down.'

Slowly she began to meet people in Holland and made friends with a few artists and experimental filmakers. She showed her films at America House in Berlin; she heard of an available grant, met the committee in charge, showed them her films and drawings (the genesis of *Asparagus*) and, on the grant, which involved a residency in Germany (eventually completed in 1978). 'Things got better. They got a little worse', she says quietly. She went back to Fountain City, where her ex-husband was residing.

'We're still very close, supportive. We share bringing up Blue. It was worth the added pain to me in trying to stay close, in touch with each other, and readjust to new separate single lives. When you have a child with someone they're a key person in your life. It'll always be that way.'

It was a production grant from the American Film Institute that allowed Pitt to start in on animating *Asparagus*. Then came an offer to teach for a year at Harvard, to be followed the next year there by a research fellowship. By the time she moved to Cambridge in 1975 she had the first section of the film drawn. 'I shot tests on the school Oxberry the summer before I started teaching. Eric Martin and Jim Shook literally showed me everything about the Oxberry camera including how to shoot bi-pack for the theatre scenes.'

At first Pitt thought she could produce the film in one year for $5,000. 'But it probably has cost at least $15,000 and that's just minimal wages for cel painters, construction of the theatre set, film processing, composer's fee, finishing costs. The production time stretched out because I was teaching, moving around, and the idea of the film just grew larger and longer.' In September 1977 Pitt had most of the film completed except for the superimposition of the cels over the 3-D theatre set sequence. She moved to New York and from September to December animated the final scenes. 'It was exhausting. I'd break to go get me something to eat, then come back to the loft and start in working again. I'd catch some sleep and wake up to start working on the film - constantly.'

Early in 1978, she flew to Germany to take advantage of the grant she had received three years before. 'It was a generous honorarium, with a studio plus another $3,000 for finishing funds. It helped tremendously and I couldn't have done it without it. Jim Shook came over from Harvard for two months to paint cels. We went to a studio in Hamburg - Cinegraphic - and spent all of Easter using a 35mm aerial camera doing the superimposition of the cels over the theatre scene. It didn't come out technically as I wanted it to. We decided it was easier for Jim to take the drawings back and edit them at Harvard, which he did.'

Asparagus was finished with filming by September 1978 and Pitt hired composer Richard Teitelbaum, who contributed a hauntingly beautiful score that equals the visual ecstasy. 'We never tried for any exact sync of music and picture. We wanted the Moog synthesizer music to create an atmosphere but not to believe the sounds were coming from the source.'

With the film finally completed, Pitt dashed, without a breath, into headlong promotion and exhibition of the work at various art galleries, but also in film shows in

Boston, Los Angeles, and San Francisco, and places in between. She has recently received another grant, so a new film will be forthcoming, although she has not had the time to formulate any ideas for the project. 'I haven't as yet put myself in a private atmosphere to start daydreaming again, which is where all these ideas come from.'

She takes a few moments to daydream: 'I'd like to spend some time making objects and pictures that don't move. I feel like I've always been painting. I seldom think about live-action. I used to think about it more when the moves and trains of my life were stranger and more powerful than any movie I've ever seen. And I'd think after a particular thing would happen, boy, if I made a film of that, that would be a great film! I make too impetuous decisions about some things, I'm drawn to unusual people.' She drifts back to her film project. 'Maybe I'll do a tighter version of *Loops*. Build a theatre, set it up and take it down after the performance. Combine screens, actors, 3-D theatre pieces, technical devices to move images, maybe not use film at all. A variety of ways of moving imagery, which all come from in and out of animation.

'And I think about making an animated feature, a truly experimental one. If I could somehow find the funding - in the $500,000 range. Ideally I'd do it all myself. Or work with two or three other independent animators. That would have problems, but the result could be good. If I could raise the money and had complete freedom to do exactly what I wanted to do, I want to do it!'

Originally published in *Funnyworld*, Fall 1979, and reprinted in part by kind permission of the author. © John Canemaker, 1979.

In fact, in the immediate years following *Asparagus,* Suzan Pitt returned to painting. After working with wood constructions she then developed a style of painting on huge canvases, using found images and the printed word, trying to represent different emotiona states as conjugated in 'new visual sentences…gestural cartooning'. When asked by an interviewer why she made her paintings three-dimensional she answered: 'That's an extremely important part of everything I've done in film and paintings… The kind of art I really want to make is in the light as opposed to the dark. It goes back to what my feelings about what paintings themselves are, that they are basically very theatrical. I've always felt a certain kind of embarrassment about making a statement that's completely bare and then putting it on the wall. I've always been drawn to the relationship between an audience and a work of art. I associate the theatre as an example of that because the audience and the art are so directly related. Between the audience and the show there is a proscenium or an architectural surrounding which physically separates one from the other. It provides a sort of comfort for one to go out of oneself into the artwork, and at the same time it provides comfort for the artists: they are behind the spotlights, they can go offstage and change clothes, then come back and be whatever the fantasy at hand is… I feel a thrill in pretending I might be able to physically inhabit that world; it's a different body sensation than viewing a flat illusion.'

Her work was widely exhibited in Germany, where 'Asparagus Theater' is permanently installed in the Ludwig Collection at Aachen. It was through this installation that in 1980 she was commissioned by innovative opera director Nikolaus Lehnhoff to design sets and costumes for a production of *The Magic Flute* in Wiesbaden. At that point she had neither heard nor seen the Mozart opera. It was the scenario that convinced her. Here she found archetypal characters - mother-queen, father-dictator - acting out archetypal roles. Above all, the sparse indications of setting provoked her fantasy: 'a rock scene', 'an intimate room', 'a palm garden'. She also experimented with four minute back and front projected animation sequences. The production aroused some controversy amongst opera purists, but was extremely successful. The project took almost three years, as did work on another German stage production, this time in Hamburg, of the oratorio *The Damnation of Faust,* a rich source, she says, of primal images. She had the opportunity to experiment with an enormous range of animation techniques, to put together an hour long compilation of animated sequences, most made in Boston with a crew of ten, including Amy Kravitz and her animator husband Steven Subotnik. The effect was that of layers of imagery, using the theatrical space, the sets and the singers to convey layers of meaning. Mirrors at each side of the stage produced a sense of 3-D wraparound.

For five years, Pitt also taught at Harvard, where she was an associate professor, teaching animation. She had some fun doing rock videos, including Peter Gabriel's *Big Time, Geneva* for Andreas Vollenweder (with George Griffin) and *Surfer Die*, for a local skateboard rap group. The latter was co-produced by her son, who also worked on the film itself. (He has recently graduated from film school and intends working in live action). She enjoyed the experience of creating a barrrage of imagery for short bursts of three minutes.

All this work, she feels, fed into the development of a new film, *Joy Street*, on which she has been working for the past two years. This will be a 23 minute epic, using a variety of techniques, and inserting three musical

A rich, densely textured symbolic narrative, it has the haunting quality of a dream perceived through open eyes. Through a range of techniques from drawings on acetate cels to three dimensional clay puppets, the film's technical scope is paralleled by its thematic complexity. The artist as woman is the focus of the film - the struggles, the loneliness, the satisfactions, the passion.

A primal erotic force embraces all, with the asparagus representing that elemental natural power. Pitt describes the film as a 'series of passages which are about the creative process as I perceive it' and throughout the film calls attention to the process of its making, to the basic fact that film is illusion, and individual images combined in sequence form an illusion trap that one should not 'believe' in.

The viewer is both distanced from and seduced by the film's imagery, just as the protagonist struggles between being enmeshed in and having control over the world around her - through her doll house arrangements, through the art she creates. Hovering in the ambiguous, fluctuating territory between the self and the other, *Asparagus* confounds distinctions between the private and the public, between the imagined and the real. Reflecting the dynamics of the creative process, the protagonist moves from the order of The Room 'her interior and private space', to the lush inspiration of The Garden.

The Garden is all she perceives as Given... everything she feels outside the Room. But there is an important question in terms of one's perception of the other - is the Room passing by or through the garden? Or is the Garden passing by or through the Room?

The Garden is so thick... It's difficult to see how far it stretches... It appears to be so rich, so dense, so beautiful, so frightening. She feels so much about it. She wants so much to see it. She wants so much to touch it, to embrace it, to make contact with it, to understand it.

She imagines she can be part of it and sees herself touching it through the window! Of course there is a curtain to open and close.

The asparagus seems so perfect.

In the Viewer Box, the protagonist then makes 'things, pictures, scenes, illusions' and chooses from the Closet 'the appropriate attitude for going out in case she is seen'. Hidden behind a mask with a 'masculine look' she takes the Bag, in which 'images she has made have been piling up and cry out to be shown. Or she is crying out to show them.' Walking through the Street, she arrives at the Theatre, 'a showing place for artists':

There is a great feeling of excitement and expectation. The audience is there to devour the images... The audience loves to be amazed. It's spectacular! It's wonderful! It moves so well and seems so meaningful!

She knows beforehand (because she's done this before) that no matter which angle she chooses to watch from she will not be able to know how the audience is seeing what she has made. Therefore as soon as the Bag is opened and the art work made visible, she goes home. In a taxi she returns home, to the intimacy she has imagined with the Garden.

It is clear from these excerpts from Pitt's notes, that *Asparagus* views the struggle to make and share art as a prism through which one glimpses other kinds of relevent issues. There is the struggle to be a woman artist, grounded in the archetypically feminine territory of the Room and the Dollhouse, and feeling compelled to circulate in the outside world disguised in the mask of a man. And going beyond the topical, the film poses the questions of poetry and myth, wondering about the bonds between eroticism and creativity, nature and art, art and life. It is a woman's experience that is at the heart of this film, yet it is, at the same time, human experience. In distilling the universal from the particular and the to-pical, *Asparagus* set a new standard of integrity for the animated film and for independent film in general.

This commentary on *Asparagus* is taken from Thelma (now Talia) Schenkel's unpublished paper *American Women Animation Artists of the 70s and the Third Renaissance of the Cinema of Animation*, 1980. See ß.

numbers to change pace and mood. She's playing with 'known styles with certain qualities which elicit certain feelings', eg. the opening section, which uses painted dissolves, recalls the imagery associated with pulp novels of the 50s, over a jazzy blues saxaphone; another section animated a monkey figure on an ashtray in a style that's like a rapid tour through Fleischer Bros and Harmon-

Ising, whilst some of the musical numbers have a similar kinetic feel to that of Sally Cruikshank's films.

Financed by grants from different sources, she has yet to find completion money, and reckons on another year's work. Although it's hazardous to make judgements on the basis of work-in-progress sequences, *Joy Street* promises to be well worth the fifteen year wait.

Kathy Rose

the transforming power of animation

From the isolating lifestyle of an independent animator in the 70s to flamboyant performance dance-artist in the 80s: Kathy Rose's creative trajectory is fascinating in itself, but also as an example of the way animation can serve, particularly it seems for women, as crucial means of self-expression and artistic development.

A family background in photography and a habit of drawing established in early childhood led to film studies at university, then graduate work in animation at Cal Arts. At college she became involved in photographing, then trained with, the dance company 'Group Motion' formed by former students of Mary Wigman, but decided to concentrate on animation filmmaking. 'I wanted to go back to drawing, something where I could work in a more reclusive space… It was exciting to me because it was a chance to dive into my own fantasy world that was under my control. It was such a personal and self-controlled type of medium'. Animating on paper 'partly because I like to feel the markers and pencils soak into the paper... I like to do all my work in the drawing, not in the camera movement, probably because it satisfies a desire to do everything by myself in solitude'. Between 1972-78 she made ten short animation films, which convey a strong sense of personality. Animation seemed to her particularly suitable to 'evolve a personal style'.

This was characterised by John Canemaker in 1977 as follows. 'Kathy Rose's insignia is the remarkable cast of 'characters' who people her films and who can be traced through *The Mysterians*, *The Moon Show*, *Mirror People*, and *The Doodlers*, made at CalArts in the early to mid 70s. In *The Mysterians*, her silly-putty creatures, capable of any transformation imaginable, begin playing their metamorphic games - which become more complex in *Mirror People*, as the figure-ground manipulations reveal space to be as much of an illusion as corporeality. To a sound-track of fun-house screams and cackles, the Mirror People, a tribe of Halloween hallucinations, fuse into each other and get absorbed into their reflections and their environment in a universe where all sorts fluctuate and nothing is stable, except for the constant delights of metamorphosis. *The Doodlers* carries the game of illusion still further. Through Miss Nose and her clan of doodlers, whose curvilinear outlines and splashes of colour come to life through a magic cat's tail brush, Rose makes some witty observations on the art of animation and on the symbiotic relationship between the artist and the characters.

'Although she was very excited by the films of Yoji Kuri, whose surrealistic pranks are echoed in her films, Rose's characters have an indescribable uniqueness. It might have something to do with the way she draws them: all her characters are drawn upside-down. Yes. When she creates them, it is as if she wanted someone sitting on the other side of the table to be able to see them rightside-up, without having to turn the drawing around. She finds that it's like 'drawing with the eyes closed, you have one less level of consciousness.' But only the characters are drawn that way; the constant swirling camera movements require tighter control and are drawn rightside-up. The battle and games between Rose's characters are at some level intra-psychic encounters; she sees her character as 'parts of my unconsciousness' and is currently working on a film in which she and her characters confront each other.' [1]

The film was *Pencil Booklings*... on which Talia Schenkel has commented, 'the integration of the artist and her art is extended still further. In using rotoscoping to depict herself in the film, Rose distinguishes the artist from the other characters as belonging to another order of being. Yet later in the film, Rose too becomes a caricatured line-drawn character when one of her characters challenges her to give up the outsider's position (indicated by her naturalistic rotoscoped depiction) by saying: 'If you really want to make good cartoons, you have to be in one first.' With these word, doors fly open to nowhere, the 'magic brush' crosses in front of her face, and the realistically depicted Kathy Rose metamorphoses into an infinite recession of concentric eyes, within which her characters appear and disappear. After returning to her realistic self again with a flick of the 'magic brush', the film ends as once again Rose transforms into a cartoon character, with her characters growing out of all sides of her - like the magical children of her imagination that they are. In this intimate charting of the creative process, the fusion is complete: the artist becomes her creation, and distinctions between art and life evaporate.

'The constantly shifting spatial parameteres of the film, the uncertain boundaries between the artist and her characters, the surreal elasticity of their bodies, and the unpredictable inter-actions between the frame, the canvas, and the screen -all parallel the mutations and flux of intrapsychic processes.

Through focussing on the relationships among the characters, Rose in these personal diaries of creation is sharing her thought processes, courageously exposing the hesitancies and the risks as well as the joys of creation. Through the apparently innocuous surfaces of the film, she shares the painful battles of artistic struggle, battles which take place deep within the imagination and which Rose is one of the few to articulate. '[2]

After *Pencil Booklings*, Rose commented 'it just seemed like there was no place to go except into some three dimensional sense'. She experimented for a couple of years with pixillation and puppet animation, but found herself dissatisfied, and blocked.

Having maintained an interest in dance, from studies of Diaghilev's Ballet Russe designs and Sonia Delauney's costumes, to further training in ballet, African dance and flamenco, in 1982 Rose toured a programme combining dance with film, *Primitive Movers*, in which she entered the world of her animated creations. The effect was described by Mara Alper... 'The animation serves as a constantly moving décor ranging from life-sized figurative dancers to cubist and abstract imagery, against which the dancer performs in choreographed and improvised movement wearing a costume designed to change throughout the piece. The film is projected on to a rear screen 9'x12' behind her, the percussion soundtrack originating from the film print. Live percussion is also played, in sync with the film soundtrack.'
[3] A reviewer of the show commented: 'The two-dimensionality of her movement, and that of the animated chorus she leads, acknowledges the flatness of the screen. The rate of change in the size, shape, composition and costuming of the chorus is rapid to the point of being mesmerising. At first Rose and her group parade in disciplined lines, as flat as paper cutouts. Gradually though she presents a more rounded, deeper space.'

Syncopations followed in 1987... 'instead of adding a third dimension to her animation, she has now achieved a holographic effect. A group of young women on film, with black lips and nails, dressed in brilliant coloured costumes seemingly dance around Rose who dances before the audience. Rose experiments with slow motion, reverse filming, split screens, repetition and close-ups. In front of us, she slouches in the mode of 30s vamps, flirts with a long scarf, and celebrates her femininity with the pride of a flamenco dancer. The event is strangely erotic and controlled with a sophisticated, graphic edge. It's as though we are witnesing a rite of passage into a celluloid, female environment.' [4]

Rose's work took a new direction in 1988. She still employs film and visual effects at times, but involves a more directly choreographic structure as a base. Her company is called KabukiMenco Visual Theatre, and her dance partner is flamenco dancer Luis Montero. *Az-Tech*, a recent work, combines ancient South American culture with science-fiction: the female wears a totem headdress mde of an electronic circuit board with flashing lights, and the male wears a belt with a light orbitting around it. The choreography employs heelwork, but in a highly original way related to futurist and Inca themes. At the end the two characters exit into time travel light beams rendered in animated film.

References
1. John Canemaker, *Millimeter*, February 1977.
2. Thelma (now Talia) Schenkel, *American Women Artists of the Seventies and the Third Renaissance of the Cinema of Animation*, op. cit.
3. Mara Alper, *An Interview with Kathy Rose* in *Film Library Quarterly*, Winter 1982.
4. Dance Magazine, November, 1987.

Primitive Movers

Ruth Hayes: Flip Book Artist

by Karen Rosenberg

These days the flip book is generally considered kiddie fare, if it is considered at all. What's a flip book? Well, the Germans call it Daumenkino, thumb cinema, because it's a form of animation: a series of sequential images on a bound stack of paper seems to move when you riffle the pages fast enough with your thumb. Its origins are obscure, but it was patented in 1868 and became popular at the end of the nineteenth century when various parlour toys with strange names like 'zoetrope' and 'phenakistascope', based on the persistence of vision, were in fashion among adults as well as children. (When a rapid succession of images still pictures passes before our eyes, our brain retains each image longer than it is actually seen. This creates the illusion that movement is perceived - hence the term 'persistence of vision'.)

In this century, flip books have been used for instructional purposes. Alongside these flip books with few if any artistic pretensions is the more recent genre of flip books by artists.

Since the 50s, when Robert Breer started drawing abstract shapes on plastic or index cards and making them move, artists have used flip books to create metamorphoses or perspective shifts. Since the 70s, women like Joanna Priestley, Kathy Rose and Lisa Crafts have produced flip books, sometimes for sale, sometimes as studies for their animation films. They provided a haven for experimentation without the pressure of high expectations, for some animators. 'It really was a cocoon - a safe place,' Ruth Hayes wrote me. 'If my medium isn't taken seriously, then no one will bother me while I work on it.' George Griffin, a leading figure amongst independent American animators, with whom Hayes studied at Harvard, has also been a prolific flip book publisher. Ruth Hayes has made this animation-related area both a successful business and a creative outlet. She has twelve books in print.

After graduating in animation, Hayes had two films taken up by the festival circuit. However, she felt frustrated at their lack of wider exposure. So she turned to flip books as a way of getting her artwork to the public. In 1979 she started selling xeroxed copies of her flip books through a Christmas store that specialised in artists' artwork. Later she moved to offset printing, which improves quality and the smooth flow of movement from page to page, and distributed her books through stores that sell artists' books in LA, New York and Seattle.

As buyers and individuals wrote to the addresses on the back of each volume, her business grew. A three year job with The Real Comet Press taught her more about the book industry, and by 1987 she was selling 10,000 copies a year of her various flip books. In 1988 she licensed six

titles to The Real Comet Press (retaining the copyright) and contracted to produce two books a year for them.

I've told the business side of Hayes's biography because I find it relevant to her creative work. Her earlier flip books reveal her training in animation; the rules are simple: make the action simple and provide enough images to make the movement smooth and easy to perceive. Hayes' experience with the artists' book movement - and particularly with multiple-edition works finely printed by a small press - led, I think, to her perception of flip books as more than animation on paper. Her later work exploits some of the possibilities of the medium of print. She published *Birthrite* in 1988, a flip book with a text culled from sources as diverse as *The Tibetan Book of the Dead* and Martin Buber's *Tales of the Hasidim*. From that date, most of her works pack the frame with so much information that they must be paged as well as flipped. It's this breaking of the usual fixed categories - and the cross breeding that results - that I admire most about her creativity.

Hayes herself, notes: '*Birthrite* has two lines of writing that move above and below the drawings. You can't read the texts and look at the animation simultaneously. You have to go back and read each text by itself at a slower pace. When you read the texts, the artwork moves on the periphery of your vision. If you stop to look at a single image, the text fragments on that page become captions. When you look at the animation after reading the texts, your memory synthesises the three elements into a complete experience of the book.'

Her later work can be seen as an invitation to find a new way of handling a bound stack of paper. In *Paranoia* an open book falls toward a brown-shirted figure. Your fast-flipping thumb must adjust its motion to satisfy your mind's curiosity about the book's title and author (*Democracy in America*, by de Toqueville). Hayes' work cautions the modern reader against imitating the regularity of the projector.

Hayes exploits other advantages of the flip book format. While the film is confined to images of invariable dimensions because it must fit through standardised projectors, the flip book frame can be fluid and shifting. In *Paranoia*, the upper edge of the rectangular image expands and then breaks open, allowing bullets out and objects in, like de Toqueville's book. In *Leash Law* a woman - Hayes' self-portrait - sketches in one corner, jettisoning blotches of colour that become the curved border of a world. But when a cat, dog and man in that world lean over and lick their genitals (in one of Hayes' works about active tongues), both the illustrator and her male character are yanked from the picture. In short, the 'off-frame' illustrator turns out to be onstage - implicated in and guilty of the breaking of a societal taboo.

In her unabashed exploration of the body, Hayes stands within a tradition of women animators in the US that began in the 70s. Suzan Pitt's *Asparagus*, the dancing penises in Mary Beams' *Seedreel*, and Hayes' own languid journey around a female and male nude in *Body Sketches* challenged and changed the permissable content of 'cartoons'. *Leash Law*, like many classics of feminist animation, gets light images to carry weighty implications. Much of her work is sparked by her wide reading. *Leash Law* came partly from her encounter with Klaus Theweleit's *Male Fantasies*, a psychoanalytical study of the Freikorps officers during the Weimar Republic. The throttling society Theweleit describes - with its fear of following one's desires and of doing what feels good - reminded her, she says, of a dog's choke-chain. In this book, as in *Birthrite*, *Paranoia*, and her 1990 *Flip Book of the Dead*, Hayes doesn't illustrate a text but employs it as a jumping-off point. In short, these are not artsy Classic Comics.

The major dialogue in Hayes' books is between the body and those who would like to repress it. And unusually, unexpectedly, her bad guys are the less interesting half of this opposition. The child-killing television in *TV Dinner*, the enraged male sharp-shooter in *Paranoia,* and the money hungry, jingoistic and militaristic preacher in *The Flipbook of Revelations* are familiar enemies. But when Hayes enters the realm of the flesh she's generally on less conventional territory. The 'horny' frog in *Frogs in Heat* is a visual pun, but Hayes isn't a dirty jokester: again she's fascinated with the way a tongue tickles, as an excited amphibian licks his/her mate. In *Roses are Red, Violets are Blue, My Cat's in Heat and I'm Thinking of You*, a drawn cat turns over sensuously, as a woman, photographed in close-up, pulls up her fishnet stockings. The pages are printed on both sides, so you see both left and right legs from painted toenail to thigh. Although I find black fishnets and painted toenails stereotypical and all-too-easy signs of female sexuality, I like the way a cat rubbing a high-heeled shoe represents and heightens the erotic in this flip book.

When I compare her flip books to those that come out of the conceptual art tradition - like *Scheherezade* and *This Book is Extremely Receptive,* by artist Janet Zweig, I'm struck by the emotionality, the heat of Hayes' work. Despite Hayes' recourse to over-used symbols, I find my hand reaching out again for her flip books - my eyes get a little more out of them each time.

Wanda

'Flip books forced economy of ideas and images which has fed back into my film animation', Ruth Hayes wrote me recently. 'The intensity is there, now I'm working on duration and pauses - the down time - while everything sinks in. You have to build that into a film but books don't need it.' Her 4 minute film *Wanda* (1990), produced at the Department of Experimental Animation at Cal Arts, where she is studying, also uses time to add depths to her characteristic themes.

Wanda, an adopted cat, licks herself, a bit like the feline in *Leash Law*, and rolls over, or around a high-heeled shoe, just like her counterpart in *Roses Are Red...* Such brief animated sequences are inserted between and superimposed over live-action footage which often recalls home movies. The animated cat sometimes repeats movements of the filmed one, and this doubling suggests how memory preserves and transforms small events.

The narrator, who we see as a foot with painted toenails getting into a black fishnet stocking, starts out talking calmly about the homey habits of her new pet. But her tone turns ironic as she relates that Wanda had more success with the opposite sex than she. Newspaper sex ads and old erotic pictures accompany her tale of Wanda's love life, and the human and animal realms coincide again when Wanda, in heat, brings a mate home.

As in many animated shorts, the punch is at the end, in the lines, 'I am just a little jealous, too, because that is my bed, and when was the last time that I lay up there with a hard tom, both of us wet and spent, and for a moment the only two creatures on earth?' Although Hayes explores women's sexuality indirectly here, through metaphor, she achieves an openness which is still daring.

The article on flip books is adapted from *Moving Picture Machines; Flip Books, Phenakistoscopes, Zoetropes, and other Optical Inventions* in *The Independent, Film & Video Monthly*, March 1991, published by the the New York based Foundation for Independent Video and Film; another version was reprinted in *The Women's Review of Books*, September 1991; and in the UK bi-annual magazine *Animator*, no. 29. Reprinted by kind permission of the author. See Notes on contributors.

HOW SOME INDEPENDENT ANIMATED FILMS ARE MADE

by Joanna Priestley
© 1988 Joanna Priestley

The creation of animated films as an art form started with Emile Reynaud's Théâtre Optique in France, in 1892. Dozens of pioneer artists/filmmakers followed, leading to the current efflorescence of independent animation.

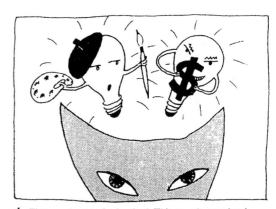

1 First you have to be inspired. This sounds easy, but it may actually require years of intense concentration.

2 Methods include long walks in the fog at twilight, visiting museums, taking classes and reading tons of books, short stories and poems.

3 Personally, I get most of my ideas lying in bed in the early morning.

4 Next you need to figure out how to fund your film (if you are rich, you can skip this step). You can borrow the money, or you can work at another job and save as much money as possible.

5 And/or you can write grants: arts grants, foundation grants, federal grants, state grants, city grants, neighborhood grants . . .

6 Now you need to find a place to work. If steps 4 and 5 were a success, you can rent a studio, or you can work in your kitchen or bedroom, like lots of independent animators.

7 The fateful day arrives when you approach the drawing board and courageously face the blank piece of paper (block of clay, box of pins, etc.). With luck, you'll still remember your original inspiration.

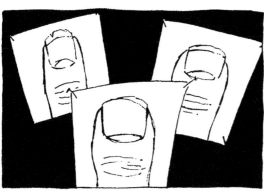

8 Some filmmakers make thumbnail sketches to organize their thoughts and ideas. Others make elaborate storyboards that plan out all the scenes or shots in the film. You might also begin with a soundtrack and create the images around the sound.

9 Some filmmakers work "straight ahead" – beginning a drawing as the inspiration hits, and then letting the drawings (sculptures, etc.) take you where they want to go. This method requires courage and open-mindedness.

10 Now you draw (paint, sculpt, move sand, etc.).

11 And draw (paint, sculpt, move pins, etc.).

12 And draw (paint, sculpt, move cutouts, etc.).

13 And draw (paint, sculpt, move puppets, etc.). Don't forget to continue to work on steps 4 or 5, or you won't make another movie after this one.

14 Of course, you could draw forever – some filmmakers take a decade to complete a piece – but at some point, you'll probably want to finish this film and move on. Sometimes you are such a different person than the one who started the film, years ago, that you can hardly relate to the early art work.

15 Now you can attach your flea market camera (Bolex, Cine Special . . .) to a poorly constructed frame that wiggles too much, and you can shoot with your cheap lights that burn your arms.

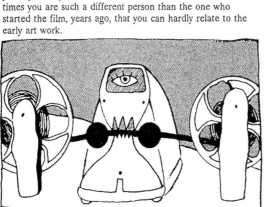

16 Now you are ready to edit on your cheap viewer that is very dim and doesn't focus. This results in a workprint.

17 Unless you did the soundtrack first, you need sound. You can make your own sounds, you can beg your musician friends to work for you, or you can hire a composer.

18 If you hire a composer, you may try to explain what type of sound you think the images need, using words like "big," "delicate," "powerful," "punctuated" and "dark." The composer won't have the faintest idea what you are talking about. If all works out well, you'll have several tracks of sound that you then edit and mix down to a master track.

20 After you make an internegative, interpositive, test release prints and final release prints (wheh!!), you are ready to premiere your new film. Of course, you have to organize the whole thing and do all your own publicity. You may have to be the projectionist too.

22 Now you have two or three glorious years of distributing your movie: filling out festival forms, paying fees, schleping it to the Post Office, UPS and Siberian Express, groveling over the tidbits that cable television has to offer, wondering if you'll ever be able to pay your lab bills.

19 Now cut your original footage to match your workprint and trot off to the lab with workprint, cut original and master soundtrack. Using arcane magick and newts feet, they make your fullcoat soundtrack into an optical soundtrack and print that with your original to make an answer print.

21 The BIG MOMENT arrives: the Premiere. Chances are 20 to 1 that your film will be out of focus, the academy leader will show, the sound will be too low, the framing will be off, the film will break or burn, or it will get turned off before the credits are over. No one may notice this except you.

You did it!

What an accomplishment!

No one knows (especially your parents – they may never understand what you do all day) what an accomplishment it is to make an animated film – except the rest of us filmmakers. Congrats!

Joanna Priestley makes movies and teaches animation at the Pacific Northwest College of Art in Portland, Oregon. She is at Step 18 on Hand Held *and Step 14 on* Ageing Grace.

Mary Beams

Mary Beams has been described by Talia Schenkel as 'a pioneer' amongst American women independent animators whose work in the 70s 'broke through conventional notions about women's imagery with her dazzling depiction of female eroticism in *Seed Reel* and her moving confrontation with her family in *Going Home Sketchbook*... and her work has already influenced the succeeding generation.' [1]

Her themes are drawn from a variety of sources, including childhood memories, erotic fantasies, and feminist issues. Most of her pictures are drawn on paper using ink and watercolour. Those cels are shot on negative film, producing Beams' characteristic floating images in eerie colours and bold white lines on black backgrounds. Beams often uses live-action as a source of her images, selectively rotoscoping frames one at a time as she chooses from each shot those elements that distill the essence of light and movement. [2]

She made her first animated film, *Tub Film*, in 1972 at Harvard's Carpenter Center, where she also went on to teach, as well as at several other academic institutions. A whimsical view of a bath from a bather's perspective, done in rough line drawings on paper, *Tub Film* ends with a slurp as the woman disappears down the drain, after the cat pulls the plug. *Seed Reel* , a series of 3 sexual haikus, is done in the same rough outline style: in *Hungry Poem*, (reverse printed with white lines on black), a peniverous flower devours its mate and swells into a pregnant belly; *Sniff and Lick* portrays the encounters of some very erotic flowers, and *12 Dancing Penises* dance to the tune of Turkey in the Straw. In *Going Home Sketchbook* and *Paul Revere Is Here* she experiments with rotoscoping and shows her deftness in handling a technique that, in other hands, can become tedious, but which for Beams becomes an exciting way of recapturing the spontaneity of the hand-drawn image. [3]

A scientific whaling expedition provided source material for *Whale Songs* from which she creates a lyrical interpretation of whales int he sea. 'She works her rotoscoped line into a nervous calligraphy, identifies the screen with tthe surface of the sea and makes compelling use of repetition.' [4]

In her last independently made film, *School in the Sky*, a girl dreams she flies to school in the sky: a boy dreams he falls off a cliff, the girl dreams she rescues him. The chalkboard-like colours come from the negative film used as reversal, making the colours and values opposite on film from what they were on cels. [5]

In the 80s Beams turned to the commercial sector and began working with computers, both for animation, computer graphics and interactive communications.

In 1987 she began working on a programme for TV, *Meet the Pundit*, 'a collection of interviews with, and cartoons from, the top ten political cartoonists..and a daily series of cartoons for television news..the animation is limited, the idea is exciting, and has a large potential audience.

'In our process of finding a camera person, we ended up finding Al Stahl, who's an old time animator. He was the original Popeye animator and he's gotten into all this video equipment. He's an old guy who's embraced the new world. I would never have run into that if I'd still been working independently. Working in a job, I've run into other areas that I didn't know about and I've been able to learn about things like advertising, how business works, what a media department does, all these people who I would never have met…it's been a real expansion…

'I've been taking a break from independent animation for quite a while. But I'm getting back into it. I don't know if it will be animation. It might be video or it might be computer art…

'I ran into a real problem with not having an audience. In the old days it was so cheap to make animation that that wasn't an issue. You made films for yourself and eventually you'd find a small audience. But that's not possible, at least in my estimation, any more. I know people are still doing it but I've had to think more what might be commercially viable and I've had to find other outlets for practising…

'The declining audience seems like it started with Proposition 13 in California… the first result of that was that they yanked all the budgets from the schools for film rentals, among a lot of other things. But that really pulled the rug out from under the distribution of independent work and things went downhill from there.' [6]

References
1. Talia (Thelma) Schenkel, op.cit.
2. Museum of Modern Art, New York, Circulating Film Library Catalogue..
3. John Canemaker, *Millimeter*, Feb.1977.
4. J. Hoberman, *Village Voice*.
5. MOMA, op cit.
6. Excerpted by kind permission of the author, from an unpublished master's degree thesis by Maureen Furniss: *The Current State of American Independent Animation and a Prediction for its Future,* presented to San Diego State University, Fall 1987.

The Woman's Voice in Contemporary American Animation: An analysis of Suzan Pitt's *Asparagus* and Joanna Priestley's *All My Relations* by Sharon Couzin.

To describe the woman's voice in contemporary animation requires a brief historical note on the representation of women in animation as well as their lack of participation in the planning and execution of these works. In addition we must look to the role the feminist movement has played in both understanding and articulating the place of women in art in general - how at this point we may say the movement has re-politicised art, in this case film.

To address these issues I wish to refer to two animations: *Asparagus* by Suzan Pitt and *All My Relations* by Joanna Priestley. While we may debate the defintions of feminist theory and female imagery, I do not think we will deny the issues, concerns, nor subject matter of these two films. I have chosen these two films, one which uses language, one which does not, because I am particularly interested in the iconographic qualities of animation in a field where the ruling ideologies of language have, in many cases, reduced or limited critical discourse by narrowly inscribing meaning.

I do not quarrel with the ideologies of feminism - the close linguistic reading was a necessary imperative to construct a field of inquiry. Laura Mulvey's seminal essay as well as the work of Julia Kristeva and Gayatri Spivak (among many, many others) advances our understanding of art, as well as ourselves. However, they address the visual arts mainly as a subset of language.

I am interested here in exploring visual language, and suggest that by examining the iconography of these films we may give a re-reading which renders both of these films powerful feminist works hingeing, not on text, but on image alone in the case of *Asparagus*, and on the collaborative process between text and image in *All My Relations*. In the latter film there are two sets of images going on at all times, one functioning as a frame while the referential quality of the inner and outer narratives in the image create their own dialectic and in so doing respond to the political agenda of feminism in this case, rather than being part and parcel of the illusionism assigned to the Hollywood studio style, which is the primary focus of feminist film theory.

Historically the woman had no voice at all in animation. The field was occupied by men in the conception, rendering and distribution. The very early individual artists who animated - Winsor McCay, for example - revealed an obsession to identify themselves as having magical creative powers. Self-figuration was as popular with the filmmakers as with the audiences. No woman figured in those early films. Studio productions depicted female characters as either unimportant, caricatured, objectified or as lazy, stupid and aggressive, or as idealised, fantasised sex objects. *Red Hot Riding Hood*, or Coal Black (from Robert Clampett's *Coal Black and De Sebben Dwarfs*) and of course Betty Boop are obvious examples of the sexual stereotypes.

But as early as Farmer Alfalfa the wife was depicted as a nagging, nasty one-dimensional figures. Other characters developed somewhat more rounded natures; Olive Oyl, for example, or Little Lulu, both had some spark of independent thought, but quite clearly the social mores of the time dictated that the mythology position the male in the heroic lead.

Ideas of representation of self figure not only in the two animated films considered here but were absolutely central to the avant-garde film movement in America which came to prominence during the 60s. Working in many cases against conventional narrative, animators like Mary Ellen Bute (mid 30s) and Marie Menken (late 50s) set the stage for work done in the last twenty years.

The avant-garde filmmakers worked poetically, graphically, and metaphorically, often bridging the areas between animation and live cinematography. Men as well as women worked abstractly, establishing territory which, in many instances, was only much later explored by women and then in a radically different way. Key animators like Viking Eggeling, Oskar Fischinger, Fernand Léger, and Man Ray focused on the graphic, iconic order of things - allowing composition, colour, and other formal elements to outweigh a secular narrative, ever popular in the studio animation film.

How did this secular narrative affect women artists? 19th century writing provides insights. As an art form it allowed the development of the woman's voice for self-acknowledgement. The stories written by women and about women were ones which valued domestic power, necessary for the rise of a middle class. However, that same power existed in a separate realm from the important decisions of society. Women's relations to objects, especially domestic objects, served as a surrogate region of legitimate focus, objectifying people as well as things. Without real power women became marginalised, objectified. Their creative voices were expressed in many cases through 'women's work', quilts, weaving, embroidery, the handicrafts. In the 20th century we can trace great interest in the soap opera and various forms of confessional fiction.

'But', points out Lucy Lippard, 'women also care more about variety than men, and variety connects to fragmentation and to the autobiographical aspect, too - as a sort of defiance.'[1] The women's movement made questions of female imagery and feminine aesthetics central to any discussion of art made by women. What is female imagery? Is there such a thing as feminine aesthetics? Like women working in other media, by 1970 women animators began to question the common modes of representation. The idea of 'female imagery' was first used to mean 'sexual imagery'. In the world of art, body art, happenings, performances, dance, and painting all used sexual imagery. Judy Chicago's work, Carolee Schneeman's films and performances, Eva Hesse's organic sculptures were all central to the iconographic background of filmmakers like Pitt and Priestley. On female imagery Lippard states:

'I prefer (the term) female sensuality because it's vaguer, and broader. There's lots of sexual imagery in woman's art - circles, domes, eggs, spheres, boxes, bimorphic shapes, maybe certain striation or layering. But it's more interesting to think about fragments, which imply a certain antilogical, antilinear approach common to many women's work.' [2]

Early feminist theory thus concentrated on the representation of women and on the gender of authorship. Feminist intellectuals have engaged in increasingly sophisticated forms of theoretical argumentation and textual analysis. However, the feminist movement is also, and perhaps more importantly, a movement linked to a political ideology and a social movement involving a process of change. How the theoretical concepts come to be used in cultural practice cannot happen through language alone as many literary and philosophical voices have seemed to assume.

Films like *Asparagus* and *All My Relations* are solid examples of avant-garde feminist films which are embedded with numerous political issues. Feminist art is art which acknowledges the difference of being a woman – i.e. what it is to be a woman – and then integrates that consciousness into the art. It may involve a set of imagery or it may function metaphorically or poetically. Many women deal more openly with feelings, with their own and with others' and, as a movement, feminist art tends to be more humanistic than formal. Making people aware through your art is a political act even if the work of art itself is not directly political.

Asparagus by Suzan Pitt is a film of social critique and a deeply personal visual narrative on identity. The theme of identity spirals around gender, fetish, sexuality and nature. In many ways the film fulfills the requirements of 19th century confessional literature. It is 'about' domesticity, power and sexual politics. Pitt's major themes of identity and gender are explored through three major motifs: the asparagus/phallus, (which she equates to nature and wholeness), the faceless woman, who is both a magician and mother figure, and the relation of

objects to self (which conjoins narcissism and fetishism). Let us examine these three motifs more carefully.

The asparagus/phallus (which Pitt equates to nature and wholeness) is a contradictory image, problematic for feminists because it clearly carries possible readings of penis envy, and acceptance of the patriarchal order. The artist herself would not agree to this and reads the asparagus as an almost primeval plant with both a male and female stage in its development. After planting asparagus seeds Pitt watched the miniscule phallic shoots grow into delicate fernlike fronds – definite female images. The phallic 'other' would be claimed by many to not refer to the phallus icon but to the desire or longing to have, or possess that other (which in any psychoanalytic reading would of course refer to the original 'other' - the mother. Logically then, a simple psychoanalytic reading could position the asparagus, as Pitt does, as faeces, as the castrated penis, and as the powerful desiring impetus which embodies the inability of both male and female to ever completely replicate that infantile empathy at the mother's breast.

The second motif, the faceless woman, also holds the possibility of a variety of interpretations – the necessary polysemic quality – consistent with Pitt's requirement of herself in the making of the film. Pitt desired each frame to contain 'everything', every colour, every shape, for all of the space to be compositionally occupied; for each 24th of a second to be trembling with movement. The artist here positions herself in the all-powerful role of magician/creator. But it is also the role of the all-providing mother and to the extent we accept her argument that the phallus represents nature, here the blank face could also represent the universal mother figure. This countenances the linguistic notions of 'mother nature', 'earth mother'. The blank face can be described as representing a loss of identity, but equally as abstract neutral terrain onto which the voyeuristic viewer must place an interpretation. By this account there are many possibilities, all of which force us to become an active participant in the viewing process.

This film is not presented as entertainment. It is a process, not a set of pre-existing conditions. For example, the blank face could be said to represent a lack of detail. And in the reading of Shor's book 'Reading in Detail' the claim is made that, historically, details in art have been gender-attached to women. They have been equivalent to deformities and aberrations while the larger, abstract universal ideas in art have always been ascribed to men.[3] Is the artist refusing such an interpretation by reducing the face to an abstract representation of idea of face? Is it then like the asparagus, both male and female? Or does it simply make a political statement validating the worth of the female by pointing to the contradictions in the art historical system (since that same system embraces realism which is completely dependent on the veracity of the detail...).

We could go farther with our inquiry into interpetation. Is the loss of identity accomplished by the destructive effects some women feel because of their desire to merge totally with a partner? We do not see a partner in Pitt's film, but then the entire film seems to represent some interior space, some stream of consciousness and to reflect mainly the protagonist's feelings. For many women the overwhelming desire for fusion (with a partner) followed by rejection, is indicative of the problem of 'feeling too much'[4]

Or does an artist experience a narcissistic dependency reliant upon others as a means of self-validation through their art? Or, even more directly, is the lack of detail in the face a request by the artist for us to give back to her, to 'fill in the detail' as it were, with as much richness, color, and charged emotions as she has given us in the rest of the scenes? I would suggest that it is as important to recognize the array of possible interpretations as to choose a 'correct' interpretation.

The third motif, the relation of objects to self, shifts curiously from a self absorbed narcissism to an almost fetishistic involvement with personal and domestic objects. A qualified 'domestic', however, because the site of the film is clearly an interior space; the space of dreams and fantasies. The objects in the space are all stylized, kitsch déco, often in pairs, usually decoratively detailed. The constraints of cause and effect are minimal, a feature of animation used in a manner that again directs our attention to the artist -ironic, since the artist both denies or conceals her identity within the film but clearly

has created a film of spectacle and power. In this case, through unusual objects and bizarre relationships: we are consistently asked to see the protagonist as the filmmaker or creator of the film. The protagonist's relationship to the space is highly charged: the soft organic shapes of the furniture, draperies, wallpapers, lighting fixtures, etc are all shaped and coloured in a similar manner. All seem to be a homogeneous extension of the main character.

The garden is of central importance and repeats the basic binary structure Pitt uses throughout: inner/outer. As the deep red curtains are pulled back they reveal a garden of fantastic exotic plants which begin to slowly revolve. We see two very large feet step into the garden and we watch from inside with the faceless woman as a large hand reaches down and caresses/masturbates the asparagus stalk.

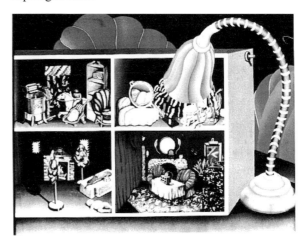

This dreamlike observing of the self is echoed in the doll house scene. The protagonist walks up to a table on which sits a dollhouse with rooms open in front. As she reaches over to turn a knob a close-up balloon shows her hand in detail twisting the knob. As the knob turns, the camera zooms up to one of the rooms in the dollhouse which is furnished exactly like the one the protagonist has been standing in just before the camera zoomed up. Pitt creates an infinite regress, an ultimate déjà vu experience through a looping of the scene. The dollhouse regress displaces memories of the childhood dollhouse with the role of the mother and suggests two or three possible interpretations. Is it merely a comment on family rituals-the middle class doll and the attendant dollhouse accessories? Does it overtly connect to the lack of other people in this internal space? Or does it speak of the alienation and isolation of the artist's work? Or the solitary nature of subjective work, as opposed to Hollywood studio narrative production where hundreds of people may be involved? Certainly there are no children here. Is it a suggestion that infantile desires or anxieties continue to be played out in adulthood? Is it a formal device, a play thing of the adult which uses time rather than objects? Is the dollhouse a fetish object?

As social critique, *Asparagus* is a highly personal narrative: melancholy, evocative and enigmatic. It clearly questions the relation of inner life and outer world and presents the dilemma of the female artist, at one with herself in search of a voice. The film is not only a stunningly beautiful work of animation, but also an important document of the struggle to articulate through the image the role of the woman.

All My Relations by Joanna Priestley was completed in 1990, a good twelve years after *Asparagus*. The film reflects many changes in American society and the woman's movement. While *All My Relations* is filled with social critique it is more importantly a film made by a collaborative process in which Priestley allowed the meaning of the film, in large part, to be determined by the voices on the soundtrack.

The two narrators, Scott and Victoria Parker, were shown the film approximately fifty times and asked to improvise with no directions from Priestley. The resulting dialogue is their interpretation of Priestley's animation. Initially the narrative describes the mental and emotional states of the two main characters, represented by two abstract shapes, one a man, one a woman. The dialogue between the two begins as they walk toward and then past one another and follows a fairly typical girl finds (saves) boy narrative and humorously depicts the rapid and excited thrills of early romance which lead in the film to love, marriage, a child, a house, job, money, etc. At some point the path twists and each of the characters begins to blame one another and an extended argument/ row begins with rapidly cut images to reinforce visually

the emotional trauma. There is none of the personal mystery, as in *Asparagus*. Instead, a fairly public collective unconscious seems to shape much of the chronology and morality of the film, which is where the gender roles assume larger significance.

The animation formally has a particularly interesting structure - a central image composed of drawn figures which are symbolic shapes - and a surrounding frame which actually constitutes an outer film. The outer film consists of various collections of objects and artifacts, animated by eight different people. The dialectic between the two parts of the film, the inner drawn one with the more conventional narrative text, the outer 'frame' silent, but reacting to or commenting on or creating an alternative to the central story, provides an oddly satisfying narrative of its own. It is as though we hear what we are supposed to in the central narrative but are also free to construct our own interpretation of what is going on in the border. In a manner parallel to the way Priestley worked with Scott and Victoria Parker, and with the collaborators of the frame section, she is also permitting, perhaps even requiring that the audience also engage directly with the content of the film.

As in Pitt's film, colour, texture, and composition give notice that a sensuous, tactile story, filled with emotion - the outer a subjective response, the inner a painful, angry and also humorous set of emotions - are both 'confessions' of an intimate personal space. Both parts of Priestley's film construct their own worlds and set up in the image a language of representation which we must accept in order to engage with this film.

Piaget in his basic research with children explored at great length how systems of representation develop. Initially representation can occur only after imitation.[5] Sounds and phonations are his primary examples, but interestingly, image symbols develop before language symbols. Piaget describes an example of how the 'mental image' which must occur before representation takes place must first be an interiorization.

'When L. wanted to open the box which was almost closed and tried to anticipate, through representation, the future development of the situation, she resorted to opening and closing her mouth.' [6]

This mental image was clearly not an imitation of external events because the event had not yet happened, it was in process. This image-forming process develops much like the processes of intelligence development. The transformation of imitation into images involves a much larger degree of interiorisation than language. Even in daydreams and dreams themselves, the imitation of experienced situations and of people and things are strikingly exact to the smallest detail, is translated into images. Visual representations which spring from quite primitive (but quite basic and powerful) understandings form the basis of the central story in *All My Relations*. The story is full of detail and nuance but the drawings are really quite simple and in their simplicity I would suggest they have their strength.

Piaget further claims that because images remain private interiorisations, while language becomes public, we can never share images to the extent that and with subtlety, we can language. These considerations help explain, I think, why the imagery in this film is given meaning by the language and felt as strongly as it is. I would suggest that Priestley has chosen images and scenes that are very basic and symbolically common - we can all respond to them in addition to, even despite, the emotional chaos of the narrative.

Which brings us to the narrative. The film clearly asks for both social and personal change. It shows us the process of it's making. At the moment when the camera first pulls back to reveal the frame around the picture (the drawn cels), any sense of illusionism we may have imagined is gone. While this cannot be explored here, I would suggest that many successful animations create characters and situations which attain a state similar to the mimetic qualities of film without actually being so. In any case, in *All My Relations* the frame is important (the frame changes, dissolving from one to another) because it/they retain a kind of Romantic individualism; subjective, personal and separate yet part of the collaborative process in this film - much like a community quilt. The various frames include: candy, buttons, crayons, rubber dolls, fish lures, primitive paintings, flowers, cloth, crushed metal, wadded up newspapers, etc.

The narrative places the voice in the same place as the face in *Asparagus* but fills in the details i.e. we see the female character change from nurturing, supportive, to helpless, overwhelmed, to aggressive, angry, hurt, disappointed, to paranoid, determined, etc. A quite naturalistic scenario is played out by the central characters, mainly through the sound. In the image Priestley uses abstraction and playfulness, a combination which is rarely seen among feminist art and is extremely successful here.

Simple drawn shapes combined with a deceptively sophisticated soundtrack are especially effective in large part because the soundtrack is a fragmented and somewhat hysterical piece of realist narrative which touches on most of the topics relegated to 'women's films' of the 40s and 50s: sacrifice, affliction, and competition. The hysteria of the woman provides a critique of emotion, of the shifting patterns of middle class marriages - who is responsible for what - and presents a reworking of melodrama.

In this version the man at some point says 'I'll just leave' and does, taking the child with him - probably the most obvious marker of real change in the nuclear family. The dog functions as the 'enabler' in these dysfunctional interactions and while we may or may not wish to interpret the dog symbolically, we must notice that he is always male and by biting the female provokes a sense of helplessness, anger, withdrawal and feelings of victimization.

The female character is, however, in the process of self-transformation. She is struggling toward autonomy rather than identity and as such reviews the array of problems which face women in just the personal, domestic arena (never mind the workplace, etc). The self-transformation evident in this film echoes the emphasis in the women's movement on the 'necessity of changing consciousness through personal recognition of the all-pervasive nature of female subordination. In so far as narrative constitutes one of the most important ways in which ideologies are concretized in relation to life experience, the emergence of new plots for women which emphasise autonomy rather than dependence should be welcomed as an indication of the influence of feminism upon the cultural and ideological domain.'[7]

What is important at this point in animation is to recognise the significance of women artists who take risks in creating work which radically intrudes on conventional forms, traditional 'plots', especially for women and conventional expectations from cinema.

I would hope for a more direct investigation of the role of representation through the image and for more involvement by women at every stage of production and reception of animation. Films like *Asparagus* and *All My Relations* reinforce, enrich and privilege the opening up of representation, a process which affects all of us by building bridges between theory and embodiment.

References:
1   Lucy Lippard, *From the Center*, Reprinted from MS 3, No. 11 (May 1975) p 88.
2   Ibid. p 81.
3   Naomi Schor, *Reading In Detail, Aesthetics and the Feminine*, (Routledge: New York and London 1987) pp. 11-22.
4   Rita Felski, *Beyond Feminist Aesthetics, 'On Confession'*, (Methuen, 1987) p 109.
5   Jean Piaget, *Play, Dreams and Imitation in Childhood*, (WW Norton and Co, Inc. 1962) pp. 6-86.
6   Ibid. p 71.
7   Felski, p 152.
© Sharon Couzin, Chicago, 1991. Presented as a paper for the Society for Animation Studies, October 1991.

Monique Renault: feminist pioneer

In the introduction to this book, the relative paucity of women animators in Europe in comparision with the situation in the UK and the United States was noted. It's somewhat ironic that one of the earliest pioneers of feminist animation should be French, although Monique Renault has chosen to live and work largely in Holland.

Although some might see her work as didactic and, like many issue based films, not always wearing too well, the strength, wit and inspirational effect her films had for many women, both as animators and viewers, cannot be denied.

Her films have dealt with such contentious issues as the church's historical endorsement of the repression of women, historical rendition and its male bias; women working in a male working world; wife battering; women

and the law. Much of her work has been made in collaboration with other women, although in 1988 she made the multi-award winning film, *Pas à Deux*, a fast-moving comedy sketch with an edge of social satire, with Dutch animator Gerrit van Dijk, who has been accused of misogyny in his films. It's a sad reflection of how women animators tend to be seen in Europe that, through no fault of van Dijk's, most of the press coverage assumed she was his assistant; her drawings were used for articles on the film but credited to him – even, she notes wryly, when the journalists were women.

She was born in 1939 in Rennes, France, and in the letter excerpted below, she describes, with characteristic wit and warmth, her trajectory and development as a feminist filmmaker.

"My mother was very conventional, very Catholic and also very funny. With me, she was completely different than with my four older sisters. They had to get married as soon as possible. I did not. I was able to study art. First in Rennes, then in Paris, in 1962. I studied painting. Always with the idea of one day working in animated films. That was the only thing I was sure about. And also not to get married and not to get any children, before…long time! There were enough in our family! I was not at all involved in feminism. For about ten years I have been looking around me, a bit stupid and passive, I think! I was very interested in men. Only their opinions were valuable. Only 'they' were interesting. Women? Pouah. Competition. After 68, like many other people, I started to look at it differently. That was also my first experience with an animated film festival, in Annecy. I got very upset to see the way my colleagues were depicting women. I thought it was very unfair! And I decided to do the same, but reverse. Still refusing to join or be accounted part of any feminist movement. Still devoted to men!

I started doing my first animated film, *Psychoderche*, a very short one minute story of a woman kissing a man's bottom and laughing. My male friends were very shocked and advised me not to show a film so bad for my reputation. I was not able to make films. I had to stay a good disciplined assistant. I said 'thank you…I did not mean to hurt…'

But, ironically, without me knowing, Marco Ferrari chose the film to be shown with his feature *La Grande Bouffe*. All France saw it.

I started to think differently…Then one day, I met Nicole Lise Berheim. She had founded Musidora,

with other women cinéastes. Then I realised I was not alone any more. I did not need to be sorry, and feminists were not those terrible Amazons…and yes, I was a feminist. And I was still beautiful and did not turn into a bad imitation of a male figure…Together we organised the first womens' film festival in Paris, in 73. It was a beautiful time.

I started a new film, *A la Votre*, working by day in a studio (A.A.A.) as head animator, and making my film during the weekends. And then another one with Jacqueline Veuve, *Swiss Graffitti*. A film I like personally very much. Then with my feminist luggage I came to Amsterdam to work for a few months. It's now 12 years. I have made a child, some more films…I have been working freelance for Dutch TV, making animated sequences for a feminist discussion programme. I got money from the government not only to make my own films but also to make one about battered wives, *Hands Off*. Last year Channel 4 in London gave us the money to make a series of films about women and the law (see feature), called *Blind Justice*. Honestly, I do not think I would have had all those opportunities if I had stayed in France. It's a bit sad to say…but it's so.

I like very much to be in Amsterdam. What I do find difficult is to educate my boy as a feminist mother…a question of love, I guess, and I do love him. I often have the feeling my mother, my dear mother, took her revenge through me, she wanted me to be different from my sisters, to have more chances to accomplish myself than she had. I thank her. Amen!"

From a letter dated October 27th, 1987, to Liz McQuiston, sent for her book Women in Design: a contemporary view, *see ß.*

Her interest in animation was sparked at the age of twelve, by a school screening of McLaren's *C'est l'aviron.* But there were no opportunities to learn animation at the art colleges she attended, so she got a job at a Paris animation studio Praxinoscope as a paint'n'tracer…wryly noting she never saw men doing this, only women.

'I felt very alone when I started to express myself in the 70's, and was ridiculed for my feminist ideas. I think only Gillian Lacey and Vera Neubauer know and understand what it was not being considered professional…I must say talented women working in animation did not dare to be considered disgraceful by making feminist films.'

Borderline 2

A laVotre

Kitty Taylor, an animator, wrote the following for the 1985 Cambridge Animation Festival's Monique Renault retrospective.

Over the past ten years independent animator Monique Renault has skilfully used the medium of animation to make a series of pertinent social and political arguments. The recurring themes of pacificism and feminism are not so much the subjects of her films as their motivation. Eschewing the self-indulgent display of spectacular visual effects that too often passes as a substitute for content these days, Monique Renault has concentrated on the potential of animation as a powerful medium of information, instruction and debate.

Since moving to the less hostile environment of Holland, she has been able to find funding for a series of films aimed directly at minority audiences. This has come from both private and public organisations, and from government bodies and Dutch television companies.

Her films have reached substantial audiences thanks to a comprehensive distribution network set up by a group of women who saw the potential demand for such work.

The films are stylistically interesting as well as polemical. A number of them were commissioned for educational use, and are therefore fairly straightforwardly didactic. But much of her more personal work takes the form of visual metaphor. *Weg Ermee*, an anti-nuclear film, uses the rousing image of a pair of hands squeezing the violent energy out of a missile - which bears a fleeting resemblance to a male phallus. *A la votre* uses rather less alarming images, but is also a metaphorical illustration of the real uses of men: 'take one regularly with a glass of water', perhaps! *Borderline 1 & 2* deal with the different sets of values held by women and men. *Borderline 1*, for example, is set in an office and highlights the problems faced by women in a male working world.

The *Borderline* films also display another characteristic of Monique Renault's work: humour This too has a particularly feminist edge, as is displayed by the periodic reappearance of a jaunty but slightly incompetent penis. This has a starring part in *Swiss Graffiti* where he plays many roles in the story of the Creation and beyond.

The western Church is a regular object of her sometimes virulent comical assaults. *Swiss Graffiti* and *In Nomine Domini* deal specifically with the Church's historical endorsement of the repression of women. *In Nomine Domini* includes a particularly striking image of a dancing pope [interestingly, this reappears in *Pas à Deux*, ed. note]. *Salut Marie* describes a feminist version of the rendezvous between Mary and the Archangel.

Her most recent work. *Blijf van m'n Lijf (Hands Off)* is her most ambitious project so far. It is intended as a stimulus for discussion, within the broader campaign against wife battering. As such, it is being used in police stations and refuges, as well as being shown in cinemas and on television. It was funded by the Dutch Ministry of Welfare, Health and Cultural Affairs, and made in close collaboration. with the Blijf m'n Lijf association. It combines drawn and photographic images, and incorporates recorded interviews with women in refuges.

This film in particular illustrates the strength of this type of animation, and Renault's sensitivity and dedication in creating it. It also indicates the benefits of the positive policies towards independent films in Holland, which contrasts with the general timidity and conservatism in this country. Her work is direct and uncompromising. Her political comments and the often discomforting images through which she presents them have provoked critical resistance as well as praise and support.

Pas à Deux

Equal Rights

Monique Renault

The situation in Holland has changed since the above was written. One writer has noted 'Commitment in the sense of drawing attention to problem areas or social abuses has certainly not disappeared from Dutch animation; it is just mainly restricted to commissioned films and no longer found in independent productions.' Renault herself feels the situation is difficult again now, and in terms of the problems facing women in animation cites the experience of how *Pas à Deux* was received.

In *Pas à Deux* a constantly changing processsion of historic characters, symbols of the images of men and women (Superman, Popeye, Marilyn Monroe, Betty Boop) perform a number of different dances, from the java, via tango and waltz to breakdancing. The film's theme is still in line with Renault's earlier work, but it is very much implied. Throughout the history of dance women have increasingly danced further away from men. The man lost his leading position, the woman has gained more freedom.

Elsewhere in Europe...

It's hardly surprising that there are so few women animators in Western Europe, since there are few opportunities - for men or women - to make art or personal animation films. The European Community's Media initiative, Cartoon, has done much to stimulate the animation industries, but the emphasis is on commercial production, mainly TV series for children and animated features, and is prompted by a fear that indigenous production will disappear in the face of cheap imports of American product, and the far cheaper costs of animation labour in the Far East.

Whilst the relative paucity of animation production is clearly related to economic factors, and state arts funding policies at national and local levels, opportunities to learn animation are equally limited, as it is rarely featured in art college curricula.

Holland has, through state support, developed an interesting range of animators, such as Paul Driessen and Gerrit von Dijk, but apart from Monique Renault, Ellen Meske and one or two others, there are very few women making animation.

In France there is generous state support for short films - both in terms of production finance and distribution support via the Agence du Court-Metrage, plus a number of short film festivals. Although animation films are made, they tend usually to the 'cartoony'. Television, particularly the popular pay-TV channel Canal Plus, makes a point of regular and imaginative scheduling for short films, and also occasionally invests, as does the arts channel, La Sept, which has funded several more experimental or innovative animation films. Few are made by women. There are, however, some exceptions. Marie-Christine Perrodin made the delighful mix of live-action and animation, *Porte Plume*, about a schoolboy's imaginative daydreaming through an art lesson. The film was made in collaboration with a group of schoolchildren and is a creative exploration of animation itself. Animator Jean-Francois Laguionie's studio in the south of France, La Fabrique, attempts to use TV series' commissions to finance more individual films, and Nicole Dufour has made some films there.

Solveig von Kleist, a successful painter and designer, was born in Germany and studied film graphics in the US, at Cal Arts, but has been living in France since the mid-80s. Her first film, *Criminal Tango*, was an extremely accomplished scratched-on-film narrative of paranoia, drawing on the iconography of film noir, with a heroine who is part cat-woman. *Panta Rhei* is completely different in style (drawn and painted). The animation is fluid and fast-moving, and the film integrates formal play on animation's properties into a witty conceptualisation of

the Heraclitean proverb. She is, sadly, somewhat pessimistic about opportunities to continue filmmaking in France.

Belgian animator Nicole von Goethen's films are traditionally cel-animated and cartoon-styled. Her hilarious Oscar-winning *Greek Tragedy* is a comic allegory of women sheding the burdens imposed on them by the (male) cultural traditions of Western civilisation. Religious ecstasy takes on a whole new meaning in *Full of Grace*, in which two nuns find a new way to feel the love of God after a mistaken purchase (vibrators instead of candles) after a power cut at the convent.

Since the early 80s there has been some development of animation in (what was) West Germany. Animation courses have been set up in Kassell (led by Polish animator Jan Lenica), where Paul Driessen also teaches, and in Hamburg and Stuttgart. Stuttgart has a bi-annual Animation Festival, whose reputation has built rapidly through its innovative programming and hugely appreciative audiences. Bettina Bayerl combines commercial films with her own work; Sabine Huber and Annette Wragge are promising student animators. American Kathy Joritz, (*Negative Man* and *Give Aids the Freeze*) has lived and worked productively in Germany for the past eight years.

It's interesting, however, that although there are few women making animation films, there are quite a few who are very active as producers. In France, Nicole Jouve and Marcelle Ponti have produced and encouraged animators; the latter also gave British animator Sheila Graber the chance to pursue filmmaking full-time. Celia van Dijk in Holland has produced all of her husband's films, and Borge Ring's *Aina and Bella*. She has, almost single-handedly, been extremely active in promoting art animation, running a 16mm distribution company, Little People, which is almost entirely self-funded. Given the gradual decline of 16mm distribution, however, and the strain of doing it all at home, Celia is currently lobbying for funds to establish an Animation Centre, to provide training and develop 35mm distribution on a less precarious footing.

In Austria the Studio for Experimental Animation at Vienna's School of Applied Arts (Hochschule für angewandte Künste) appears to be producing a number of women animation filmmakers.

Computer animation, in Italy, seems to be the main area in which women are working. Raffaella Filipponi studied in Canada, where she made some films, and has since been been working in computer graphics in Milan. Elena Chiesa, with Todd Ruff, made the highly regarded computer animation *Green Movie*.

Animation in the UK

an introduction

The 80s saw British animation generally make a dramatic impact world-wide, celebrated for its wide range of talent, technical achievement, and innovative subject matter. Women making animation films in the UK have been as prominent as men in the field, and have shared in the acclaim, and international festival awards.

The following is a brief overview of the situation of women animators in the UK. Most of the filmmakers cited are discussed further in subsequent chapters, or in the A - Z section.

There have always been a lot of women working in the animation industry. Very few, however, had the opportunity to make their own films. Vera Linnecar, Nancy Hannah and Kathleen 'Spud' Houston were amongst the earliest to make the transition from animating to directing, but only towards the end of their long careers.

In the 70s Alison de Vere produced the award winning films, *Café Bar* and *Mister Pascal*. The London Film School, at that time much less expensive to attend than now, also provided opportunities for Antoinette Starciewicz and Thalma Goldman to make a name for themselves. Starciewicz's *Puttin' on the Ritz* and *High Fidelity*, were both highly accomplished, retro-styled homages to 30s American song and dance. Goldman's work was somewhat controversial for its frank and disturbing explorations of women and sexuality, particularly in *Stanley* and *Amateur Night*

Vera Neubauer also began her prolific career in the mid 70s, and her films *Animation for Live Action* and *The Decision* must be considered classics of early feminist, and avant-garde, animation.

The reason so many women have emerged as an exciting force in British animation in the 80s is bound up with the development of art, or adult, animation generally - although the impact of feminism on arts funding policy, and latterly in television practice have played a role. Several inter-connected factors are relevent. The growth of inter-disciplinarity in higher education, and the development of animation as an option in a wide range of degree courses, (e.g. Fine Art, Media Studies, Graphics, Illustration, Film and Video) has built on the strength and diversity of art colleges around the country. Each provides a very different approach to the teaching of animation, in terms of techniques and theoretical approach.

Channel 4 televison was created in 1981, with a specific remit for innovation, and to cater for minority interests. Jeremy Isaacs, who ran the new channel, included animation for adult audiences, and as an art form, as part of this brief, and hired Paul Madden as Commissioning Editor for this area. For the first time animators were able to obtain funding for developing, and making, entire films, as well as, in some cases, completion money. Although scheduling didn't really do justice to the work when finished, this is starting to change, with attempts by Clare Kitson, Madden's successor, to programme regular animation strands, which have achieved press coverage and very appreciative audiences. Kitson, a figure well known and admired in the British and international animation community, has also set up a joint funding venture with the Arts Council of Great Britain for more experimental or innovative films. Another of her initiatives has been the highly successful 'Animators in Residence' scheme at London's Museum of the Moving Image. This provides a wage, and work space, for animators to develop a project, and so far several have justified commissions.

During this time, the animation industry has flourished, with British studios in great demand both here and abroad, particularly for television and cinema commercials. TVC make childrens films that achieve almost instant classic status - e.g. *The Snowman*, and *Granpa*, both directed by Diane Jackson. Ads, in comparison with many other countries, are extremely sophisticated, allowing a degree of experimentation and play on self-referentiality that many animators find rewarding in itself. On the most basic level, working in commercials pays the rent (and can be a very good living). But it can also provide opportunities to try out new techniques and equipment, which would otherwise be prohibitively expensive, as well as demanding a discipline which feeds back into more personal work. Pop videos are another source of work and creative challenge. Annabel Jankel and Rocky Morton at Cucumber Studios were pioneers in this field, demonstrating how creatively animation could be used.

The revival of the bi-annual Animation Festival, (part funded by C4), under Irene Kotlarcz' direction, and held at Cambridge, Bristol, and Cardiff over the last eight years, has helped build animation's public profile, and develop audiences, as has the regular programming of animation in British Film Institute-associated and art cinemas around the UK. More recently, the BFI has ventured into video publishing of adult animation, in addition to cinema and non-theatrical distribution, with an encouraging degree of success.

It's a commonplace that critical mass is necessary to allow diversity and growth, and that seems to be happening in the UK. The Aardman Animation studio's success has increased employment opportunities, and helped develop Bristol as a productive animation centre, as did David Anderson's Redwing Studio. BBC Bristol funded some

Joanna Quinn's Girls' Night Out

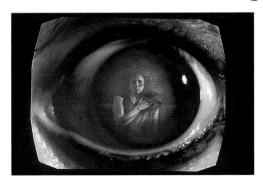

Chitra Shriram's Maya

Antoinette Starciewicz' Pianoforte   *Antoinette Starciewicz' Koko Pops*

Petra Freeman's The Mill

Sabrina Schmid's Middriffini   *Sabrina Schmid's Once as if a Balloon*

Caroline Leaf's Two Sisters

Joanna Woodward's The Brooch Pin and the Sinful Clasp

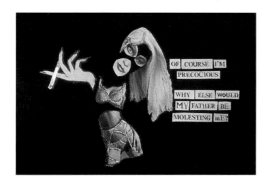

Karen Watson's Daddy's Little Bit of Dresden China

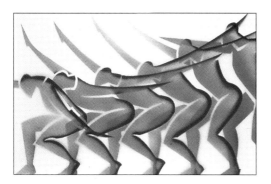 

Erica Russell's Feet of Song

Nina Shorina's Door   *Rimmimen & Roche's The Stain*

Alison de Vere's Black Dog

 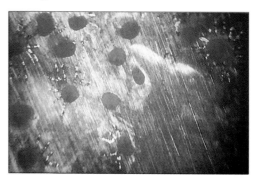

Emily Hubley's Emergence of Eunice   *Kayla Parker's Unknown Woman*

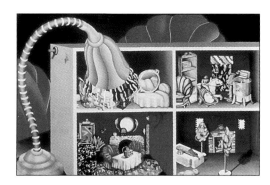

Suzan Pitt's Asparagus

Thalma Goldman's Stanley

Alison Snowden's Second Class Mail

Marjut Rimminen's Some Protection

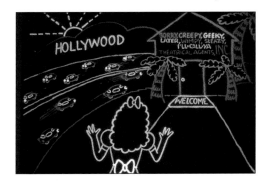

C. Kugel & V. Cafarelli's Snowie & the 7 Dorps

Sally Cruikshank's Quasi at the Quackadero

animation via *10 x 10*, a series encouraging new filmmakers, and have begun to commission animation specifically, although they have limited budgets as yet. Maya Brandt is a successful Bristol-based independent animator. Cardiff has several commercial studios that have developed alongside the Welsh TV Channel; this, and the work of Chapter Arts' Film & Video Workshop, have helped develop independent production locally.

Given these developments, it's interesting to look at how many of the emerging students have fared since college.

Susan Young, who made the stunning film *Carnival*, has been working in commercials and rock promos for the last six years. She is currently running a studio called Mojo Working, with two other women, which aims to provide a working agency base for like-minded animators, but where their work as artists will be respected. Karen Kelly, who as a student made the impressive *Egoli*, about black mine workers in South Africa, will be part of this set-up. Young would like to make her own films again, but only when she has created the right conditions to do so. She feels her experience in commercials and rock videos has developed assertiveness and an ability to defend the quality of her work, as well as developing her craft skills.

Young first studied animation at Liverpool Polytechnic, which under Ray Field's direction inspired a whole generation of students. Partly because of extremely limited budgets, but mainly because of his emphasis on animation as an art form, and encouragement to experiment, a distinctive style emerged that celebrated the power of line and colour, a richly suggestive minimalism. Susan Loughlin, who made *Grand National*, a graphic evocation of a day at the racetrack, was also a Liverpool Poly graduate, and is now at the NFTS.

Other Liverpool graduates include Yvonne Eckersley and Strinda Davis, who with Laura Knight formed Jackdaw Media, whose commercial commissions fund their education and production work, aiming to demystify animation and introduce it to children and adults. 'After we graduated we just didn't want to be based in London and be gobbled up. Instead we wanted to encourage the talent that's here in the city.' They call on a pool of freelancers, to help run workshops in schools, particularly those with special needs, and community-based courses; produce education packs and do outreach work beyond Liverpool. A recent commission to produce animated inserts for a C4 series, *Female Parts*, in collaboration with feminist cartoonist Angela Martin, has led to a project about the experience of teenage girls.

The National Film and Television School, richly resourced in comparison with most art colleges, has never had a well developed animation course, but has turned out several successful animators, from Nick Park and David Anderson to Joanna Woodward - all with very different styles.

Alison Snowden made her first animation, the Oscar-nominated *Second Class Mail* at the NFTS where she met her husband, David Fine, with whom she co-directs, and they now have a studio in South East London, after some time spent in Canada. Their films to date are characterised by fairly traditional cel animation with a gentle but idiosyncratic touch of humour. They are currently working on a film for C4, about the male menopause.

Joan Ashworth, who made *The Web*, a mini-epic, model-animated Gothic comedy based on Mervyn Peake's Gormenghast trilogy, at the NFTS, went on to found one of Britain's most successful model animation studios today, Three Peach. Although she is keen to make her own films, the capital investment and studio overheads make it difficult simply to take a break, especially with people on staff. She is hopeful of funding from C4 for a 12 minute film, *Pearls & Swine*, about a mermaid discovering her fertility, (with the barest of nods to Hans Andersen).

Karen Watson, who made the ground-breaking *Daddy's Little Bit of Dresden China*, on sexual abuse, graduated from West Surrey College of Art & Design, unique in offering a full-time undergraduate degree in animation. WSCD is known for its encouragement of innovation, in both form and content, with the emphasis on ideas and personal expression rather than purely technical proficiency. Department Head Roger Noake also brings his students into contact with a wide range of British and international animators as tutors.

A more recent graduate is Maybelle Peters, whose film *A Lesson on History* used text, music, and haunting aerial imaging to revise traditional British history, as told in schools, to one of colonial slavery and the strength of Black resistance. She is currently a MOMI Animator in Residence, developing *Mama Lou* (named after the famous 1880s Black American brothel singer), a tale of myth and superstition told across generations. She is part of the second wave of independent Black British filmmakers. She sees animation as a means of personal expression and her unique choice of this medium offers her even greater independence to do what she wants in the way that she wants to do it.

The Royal College of Art's post-graduate course has developed a strong reputation in recent years. Emma Calder's student film made there, *Madame Potato,* featuring a potato-print woman who achieves fame and fortune only to return to the earth which produced her, brought Calder press attention, and several offers of work. In 1989 she formed Pearly Oyster Productions with Ged Haney, a college friend and composer for her films. The company works with both cut-out and model animation for commercials, rock videos and their own films. Her work is characterised by an earthy off-beat sense of humour.

Amongst the most promising recent RCA graduates are Ruth Lingford and Petra Freeman. Lingford, a mature student, worked as an occupational therapist and raised two small children before taking a Fine Arts degree. Largely self-taught in animation, her work is concerned with sexuality, the body, and subjectivity.

Freeman came to animation, like Lingford, from painting. Her MOMI/C4 residency resulted in *The Mill*, a beautiful and densely packed evocation of childhood memories and emotions, painted on glass.

In the area of experimental, or avant-garde animation, Kayla Parker has produced a substantial body of work, remarkable for its resourcefulness - in both the formal and economic sense of the word. Her sources are often autobiographical, and some deal with women's experience: *Cage of Flame*, a recent Arts Council/C4 commission, explores the mythology of menstruation. Jayne Parker, one of Britain's most interesting and provocative avant-garde live-action filmmakers, has made an intriguing foray into animation with *I Cat*, which 'uses a savagely unpolished graphic style to explore women's sexuality and psychic castration'. Benita Rapham, a highly regarded young American designer working in graphics, photography, fashion and architecture, made *The Immediate Subject* at the RCA, a powerfully haunting film which used animation, collage, photography and text, and is currently working on *Within/ Without* via the Arts Council/C4 scheme.

There are, however, women making animation who've come through without the benefit of art college support. Erica Russell was 37 when she finished her first film: and *Feet of Song* , a stylised celebration of African song and dance, was a truly stunning debut. It's difficult to believe, but she had no formal training in art or animation, and learned her craft working freelance for some of the top commercial animation studios, working in her own time on *Feet of Song*, which was then given completion money by C4, who have funded her new film.

Leeds-based Joanna Dunn is another entirely self-taught animator. Intending to be a painter, she graduated in Fine Art and only discovered animation accidentally, through a friend who was working at Leeds Animation.

As she couldn't afford rostrum camera work for her film, she took a course so she could do it herself, and this generated some freelance work helping to finance her film. A small grant from Yorkshire & Humberside Regional Arts Board helped, as did access to Leeds Animation's facilities; just as crucial was their support during the four years the film took to make. *Watercolour* is, as its title suggests, an evocative, fluidly animated sea and landscape film. She is currently working on two new films, although she has to do part-time office work to support herself.

The growth of feminist publishing, and its input to the mainstream, has encouraged the emergence of several feminist cartoon strip artists, e.g. Posy Simmonds, Claire Bretecher, Angela Martin and Christine Roche, some of whom have crossed over into animation. There's also the television take-up of alternative comedy, in which several women have made their names. Their sometimes taboo-breaking exploration of womens' experience, and the use of the comic confessional mode, have also influenced animators Joanna Quinn, Candy Guard and Sarah Kennedy (all of whom have received C4 funding). Although quite different in style, their films all have a strong narrative drive, brilliantly observed characters and a well-developed sense of comic timing. Although they reject the agit-prop feminism, and aesthetics associated with Leeds Animation, their work centres around women's experience and point of view.

In the field of computer animation, Scottish filmmaker Lesley Keen has for some years been developing systems, used in some of her films, and is active in trying to develop the animation scene in Scotland.

Animation is producing some of the most exciting work in British film today. And women animators are right there at the cutting edge. What's also striking about women animators is the number who see teaching, adults and children, as an important part of their work. Sheila Graber has already done a great deal; Marjut Rimminen, Kayla Parker, Karen Watson, Sue Laughlin, Jessica Langford and Jackdaw Media are all keen to develop work in this area. This is encouraging, in terms of inciting interest in the form itself, developing audiences, and providing useful role-models. It might also result in more interesting films made for children themselves.

Although theatrical and video markets are developing as sources of revenue, it's true that, at present and for the foreseeable future, a great deal depends on Channel 4's continued support for animation. Hopefully, this will continue, given the international acclaim and festival awards their films have received, and the high appreciation index ratings from domestic audiences.

Alison de Vere

an interview with Lorenzo Codelli

After working in publicity and information and educational animation films, Alison de Vere made her first personal film, *Two Faces*, in 1969. Her career as a filmmaker took off in 1975 with *Café Bar*, which won the Grand Prix at Annecy, as her later *Monsieur Pascal* was to do in 1979. In 1984 Channel 4 put up the money for *Silas Marner* (a literary adaptation from George Eliot's novel), then commissioned a much more personal film, *Black Dog* which won several prizes at Annecy in 1987. It's a film full of symbols and psychoanalytic sources, that she has described as a 'soul journey…a death journey even', in which a woman traverses a desert accompanied by an Egyptian looking black dog (cf Anubis figures in Egyptian mythology), who is both menacing and protective. She comes to a city inhabited by the three fates 'three monstrous aspects of the woman herself'. The film draws on Martin Buber's distinctions between destiny and fate, but is also about sexual initiation and being female. - Ed.

Lorenzo Codelli interviewed one of the leading figures in British animation in 1987.

How did you become interested in animation, and who did you work with at the beginning of your career?
I started off wanting to be a painter. From early childhood I used to draw all the time. I studied painting at the Royal Academy in London but I never finished the course, as I married whilst still a student. Then, since I was really hard up for money, I took all kinds of different jobs (and some of those experiences are used in *Black Dog*) and finally I ended up working as paint and tracer on Paul Grimault's cel-animated *The Shepherdess and the Chimney Sweep*, which was released years later as *The King and Mr Bird (Le Roi et L'Oiseau)*. I hadn't been at all interested in animation before that, but seeing the marvellous drawings for this film made me want to work in the industry. I worked for a few years at Halas and Batchelor, beginning as a colour paint mixer and ending up as a drawer. This was around 1956, I had a son, and my marriage to the artist Karl Weschke was over, although we still remain friends to this day, and sometimes still work together.
In the next few years I worked a lot in commercials, for the cinema and for television, also for instructional films, credit sequences, special effects etc. None of this allowed for much personal expression, so I used to make notes of my ideas, sometimes as poems or stories. Some of my poems were published in underground magazines of the time. *Two Faces* began like this - and my first attempt to make a personal film. I made numerous monotypes, and I practised using dissolves from one to another. I thought that a poem spoken aloud with visual effects couldn't be considered as a real film. Then I had the opportunity to make a ten minute film for the World Health Organisation, about drug addiction, heroin. The script was already written, and it was rather naieve. The film is called *False Friends*. For the first time I experimented with animated silhouettes, but using realistic proportions, instead of the usual characters with enormous heads and tiny bodies. I think it was the first time that I made any connection between my working life and my earlier studies and the hopes I'd had then. Looking back, I'm amazed at how I could have made such a rigid distinction. It was as though I was two people, one who worked to earn money and to survive, and the other was a secret poet who never got anywhere, scribbling in her notebook whilst making dinner.
I then worked as supervisor on backgrounds for *Yellow Submarine*, under art director Heinz Edelman. He was very impressive, but obviously I worked in his style, not mine. Then I spent ten years working for Wyatt Cattaneo where I made *Café Bar* and *Mister Pascal*.

Was Café Bar *inspired by something in real life?*
Café Bar is a real place. I tried to draw it as it was. It's a place you could spend time in, when out of work, as it was very cheap.

And the idea for Mister Pascal*?*
This also was anchored in real life. I was living in Kensington High Street, where there's the Carmelite Church, and outside it there's a bench next to a giant crucifix on the church wall. As a child I'd always wanted to liberate this tortured figure; I couldn't bear looking at it. A lot of ideas started connecting up in this film about

an old man, an innocent and iconoclast. The musicians were real musicians, buskers I'd met at Hyde Park station, and who did the soundtrack for the film.

In Black Dog*, you're constantly mixing dream and reality.*
Yes, I often use dreams for my films, and particularly with *Black Dog*. The dog itself used to haunt my dreams, which is also where the ship with eyes, the wheel that becomes a child come from. But once the script is almost finished, then it's a case of working consciously on the meaning, at least as far as I can see. In any case, a work of imagination is always difficult to pin down, as sometimes images just appear from nowhere, then other times it's the result of laborious trial and error.

What's the process from conception to animation?
I work on a story a long time, until the narrative and the meaning are fully worked out in my mind. The visual treatment, essentially, isn't decided till I start drawing. The script can be in storyboard form, which only has a written counterpart for convenience. The story doesn't develop during the animation and the filming, the end is already worked out right from the beginning. It was absolutely essential with *Café Bar* and *Monsieur Pascal* as both were done over a long time period, in my free time. If there hadn't been stories, with endings, I'd have lost the thread and tiredness leads to loss of concentration.

What's the relationship between your commercial work and your own films?
Technically, commercials work imposed such a tight discipline that it was actually quite difficult to free my hands of certain conventions, and to base my work on my own vision of life.

How ideal is your relationship with your funder, Channel 4?
Working for Channel 4 has been easy, since I've been left quite free and simply encouraged to continue. *Black Dog* was accepted (by Paul Madden, then commissioning editor for animation at Channel 4) after seeing three minutes of fim that I'd done by myself, and reading a short synopsis. That said, there was a year's wait whilst the finance people looked at it. My producer, Lee Stork, was very persistent and so they financed the film, although for less than we'd hoped for. Since I'd made a half-hour film for them the year before, they knew that I could bring it in on time and on budget.

Are there films or filmmakers which have influenced you?
It's difficult to say, in terms of animation. There's been more influence in terms of live-action and, for sure, the art of mime, as I prefer to tell stories as far as possible without using words. Image and gesture can achieve communication with an audience without the language barrier. And the difficult art of timing, the sense of rhythm are most probably best studied watching good actors. In any case an animator has to be some kind of actor.

Reprinted from *Positif*, December 1989, by kind permission of the author.

Alsion de Vere is currently working on a new film, *Eros & Psyche*, her own version of the classic legend. 'On one level, it's about the difficulty of growing up as a woman, on another, about equality.' The film has presented her with something of a new chllenge, that of animating the nude female body. However, she stresses that in the end, technique is only a means to an end, that of communicating a story… 'If the emotions are not engaged… all the technique in the world doesn't hold the audfience.'- Ed.

Joanna Quinn

an interview with Linda Pariser

Joanna Quinn's films have delighted audiences - and festival juries – wherever they have shown, with their anarchic humour, brilliant observation of everyday (only slightly larger than life) characters, and superb comic scripts. It's rare to see working class women portrayed in animation with such warmth and humour. Girls' Night Out *is a raucous comedy in which Beryl, a quiet middle-aged housewife, is transformed into joyful hooligan on a ladies-only night at the pub, the highlight of which is supposed to be a male stripper. In* Body Beautiful, *Beryl is now working in a Japanese electronics factory in the Welsh Valleys, and is provoked by narcissistic macho nerd and colleague Vince into competing at the works' annual body-building contest.*

Joanna came to live and work in Cardiff, attracted by the lively independent film and video scene, after frequent visits whilst working as an illustrator and graphic designer in London. Plans to work on a magazine based at Chapter Arts Centre's then Film & Video Workshop fell through due to funding cuts, but she stayed to make Cardiff her work base. She works closely with Les Mills, director of the Film School at Gwent College of Higher Education, and a live action filmmaker and activist in the independent sector.

Girls' Night Out

How did you get into animation?
I went to Middlesex Polytechnic. I really wanted to draw cartoons in the *Beano*. I wanted to do strip cartoons, because I really liked Posy Simmonds' work. I thought 'I want to be her', so I went there. By chance they did

animation in the first year and all the first year students had a go at animation. It was fantastic! I loved it. I did this terrible film called *Superdog* which was appalling. I quite like it actually; it's so awful. It was good because the bloke who was teaching us said don't do anything with walks in it. So I chose a dog which had four legs, so it was really complicated. It was like magic. So that was it then.

Was Girls' Night Out *started when you were still at the Poly?*
Yes. I can't remember how the idea for *Girls' Night Out* came about. It started with a strip cartoon I did of it in the second year of college. But it wasn't coloured in when I left - it was just drawn.

Did it have any voices assigned to it then?
Yes, my voice and the woman from the canteen - she was Beryl - I dragged her down to be recorded. There were a lot of different people in it. Les was Tarzan. It's got quite a lot of energy in it. I showed that in my degree show. That was the end of that. Then I left it for a year. I'd given up on animation because it took so much effort. Les and Phil Davies from college (a technician there) kept ringing me up and forcing me to finish the film. So eventually I did, and I asked for some money to redo the soundtrack because I realised it would cost more. It had to be Equity. So I got money from Channel 4 then, wrote them a really cheeky letter, 'Dear Paul Madden'... I got about a thousand. I thought this is it - Big Time!

Straight out of college that must seem a lot of money.
They asked for a budget, and I wrote this absolutely pathetic budget - total cost of materials: fifty quid. Then I thought I better reduce that: thirty quid - fifty was a bit too much. I thought I could do it for twenty. I had no idea of real costs. That was a really good lesson. Then S4C as well put money in so I was able to do a Welsh version. I didn't make any money out of that because the money just went straight away because I under-budgeted so much.

But you got lots of trips around the world to film festivals out of that film.
Yes, no money but lots of fun.

How did Beryl end up being from the [South Wales] Valleys?
The state I'd left her when I finished college was she was this canteen woman who looked just like her. She was sort of based on her. She was really full of character until

you put a microphone in front of her - and then she'd put on this posh voice, go all tight and perform. When I came here [Cardiff], doing it for S4C [the Welsh TV channel who also put up completion money] I had to get a Welsh speaking woman to do it, and she did the Valleys and it seemed to fit really well.

Then Body Beautiful *came out of what was happening locally. Beryl changed her profession quite a bit, didn't she?*
It wasn't her choice (laughs). It was supposed to reflect what was going on around here.

You were saying before that you admired Posy Simmonds. Her work is quite feminist orientated and yours is as well.
That's what I like about her work . It's got really strong women characters - some of whom you loathe, but they're still strong and they're great. But it's not feminist in that brow-beating way. I suppose that's what I like. I'm a feminist but I'm not... I get angry, but I think humour's a great weapon. I like using humour to say things.

Beryl's a really attractive character, isn't she?
I'm so lucky I found her, really. You can do anything with her. We were watching a documentary last night on Ecstasy drugs. So the next Beryl is going to have Beryl on Ecstasy...Raves... Beryl gets into the drug scene...Right now we're writing. We've got about thirty ideas - all Beryl.

Who's 'we'?
Les and I. Well, Les is writing them actually. I just giggle when he shows them to me. There's a bit of interest in doing a Beryl [TV] series - within Britain. She'd be an obvious choice because she's such a good character and you could really build something around her. But I have a slight fear that once that happens it's 'Bye Beryl' - I'll lose her... She'll end up all horrible...banana fingers with stripes on... Mickey Mouse hands done by loads of in-betweeners.

Could you describe how you work as a creative partnership?
We are a team. It works so well 'cos he's more abstract, free thinking, very willing to experiment and encourage me in this direction. I'm more rigid, more conservative. Perhaps it's our different backgrounds: he's from Fine Arts (splashing paint freely), I'm from Graphic Design (straight lines, rulers, T-squares). Together we work well, I keep Les from going too wild, I experiment more

than I would. We do have 'lively discussions' but usually end up both pleased with the final result.
I do the art (drawing), Les scripts, produces and organises. He does storylines. His roots are in South Wales so he's good at bringing out the local element. He thinks it's important to make it Welsh. We create and refine charcters as well as collaborate on soundtracks.

Apart from Girls' Night Out *and* Body Beautiful*, I know you've done a three minute short based on a Toulouse-Lautrec painting. Can you tell us about some of your other work?*
I've done title sequences for televison. I did a piece for a series about Goya. I had to draw like Goya, do his etchings - and animate them. I animated a bull lunging which was cut together with a live action toreador waving a red rag. That was fantastic.

Have you actually been able to support yourself by doing animation?
Yes. I also got asked to direct a film based on some work I really admired. I had to do the storyboard and pre-production before all the finance was in place. But that was a new experience, working with an established group of studio animators. It was a bit awkward sometimes, a 'little girl' just wandering in and being expected to tell all these long-time animators what to do. But I learned a lot. That was a taste of what it's like to work with a huge team. I decided I really like to work on my own.

You work quite independently don't you? Even within Home Movies. *Could you describe* Home Movies *?*
Home Movies started as a sofa and two chairs and since then has grown. It's basically a shared studio space housing seven artists who also serve as a constant support group for one another. There's Candy [Guard], Jane Hubbard (who makes live action and animation films), Gerald Conn makes animation using sand, Chris [Elliot] is the artist among us. He got one of those BFI/Channel 4 awards, and he's making a film called *The Cabinet of Curiosity* with bones and skulls in it. It's hysterical seeing him with all his bones, making this strange music using homemade pipes. He's really into weird things. And then next door there's Candy making films about women and lavatories! They're always fighting for the radio 'cos Candy wants Radio One and he wants to put on all these weird tapes from his travels. I work at home; I get too easily distracted. It's lovely having such a peculiar mixture of people. It works really well.

Is it a production company or just a sharing of a space?
It's a sharing of space. But also because there are a number of studios in Cardiff - Siriol and others- we thought if we all stuck together and gave ourselves a name we'd be taken more seriously. Especially being women as well. We do tend to be treated as 'the girls'. It's seen as very much like a cottage industry - those 'sweet' girls who do it on their kitchen table.

Do you seek your funding separately?
Yes. We don't make films together, but we do teach together. After the summer we're doing five separate courses all in the Valleys, and that'll be great fun. We did one last year and just found out last night that one of the films made there has just won an award. That's fantastic because they were great kids; they were so nice. They don't get much in the way of that. None of them had done anything like that before. You tend to forget that, because I would think kids these days, they do everything. But these kids don't. They don't get anything.
Now that we've taken on more space we've got some other people joining us: Angela Hughes does some animation and textile design (and is our 'script advisor'). Some cel painters have moved in with Candy. It should be really exciting with all these people based there.

What are you working on now?
I'm working on a new film, *Britannia* about British imperialism, and we've finally got it sussed. We started it last year and it's been through loads of changes because it's such a vast area to cover. It's hard to find a focus. Claire Kitson thought it was a bit 'invective'. So I looked it up and I thought oh yeah, it is a bit.
I changed it a bit. It was all about the class system. It was too angry, too obvious. Someone suggested I show it to Steve Bell [a leading political cartoonist, best known for his brilliant anti-Thatcher *Maggie's Farm* strip]. He suggested I should start again. So I did, and we've got it now - finally cracked it. I'm just doing the last storyboards and I'm happier with it. I think C4 and S4C will be too, because it's a lot simpler. It's a five minute film about the British - with a bulldog in it.

No Beryl?
No Beryl. But Britannia's in it and she's beginning to look suspiciously like Beryl. Her glasses are getting bigger and bigger and her bottom's widening.
What I'd like to do in the future is more teaching. I'm doing some teaching and am really enjoying it.

Do you prefer teaching adults or children?
Adults, I think. Not animation students particularly, but anyone who's interested. We've got an animation club here each week which is good fun. All different types of people go to that. It consists of people who are interested in making animation and serves as a support group, offers equipment, screenings, feedback, skill-sharing and teaching. There are about ten people involved including animators, teachers, and one illustrator and ceramicist who travels each week from Hereford to attend.
If I could do some teaching and do my own films, I'd be happy then.

[Since this interview took place, Joanna Quinn has been offered a teaching job as Associate Lecturer in Animation at Gwent College of Higher Education.]

Do you have any plans to move out of animation? Into live action perhaps?
Not really. I love it. I can't stop doing it really.

Do you think there's something different about being a woman working in animation? Do you think that's a fair categorisation?
I do generally. However, working with Gerald and Chris at Home Movies, they're not typical bloke animators. I think womens' films tend to be more personal. I think it's quite new for women to be doing animation. Seeing womsn's animation at festivals - it's a lot fresher. It's as if time hasn't really moved on for a lot of these men. There's that old school of sexist jokes about women's bodies. That's what's good about women's films. They are different, and they're not relying on the same old hackneyed jokes. It's not just having stronger women characters in the films. It's a different type of film, I think.
I think it's very difficult for women to work in a big studio system. They are all blokes. They're used to working in an all-male environment and to suddenly adapt to having a woman there and not be patronising... They can be very nice, but often in a very patronising way. I think there's a lot of animosity towards people who just make animation on their own and say 'I'm an animator/filmmaker' from the people who work in the studio who've worked their way up from tea-boy and spent years becoming an animator. And then they see 'some little squirt' straight out of college who says 'I'm an animator'...

July, 1992, Cardiff

Candy Guard

an interview with Linda Pariser

Candy Guard's minimally drawn, but richly observed comic skits on womens' everyday experience, such as Fantastic Person, Fatty Issues et al, are invariably greeted with delighted, if rueful, laughs of recognition.

How and why did you get into animation?
Writing was always my strong point at school… writing and talking. (School reports always said 'Candy would do better if she spent less time talking to friends'.) When I studied Fine Art (with film and video making) at Newcastle Poly, I started to put ideas down in strip cartoon form, quite naturally, it wasn't a conscious decision. It was a quick way of dealing with dialogue visually, without having to writing it as a script. Someone suggested animation which seemed to marry my different interests. I really wanted to be a filmmaker, but I wasn't confident enough to get a film crew together. At college animation was the easiest way to make a film on your own. And with live action, you couldn't make it up as you went along.
I did more live action when I went on to St Martins School of Art. But after college, when I was taking my showreel round, people were more interested in my animation. People accept off-the-wall in animation, in live-action they don't. And people feel you have a specialised skill, a kind of mysterious technique.

Your films are all very narrative based…
Yes, which is why the animation technique of recording the script first suits me. I treat it like a radio play. If it works that way, it'll work as a film. My technique is very simple, very economical. Because the soundtracks are so busy - I use a lot of voice over, characters' thoughts - it would be distracting if there was a very full visual style. I think more in terms of cartoons…It's drawn, flat, two dimensional, narrative based, it's quick, humorous. A lot of stuff called 'animation' tends to be more difficult, all that you associate with art films. Animation attracts a lot of visual artists, it doesn't attract a lot of writers, which is a shame. Its quite scary to make the kind of films I do because its so obvious when it's failed. With a serious film, there's a silence at the end… you can't tell if they enjoyed it, but with my films, they have to laugh. Laughter is a very immediate form of communication. When you first realise you've made a film about something you've experienced and people show they feel like that too, it boosts your confidence.

What about your influences?
Comics, like the *Beano* and the *Beezer*… which I read totally seriously, I didn't laugh. I wanted quick access to what was going on, the pictures and the talking. My mum used to leave *Pride and Prejudice* lying around but I didn't read a book until I was 15…
Mike Leigh… writers and directors who deal with life as it really is, slightly exaggerated for drama. Women like French & Saunders didn't so much influence me as egg me on. I think they, and Victoria Wood are doing a kind of observational comedy that deals with very personal, day to day things which seem petty but in fact take up most of your mental time… they've touched on areas that haven't been touched on before. I feel more related to women comics, and cartoonists like Claire Bretecher, among others, than I do to to other animators.

What about your current project?
It's an 11 minute pilot for a series, *Pond Life*. Dolly Pond lives in a cul-de-sac and thinks she'd be a fantastic person if she wasn't held back by her family and friends. It's called *Pond Life* because the environment is warm and cosy, but at the same time claustrophobic, limiting. It's about freedom vs security: things she wants but doesn't dare go and get. It's structured around people's inner lives. I think a lot of people's minds are centred around what they think they're capable of rather than what they're doing… there's so much fed in via media these days, how women should be, shouldn't be… everyone thinks about it too much… Each episode poses a dilemma: I want a boyfriend, or do I? I want to be successsful, or do I? She has a whole relationship with a man who doesn't even know it's going on. I only want to do six, like a sit com series. I've changed my visual style so I can work better with other people, but it's still my style. There are a lot more characters than in my other films. It's a big transition, having a crew, letting go of control, being Big Boss Woman.

Would you like to work in live action?
Yes, I'd like to work in comedy drama. I might be scripting and storyboarding an animated film by someone else. Much better. I'm not interested in animation, it's very boring. What's interesting is telling the story. I'd also like to go back and re-do some of my Super-8 live action films on 16mm.

Women and animation?
There are a lot of successful women animators because of this issue of control, you can do it secretly, away from prying eyes, it feels more private…You don't have to deal with other people so much. A lot of women can't bear to be thought of as horrible, forceful, appear bossy, whilst men don't give a shit.

Vera Neubauer

by Leslie Felperon Sharman

If, as some academic critics like to insist, animation is, or can be, the most subversive form of filmmaking and if the work of most independent female animators represents a dissenting faction from mainstream normative narratives, then Vera Neubauer's films are the terrorist branch of the art form, the Red Brigade of the animated film.

Thematically and aesthetically, they are resonant with a heritage of female filmmakers that starts with Maya Deren and leads to Yvonne Rainer, Cecelia Condit, or Leslie Thornton, experimental filmmakers and video artists whose employment of bricolage and Brechtian mannerisms, radical feminism and repetition, avant garde montage techniques and monstrous Mother figures make them the darlings of feminist film theory.

But Neubauer's work has never received commensurate attentions, although she is probably the most prolific independent animator, male or female, in the UK, and has directed a strikingly diverse body of challenging work. One might conjecture that that it is precisely her innovative use of live-action experimentalism and animation that have contributed to her neglect.

She has said in a recent interview that she prefers her art to 'provoke rather than entertain', and the films hold good to the aim, provocative to the last frame. Brazenly unpretty, mischievously playful, they bring to mind the drawings of a wilful but clever child who when asked to draw a house depicts the primal scene in the upstairs bedroom, the dog eating the baby in the downstairs one, and the garden on fire, and then crumples it all up to throw at the teacher.

And yet, her films do entertain - the mind, with their rapidfire stream of ideas, but also by their savage wit, and irony.

Born in Czechoslovakia in the late 40s, she moved to Britain in 1968. She began studying print-making at the Royal Academy of Art, but then switched to film in which she graduated. She began to make short films using animation, which she perceived as a medium not unlike printmaking, both using techniques that generated limited series of images, and requiring a high degree of repetitious work. She soon developed a unique style, one which uses seemingly crude, thick wobbly lines to create simply drawn characters that move through a sparse background, formally somewhat reminiscent of the work of Emile Cohl.

Neubauer's work strikes the viewer as faux-naif with the accent on the faux, for the simple drawing style belies and contrasts with the complexity and sophistication of her subject matter, which uses strong, even occasionally shocking, images to illustrate her concerns. Thus, her films have a raw, spontaneous quality that enhances and underscores the sketchy narratives that they illustrate, which often draw on the imagery and elliptical qualities of fairy tales. The tension which Neubauer's draughtmanship maintains, managing to appear fresh and direct rather than merely clumsy and badly drawn, is symptomatic of the tension she maintains throughout the body of her work on a more thematic level.

Some of these are difficult films, sometimes inaccessible after only one viewing. They require the viewer to think critically and watch closely. This intransigence is both the work's greatest virtue, in terms of artistic quality, and its greatest 'vice', in terms of securing wider recognition, for Neubauer's films resist categorisation, and refuse to take predictable stands on political issues such as feminism.

Like some of the women filmmakers cited above, Neubauer's films attempt to tell stories through montages of striking images and fragmentary scenes which refuse to pull the wool of linearity over the spectator's eyes. Instead, the time of her narratives is fractured, the 'plots' cut up and reassembled on the editing table, evoking the feel of stories half-remembered, narrated by someone perhaps with the digressive tendencies of Tristram Shandy, or perhaps with an unreliable memory, or perhaps just someone trying to say not 'this and then this' but everything at once.

The animation's graphic style, which gives a sense of swift and urgent execution, does not fetishise technical perfection. Neubauer's films consciously swerve away from a tradition in animation which has elevated fluidity of movement and solidity of figure above all other artistic virtues. Moreover, in their consistent use of collage-like montage, in which fragments of animation and live action are edited together to create ironic juxtaposition instead of narrative cohesion and closure, Neubauer's films are more consistent with what Peter Burger describes as the project of the 'historical avant-garde'.

Like the work of Frida Kahlo, Max Ernst, or John Heartfield, Neubauer's films work through negation, deny the organic unity to the art object and use 'shock...as a stimulus to change one's conduct of life; it is the means to break through aesthetic immanence and to usher in (initiate) a change in the recipient's life praxis.' [1] 'The project of the avant-garde is thus an inherently radical one politically, and while Burger pessimistically insists that the 'true' historical avant-garde has been and gone, current artists still employ its strategies as a means of expressing discontent with the 'new' cinematic and world order.

Neubauer's education at art school coincided with the height of political and social upheaval of the late 60s, and she has conceded that her work was inevitably informed by that era. But the films never seem like polemical tracts or sterile exercises in radical filmmaking, like Laura Mulvey and Peter Wollen's tedious live-action film *Riddles of the Sphinx* , for example. In contrast to the worthy agit-prop of some feminist animators, Neubauer's films refuse to preach, and seem to prefer to problematise through abstraction and personalise through the use of autobiography that declines to claim for itself any universal application, while still inviting the viewer's identification.

In an interview with this author, Neubauer said that her work grew in part from the perception of telling accidents, from using what was at hand. Sometimes this use of the 'found' yielded images which are simply striking, apparently just aesthetically pleasing, or disturbing. At other times, however, an event, for example noticing that after a car crash the police tend to arrive before the ambulance, or the reaction of a crowd to a disturbed woman raging in the street, would seem to resonate with larger implications about social conditions. Her work often seems to try to address such conditions on a microcosmic scale, paying particular attention to the politics of gender, which becomes the point of origin in her films from which conflict emanates on a more macrocosmic scale. *Mid Air* is an excellent example of this movement, where a wife's use of witchcraft to subvert her husband's authority leads eventually to its use against the police.

It is while prising open the gates of the Garden of Eden, investigating the beginnings of sexual difference, that Neubauer's films are at their most shocking, pointed, and effective. She noted in an interview with Claire Barwell that her favorite part of *The Decision* is…

'The little piece every projectionist cuts off or projects against the curtain, the piece everybody turns up too late to see. It's the title that says 'That is where everything begins' followed by a close shot of the backside of a newborn female baby [later covered in excrement]. When I got the rushes back and projected them in the viewing theatre I could hear the reactions of the male projectionists. They were disgusted and angry - so I knew it was good! These men must see hard-core porn films by the dozen yet they could not take the mess of a newborn baby - something a mother has to deal with twenty times a day!' [2]

Indeed, this shot is a condensation of where 'everything begins' in a multiplicity of ways. On the most superficial level it reminds us that we all begin as babies, incontinent and helpless. But more subtly, the image of the newborn's vagina metonymically reminds one of the vagina from which the baby itself emerged - this is truly where all of us, 'everything', begins, in the cycle of matrilineal descent. Ever since Mulvey's influential essay on 'Visual Pleasure and Narrative Cinema', film theory has been obsessed with the centrality of the female genitalia as the structuring absence around which the scopic regimes of cinema are constructed, either through voyeurism or the disavowing mechanism of fetishism. Neubauer's close-up of this organ literally strips the woman, and exposes the empress's nakedness, and thus lays bare the 'lack' over which cinematic visual pleasure erects its defences. The projectionists and audience are shocked because by its clinical frankness, the elemental simplicity of the baby girl's body undermines those very defences of which 'hard-core' pornography is another symptomatic manifestation.

The film's later use of zoëtropes, old silent film footage of couples kissing, and peep show reels emphasizses the masculine power of 'the look' in cinema's heritage. Neubauer's films attempt to deconstruct these systems, but (thankfully) without denying the possibility of pleasure or humour; instead the films return to origins in order to rediscover the sources of pleasure and 'unpleasure', by an examination of the origins of sexual difference, of conflict, and, most innovatively, of cinema itself through this very melding of live action and animation which harks back to early films, like those of Georges Méliès and Cohl, which similarly enmeshed the drawn and the 'real', fantasy and the fantastic with the prosaic, myth with cultural specificity.

The Decision typifies this mixture. After the opening shot of the baby's bottom, the film proceeds to tell the story of a beautiful princess, who has to decide which prince she would like to marry. A male voiceover describes the tale in a deadpan parody of fairy-tale discourse, while animation and live action sequences intercut, now illustrating the story with drawn footage, then suddenly cutting to live action shots, to provide ironic counterpoint, e.g. as the voiceover intones 'One prince had the most beautiful words and with them he could spin dreams,' the film cuts to a washing machine spinning clothes.

A steady rhythm is gradually built on these sort of juxtapositions: an animated couple make love in blackened frame, their outlines quivering and blending into each other in vibrant colours, while a peepshow reel scrolls on in a boxed corner of the screen; the drudgery of housework and childrearing is contrasted with the images, drawn and from a 'sampled' live action film, of a couple dancing joyously. The King, as an animated character, enjoins the princess that she is free to choose, but choose she must. An empty screen appears with the words 'F*** that Freedom', written in type. The montages seem to suggest that there is really no choice, all decisions lead to the same final drudgery. In desperation, the princess seeks advice from the castle witch, who suggests two courses of action. First, disfiguring her beauty to see which suitor will still want her afterwards. But the princess rejects this nihilistic option. Then the witch offers her a zoëtrope made from a tin can, saying 'this box will show you the ending of many stories,' but all the film shows is a simple drawing of a skeleton repeatedly losing its head, as the zoëtrope revolves.

As the princess becomes hypnotised by this magic box, the film could be read to imply that all stories, especially cinematic ones, are seductive illusions, death is the only closure, and to make decisions of any importance one must try to escape the ideological control, or, as the voice over concludes, 'Let us hope that by the time she awakes she will no longer be a princess, but someone capable of making a decision.'

Such would be one interpretation, by no means the only possible one, as this film, like Neubauer's *Animation for Live Action*, not only resists but openly parodies the imposition of a univocal reading, represented by the male voiceover whose seemingly assured narrativising is undermined by the polyphonic proliferation of images. In *Animation for Live Action*, the cartoon character that is both a representation and a product of its creator 'says' in a scroll of text that passes over the screen, 'Artistically, the film is the medium which by its nature, can accommodate most easily a simultaneity of viewpoints, and demonstrate clearly the indivisibility of events.'

Her films attempt to put this observation into practice, *The Decision* especially, *The Mummy's Curse* and *Mid Air,* to a lesser extent. *Animation for Live Action* has at

Animation for Live Action

An extremely imaginative combination of animation and live action filming which explores women's roles, artist's identities, and the tension between drawing and live action photography. In the film Neubauer creates characters she then does battle with - they attempt to break out of the film, fight back, and generally act as her unyielding artistic conscience. The animator also creatively destroys the feminine ideology of traditional women's roles - her muscle-men don't look right, and her knights in shining armour do battle and then impale her. Running a gamut of self-questioning and identity-exploring ideas, this film is also a fascinating example of cinematic self-reflection. Neubauer's characters troop through myriad filmmaking machines, manipulating images on editors and examining the frames themselves.

least three 'narrators' or viewpoints, a male voice over who claims the film as his own, a 'dramatized reconstruction of the life of my ex-wife', Neubauer herself, who we observe filming in the reflection of a shop window, and the animated figure she creates, who in turns draws Neubauer herself in a parody of the Fleischer Bros' *Out of the Inkwell* series, carries a camera, and cuts film stock into pieces.

Neubauer has said that editing is probably her favourite part of filmmaking, and it is through her subtle use of it that most of the impact of these films is made, and by which 'the indivisibility of events' is suggested. By repeating cycles, returning to images already seen, and disrupting what little narrative remains in this manner, these films convey the impression not just of fairy-tales or stories told, but of dreams remembered. For this, the 'uncanny' quality of animation is well-suited, conveying as it does the primal pleasure of seeing the inanimate move and speak, of the impossible being made manifest. This was in part the attraction of the earliest cinema, and one that animation consistently replenishes.

Neubauer's use of the medium stays close to these roots, and the rejection of polished technical perfection lends her work a spontaneity that is often lacking in her peers, and adds a visceral impact to the strong images she creates. By rejecting the glib perfectionism of mainstream animation and its fetishism of fluid movement and cleaned-up graphics, these films force the viewer to confront their own expectations about the animation, and indeed film. Furthermore, Neubauer's work insistently reminds the viewer of its own constructedness as art, and thus of the construction of the themes with which it deals, such as sexuality and power relations.

Neubauer's work is strong, uncompromising stuff. It refuses to pander, patronize or reassure its audience. Consequently, Neubauer has found it increasingly difficult to find funding to make animated films in the present climate, where the spectacular is valued over the speculative. Lately she has taken a productive change of direction in her work, concentrating on live action. Her latest work was a story about skinheads and motherhood shot in black and white in Brixton, an evocative film called *Don't be Afraid*. She says that her favourite film is the one she is going to make next, about which she refuses to divulge any information. One cannot help but admire her determination to go on making small budget films independently under such difficult financial circumstances, while hoping that someday she will return to animation, to which she has contributed so much.

Mid Air
A satiric quasi-operatic soundtrack drives this elliptically told tale of a bored housewife who goes to a Further Education College to learn Witchcraft. Frightened by the implications of a fighter plane flying overhead, and musing on a piece of found graffiti that says, 'War = Menstruation Envy', the witch concocts a potion that will make men menstruate. The final images are still photographs of policemen arresting women peace protesters, the inside of their trousers staining red as the potion takes its effect. *Mid Air* stands as one of Neubauer's more overtly political films, as well as one of her most tightly structured and aesthetically polished works. The animation is predominantly cut-outs made from fabric and puppetry.

The Mummy's Curse
One of Neubauer's funniest films. Footage from an old *Curse of the Mummy* film is intercut with the representation of a story of Oedipal struggles of a woman coming to terms with her feelings for her mother, who is about to visit. As in *Animation for Live Action*, male psychoanalysts are roundly mocked, the masturbating analyst's ejaculate becoming tranquilizers, while the Freudian image of the Phallic Mother is literalized, her penis forming a skipping rope with the husband's over which our hapless heroine must jump. Although a vicious irony runs through most of the action, the film maintains a deeply personal resonance, and flirts with the autobiographical mode by Neubauer's use of her own image. Animation mainly with drawn cutouts; and contains a suitably melodramatic score by Gary Carpenter, one of Neubauer's most frequent collaborators, and drawings by her daughter Lucy Mulloy.

References
1. Peter Burger, *Theory of the Avant-Garde*, trans. by Michael Shaw. Manchester University Press: Manchester, 1984.
2. *Interview with Vera Neubauer* by Claire Barwell, in *Undercut*, Winter 1982/3

For infomation on the author see *Notes on Contributors*.

Joanna Woodward

At art school Joanna found little sympathy towards her multi media ideas, and non-mainstream approach, but she persevered, developing her interests in dance, painting and sculpture, and then in relation to film. Her art began to be shown in London galleries, and she was one of the artists selected in 1983 to work on a touring exhibition, *Pandora's Box*, which re-examined the myth of Pandora as the beautiful temptress who brought evil into the world.

Her first films were made at home with a cheap Super-8 camera. *The Poet of Half Past Three* is a lyrical and free associative tribute to Jean Cocteau, scratched and painted on film. *The Hump Back Angel*, a dark fairy tale, is reminiscent of Vera Neubauer's work, in its faux-naif style, mixed techniques, and subject. The films gained her entry into the National Film and Television School.

Her first film there was live-action: *The Discreet Call of Nature* , a story of three city gents on a country excursion and about their repressed fantasies, watched by an amused voyeuristic mermaid. *Two Children Threatened by a Nightingale*, animated on cel, was based on a painting by Max Ernst. Conveying a sense of menace and enigma, its use of screen space is particularly interesting. Her graduation film, *The Brooch Pin and the Sinful Clasp*, took three years to make, and the result was a 25 minute tour de force, combining cut-outs, oil paints, collage, live-action, and models.

BBC Bristol commissioned *The Weatherhouse*, another mix of live action and animation, produced by the IOU Theatre Company. She is currently Animation Fellow at Bristol Polytechnic, and is writing a series for television, whose working title is *Shrunken Mortals and Little People*, which uses similar mixed techniques... 'the ordinariness of the every day with the extraordinariness of animation'.

'I wrote the script for *The Brooch Pin* with a very loose plot. An early morning pedestrian sees a ballerina dancing at the top of a towerblock. He is convinced she is trying to attract his attention, so he sets out to become acquainted with her. His obsessive journey to find her takes him into a vivid world in the towerblock, where the loneliness of the inhabitants is masked by their frivolity, and an overwhelming desire for intimacy. He ends up in a lurid restaurant at the top of the tower where he finds out the ballerina was not the beauty he had imagined, but bait used by the cook so that she can include him in her elaborate recipe!

The angel aspiring to flight yet bound to the earth, the lover doomed to failure, man is shown at the mercy of fate, but the message can never be wholly dark as I believe the poetic and the prosaic are never clearly defined.

'The Brooch Pin is like the tragedy of the fly caught in a cobweb. The man has a dream of happiness which he believes is always just beyond his reach. He will spend a life devoted to obtaining that dream, but on closer examination it is nothing more than tinsel and lace. Just as we spend our lives like frustrated magpies with bottomless nests, the circumstance of happiness always just beyond our reach. Instead of being sensitive to the moment, we continuously prepare for a time not too far in the future when happiness will surely come. — Joanna Woodward.

Treatment and Technique

'Somewhere around 1987 I started work on the film in

THE BROOCH PIN AND THE SINFUL CLASP

In a city of looming buildings and scraping feet, described by a film whose sounds are as varied in texture as its visual surfaces.

Desire tugs poor man upwards from layers of noise and paper, through the layers of other's lives - locked in their buildings, immured in cells only the foolhardy will brave and break through.

Stories of anguish and joy and loss as he scales the high towers of newsprint and lonely rooms.

A lover made of paper weeps lonely at her telephone, while next door vertigo holds no fear for the couple whose kisses swing from from window to window like messages through prison bars.

Cut-out dancers bend and thrash at a party, and folds of torn paper denote a desperate tender seduction.

More textures: man changes and thickens from paper to sludgy paint to plasticine to solid padded cloth and soft face as he overcomes obstacles almost by default, the object of his desire still scraping her string sounds in his head, his dreams.

Yet he gains substance in our hearts and minds not through this physical transformation, but through what he witnesses, through what this allows us to project into his cotton-wool head. The conjuring of compassion and joy and despair from slices of newspaper, pencil stabs, smears of paint. The artifice is left bare.

Live action seems monumental and unyielding after such naked feeling, but this very quality is made use of in the story-telling. The horrid truth - that desire is so easily exploited - is made clear by the impassive face of a giantess. Poor man is helpless in this solid, heavy world. —Susie Arnott, June 1990 chronological order. The opening street scene was particularly painstaking being cel animation on a tiny model background. I had always liked the rawness of paper cutouts as animated characters. However they were a problem to animate in a fluid way, so I drew what looked like cutouts on to cel, the transparent substance used in traditional animation. The effect, I hope, is cutouts with fluid movements.

'The script was designed in such a way that it could be moulded and changed. In a similar way I moulded and change my animation techniques as I got deeper into making the film. It was unfolding to me, and gradually the cell work was replaced by oils on glass. The image is manipulated in wet paint in front of the camera to create the impression of movement.

'This technique led on to collaged found objects until the work had become so three dimensional a puppet was required for the main character. A latex puppet with wires inside was cast from a Fimo original.

Collaborating

'As the work became more and more three dimensional, I took great delight in being able to collaborate with other artists who were more skilled in some of the areas I was now working in. The Theatre Design course at Central School of Art introduced me to Samantha Jones whose amazing dressmaking skills could be adapted to the requirements of a seven-inch puppet.

'I knew of the remarkable performance artist Rose English, and that she had the most suitable legs. I was astonished when she was willing to have them cast in plaster and play the part of the Giantess in the live action sequence at the top of the tower block.

'Most people are dreadfully patronizing to animators, making comments such as, 'Can you get into real films through doing animation?'. However, directing the live action sequence I felt fairly relaxed. After all, I had been working with film , however slowly, for the past six years and many of the decisions an animator makes are the same as any film director: camera movements, framing, pacing etc.

The film's opening scene is latr projected in the cafe-bar.

'We shot the live action mute and of course all the animation was without sound. David Humpage, the composer for the I.O.U. theatre company whose work I greatly admire, I thought would be ideal. I felt that I.O.U. were dealing with visual metaphors that had parallels to the world of animation.

'I was nervous handing over what was now the nearly completed three years work to have the emotional substance that was lacking without sound made complete.His interpretation had a rawness and a compassion for the work that I could not have anticipated.

'My films have continued to be, I hope, not only cinematic, but to have an interconnected thread with my love of simple theatre, leaving enough room for the audience to make their own leaps of the imagination, unique to each of them as individuals.'

'The film seems to break all the rules, yet achieves its effect by pulling us into a bleak fantasy, where violence and pain are never far away... Gothic and witty, an adult animation film.' Nik Houghton, Independent Media, Jan 1990.

Sarah Kennedy

Sarah Kennedy is, quite simply, one of the funniest young animators around today. Until recently, she's been heard, rather than seen, as the main character's voice for most of Candy Guard's films. The TV broadcast of her latest production, *Nights*, is likely to bring her name to a far wider audience.

A hilarious series of five 10 minute films, *Nights* uses live-action alternated with model animation to chart Bob and Carol's relationship from first night, moving in together a fortnight later, a disastrous holiday abroad, break up, and a 'civilised' friendly reunion. *First Night* conjugates all the hopes, fears and embarassments of… the first night, voiced-over thoughts counterpointing the actual dialogue (and Carol's to-camera account of it all, somewhat at variance with what we see). Worried about what he'll think of her awful pink knickers, she decides to remove them and get into bed whilst he's out for a pee - which reinforces his fears about her being '*really experienced*'. Will she notice his fat belly? Will he notice her cellulite? (She brings it up anyway). As the relationship develops, Carol's impossibly romantic expectations clash with mundane realities…

The style of model animation Kennedy has developed could be described as (psychological) warts and all. Her characters verge on the grotesque, yet, paradoxically, this makes them all the more sympathetic. It also allows things that would be simply impossible in live-action (e.g. the talking penis in a leather jock-strap who Carol, newly back in the singles game, encounters). The dialogue rings painfully true - but you can't help laughing.

'I want my work to be honest, something that people can relate to. I think women are strong enough now, and should feel confident enough, to get away from the idea of positive images, to be able to explore their own weaknesses.' She feels women are particularly prone to negative self-image: 'It doesn't matter what they look like, there's always the worry about whether they're too fat, whether they should be doing this or that… in some ways, I'm like that, and my films are exploring all the worst aspects of myself.'

She made her first films in the mid-80s as a Fine Art student at Newcastle Poly, then at the RCA. *As it Happens* satirised aspects of 70s feminism: the ideological puritanism, and peer group pressures to conform. 'It just didn't seem to fit the life I was living. In some ways, it was a reaction against what I saw as the creation of new stereotypes. I was meeting men who were just as confused with who they were supposed to be as women students.' *Carol and Mary* skits the way women can be competitive with each other, in subtle but deadly ways. *On the Rail* follows two young women on a package tour to Spain.

Like all her work, it explores the gap between fantasy and reality: the unrealistic expectations of holiday romance, the desperate need to assure yourself you're having a great time, to appear to be, even if you're not.

After college, she was wary of the isolation animation can impose, 'I found it depressing working by mysel,' so decided to try television to gain wider experience, and work as part of a team. *Family Favourites*, commissioned for a C4 youth programme's Christmas edition, dealt with the nightmare that family reunions at that time of year often turn into. Fellow RCA graduate Jonathan Bairstow produced, and their collaboration has continued with *Nights*. 'He's a great sounding board, and knows everything about animation on the technical side'.

She next worked as a researcher on the much discussed series *Sex Talk*. 'For a whole year I went round the country, talking to an incredible range of people I'd never normally have come across, asking all sorts of questions about their sex lives… and getting paid for it!'

A stint researching for *East Enders* taught her a lot about developing storylines, how soaps are constructed, and how different people can input ideas and collaborate. Then *First Night* was commissioned for C4, and made in studio space rented from *Spitting Image*, whose co-creator, Roger Law, offered development money for her animated soap project. This now looks set to go.

For her, writing is the most crucial element. She aims for -and brilliantly achieves - a kind of 'edited naturalism' to the dialogue. 'I'm really perfectionist about it - I like the sound to be really tight. As long as the people doing the voices are on your wave-length, all that matters is that they don't try too hard to be funny delivering the lines: it should already be there in the writing.' She's enjoyed directing, although happily left the live-action sequences to someone else. Though she's used cutouts and drawing in some films, model animation appeals 'because it's quick… it's like creating a whole mini-world. I like working with objects you can touch. And working with a team is very satisfying, getting the right people together, letting them go for it…and come up with great ideas.' She's keen to work in different areas: feature films in the long term, although she's in no hurry, and would like to keep animation going, and maybe a live comedy show with Candy Guard.

Drawing on Experience...

Karen Watson on *Daddy's Little Bit of Dresden China*

Karen Watson made Daddy's Little Bit...*in 1987, as her graduation film at West Surrey College of Art & Design. It's worth noting that the film was begun a year before the revelations about child abuse in Cleveland were breaking on national news and placed the issue, ofr the ifrst time, on the public agenda. Karen Watson writes here on how she conceived and made the film.*

In childhood we are innocently led to believe that only people we don't know are capable of hurting us. We are told the dangers of talking to 'strangers'. Thus we are quite unable to understand, particularly as children, when the stranger is a member of our own family, an adult in whom we are expected to place our trust and our vulnerability.

The stranger, as many women know, does not resemble this monster. He is an ordinary, respectable family man who resides in their own home and has access to their bodies and minds, at all times of the day and night, past or present.

Daddy's Little Bit of Dresden China is an eight minute film which draws from my own childhood experience of living with the familiar 'stranger'. It centres on a female child who is being sexually abused by her father from within the confines of the patriarchal family home, and challenges the notion of the family as a 'safe' place and destroy the notion of the abuser as a 'stranger'.

The film also presents and questions popular myths which surround sexual abuse, of both children and women. Myths which serve only to provide a smokescreen behind which the actual abuser may hide whilst accusing the child or woman of inciting, and colluding in, the 'act'.

The film begins with the narration of a fairytale over a montage of images and text. Photographs, documents, scratched film and drawn animation are combined to give a brief family history which is centred on a female child.

But the story is disturbing. It is not a traditional, happy one. A girl's voice tells us of a possessive King who could not bear his beautiful Queen to look at anyone but him, such is his fear of losing her.

'Until one day the Queen gave birth to a daughter, Snow White. Who in time became far more beautiful and obedient than the Queen could ever be and the King doted on her.'

Through his own insecurity the King seeks to possess his wife and daughter completely and abuses his power over the Princess who, as a child has not the power to protest. She cannot say 'No'.

The wife and the daughter are the Father's property. The Queen has no right to her daughter and the King actively incites and encourages competition between them, separating them from one another.

'You are mine, he tells her, and no man shall ever have you. Only I love you. Your Mother hates you for you are far more beautiful than she. I have told her that. And what is more, you have taken my love from her.'

The Princess is unable to tell her mother of the abuse and her story remains locked inside of her.

'Unfortunately, for Snow White, no-one ever questioned the King's love for her. The Mother was blamed, the father forgiven, and the daughter silenced.'

The daughter becomes 'Daddy's Little Bit of Dresden China', a precious, pretty and fragile object belonging exclusively to Daddy and this was how I visualized her in the film.

When I was a child, this title was given to me by an aunt and was considered to be an honour, although that was not my experience. *Daddy's Little Bit of Dresden China* is a personal attempt to give voice to the reality of sexual abuse which I see ultimately as the abuse of power.

The film moves into 3D model animation, the action taking place on a theatre stage. The curtain rises to reveal the conventional patriarchal family. Father is reading a newspaper, Mother is busy sewing and Daughter is doing a jigsaw of a house. Each character is made from materials which symbolize their way of being.

The Daughter, Dresden China, is small and fragile, her head a pretty china vase and her body made of white feathers and bandages. She has been hurt. She is a victim. The Father, the abuser, is cold and metallic. He wears a suit of armour to protect himself. He has broken glass for a head and razor blades for his mouth to symbolize his sharp and cutting personality. The Mother is made from dried flowers. She is withering through hard work. She has a wooden spoon for her arm to symbolize her domestic role.

This idyllic family scene is intercut with colour photographs taken from the 'Family Album', conveying the happy, 'normal' family image, but the voiceover is ambiguous. 'It' happens in many families but no-one ever talks about it. 'It' is shrouded in secrecy.

Voiceovers like this occur throughout the film. Survivors of sexual abuse speak out on their experiences and thoughts. These women are from different cultures and backgrounds, challenging the idea that sexual abuse only happens in working-class families and certain places.

Later, black and white photographs appear which contradict those from the 'Family Album'. In these images the girl is in distress. The pictures do not fit the idealised image and are ripped up.

The Happy Family Theatre show ends, curtains closing

on the patriarchal scene where the characters 'act out' conventional family roles: Mother cleaning frantically, Daughter prettied up, and Father by the fireplace smoking his pipe.

Now we go behind the scenes, behind the 'normal' facade where the characters are naked, stripped of their respectable paper clothing.

The Mother is blindfolded. She cannot see what is happening, and her ears are also covered over. The Daughter's mouth is taped, she is gagged. A red cross silencing her. The Father has nothing restricting him, he holds the power.

Behind the scenes, from within the family home, we are now able to see particular ideas and events which enable the Father to abuse his power. The four walls of the family home, and the firm belief that what happens inside the family home is nobody else's business, conceal the misery and torment that lies within.

Dresden China is her Father's prized possession, his obsession. He has her under lock and key. She is safe with him, he will protect her.

These domestic scenes are interrupted by others which occur outside the home. They are set in a pub (public house) and convey society's attitudes toward child sexual abuse and the perpetuation of myths which mask the reality as experienced by the child in the home.

The characters and settings are a mix of rapidly changing magazine cut-outs and drawings, collaged together and animated to symbolize a cross-section of social types and attitudes.

The characters' actions contradict what they say. Male voices protest. 'The man can't be normal'. Yet in the same breath, a man throws a dart at the image of a naked woman on a playing card. Images of women's bodies, hence, women's bodies, are a target for humiliation and the release of men's anger.

The Mother and Daughter are labelled. Only the Father is forgiven. Each becomes a stereotyped image from the cutting of magazines. They each attempt to voice their story anonymously (via text).

'The Daughter is a 'Lolita'. She must be precocious. Why else would her Father be molesting her?

'The Mother is a 'Wicked Witch'. They say she is a bad wife and Mother. But she had to work to support her family. The Father is 'Santa Claus'. He gave her a gift. What's wrong with a gift of love?'

Towards the end of the film, Dresden China ends her silence and takes the tape from her mouth. Her Mother uncovers her ears and takes off the blindfold. She hears her Daughter's voice and comforts her.

The Father arrives and the Mother confronts him.

Scissors appear from her mouth and she cuts into the blades of his mouth. They are locked in a struggle, a conflict. They are unaware of the china vase, which is also used to symbolize the Daughter throughout the film, breaking.

For me, *Daddy's Little Bit of Dresden China* acted as a form of therapy, enabling me to express feelings I could not have expressed otherwise. Feelings I didn't have words for, and forbidden feelings such as anger. The process of making the film helped me to come to terms in some ways with what had happened to me as a child and locate certain patterns of behaviour in my adult life that were destructive.

The final image is of the shattered china vase. It is the child who is damaged and broken through such an experience and this can only be stopped when society offers encouragement and support to people who have to live in silence because of the ignorance of others. Sexual abuse is a political, as well as personal, issue.

After leaving art college, Karen Watson has continued making films, whilst also working with children. She was one of thirteen animators to gain funding from a nation-wide competition sponsored by Kelloggs' Cornflakes, to make contemporary versions of Grimms' fairytales (Marjut Rimminen and Emma Calder also made films for this series). The Sharpest Witch, made in 1989, reworks the story of Hansel and Gretel to give it an ecological thrust: the witch is a madly consuming housewife, and the model-character is based on Dame Edna Everage. She has done some commercial work for Three Peach Studio, animated sequences for the Natural History Museum, and for an educational video on the work of the Museum of the Moving Image. Reception and Soft Perm were two quite surreal thirty second animation films commissioned for television, for a series looking at confrontational situations, called Them and Us. These, however, proved a little too challenging for early evening broadcast!

She is now at the National Film and Television School, where she is working on a film mixing live-action and model animation. The film aims to explore the subjective experience of anorexia, and is partly drawn from her own experiences.

The most important thing about animation, for her, is that it offers total control.

She is also keen to develop her work with and for children. - Ed.

See colour pages for stills from *Daddy's Little Bit of Dresden China*.

Drawing on Experience...

Joan Staveley on her computer animation

The startlingly surreal flights of fancy that distinguish the work of American animator Joan Staveley are simply the most obvious expression of her talent. What makes her two computer animated pieces, Broken Heart, *(1988), and* Wanting for Bridge *(1991) so impressive is their emotional range and depth, disclosing feelings of pain, anxiety and loss with a sensitivity that is all too rare in the computer animation field. Both works draw heavily on Stavely's personal biography:* Broken Heart *confronting the complex tangle of emotions many women experience regarding food, diet and self-image;* Wanting for Bridge *mourning the death of a loved one, killed in a random murder, in a delicate and haunting requiem.* Steven Bode.

Broken Heart

Broken Heart crosses the terrain of the mind as one experiences a trauma. Dinner forks violate a corridor and room, stabbing vicious wounds in the architectural structures. The attack results in the symbolic death of the space.

It is about pain, the kind of pain whose cause becomes irrelevant long after the initial wound. The film expresses what I experienced through 14 years of a severe eating disorder. Through the creation of *Broken Heart*, I was able to understand something in the soup of my unconsciousness about that painful part of my life.

The initial shot is of a white room, innocence. The following shot: a hilly meadow, a photograph, with forks tumbling in the air towards the viewers. It's windy. The shot is odd, but not necessarily foreboding. When we cut to a long corridor with doors on one side that open and shut, the mood changes; it's ominous. A voice whispers, but the words are not easily deciphered. The camera tracks from one end of the hall to the other. As we reach the far end of the hall, we see an elevator. It opens as we near it. Forks shoot out of these doors of chance. The forks puncture the hall floor when they land. The punctures turn red. A fork stabs its way down the hall and enters the only door left open. The room is stabbed to death.

I want the viewers to associate the floor and wall punctures with the puncturing of their own skin by these indifferent tools. I use forks, because their purpose in our culture is to spear or stab food so that it can be brought neatly to our mouths. In the western world we see our use of forks as a sign of civilised gentility. However, the act of stabbing is violent. I see the use of forks as symbolising the sickness of our culture: the tools affirming our civilised and superior selves are the same tools of our violence and savagery. I destroy myself and the structures of society in *Broken Heart*. There is, however, a redemption and a spiritual birth after the death of the structure in *Broken Heart*. The red wounds turn white when the room dies. There is no more pain. A ghost room lifts off the dead room, a spiritual ascension. The shot fades to black and cuts to another photographic landscape of an ocean beach just after a storm. Forks are, again, blowing in the wind towards the viewers. The photograph is much darker in mood. A wall of the corridor and swinging doors cross the sky far off in the distance. The encounter with the forks is over. The wind and corridor move in separate directions away from each other. The last shot is of the death room which was also the initial shot in *Broken Heart*. No wounds are present, but the room is dark rather than white. A loss of innocence has occurred.

I borrowed the two outdoor shots from a Hollywood western. At the start of the film, men on horses diagonally crossed the screen towards the viewer. The west was being explored; it was still the 'wild west'. At the end of the film, a train crossed the screen diagonally away from the viewer. The west had been civilised; the 'wild west' had come to an end. These shots were used to cross the terrain of a changing land. The landscape also represented the change in the psychology of those who live on that land. I used landscape in *Broken Heart* to cross the terrain of the mind and track changes due to a traumatic experience.

Wanting for Bridge

A requiem for my cousin who was murdered in 1989. Hands, which become birds, cross above the ruins of a bridge that can not afford them passage, that can not sustain horizontal motion - life. The birds are shot down in a mass murder.

For a split second Bridget knew she was going to die. *Wanting for Bridge* begins at that moment; crossing the bridge between life and death. This murder victim was not just a statistic to me, but a life I knew, my cousin. She was 23.

The Christian concept of life after death is a struggle for me intellectually, and yet it is part of my body. I was raised in that faith. In reality I think there is no afterlife, and yet somehow I can not bear that thought; it offers no peace. When I cross moments of transcendence in my life, usually caused by overwhelming joy or grief, I talk to God. I even feel that God listens and guides me. But where was God when Bridget needed him? Who is comforting her now? I dream of holding Bridget across my lap and stroking her hair, comforting her broken skull. Other times I imagine Jesus holding Bridget on his lap, a reversed Pietà of sorts. Jesus heals her head with his soothing hand and looks at her the way my mother gazes with adoration at her babies in old photos. I see the hands of Jesus on the cross, wondering at the purpose of martyrs. Bridget's death is senseless: just another murder in an American city.

Shortly after Bridget's death, came the Tiananmen Square massacre. With every newscast of the total number of dead, I was acutely aware of each body required to make that sum. Each individual had to die – suffer to die – fight to live – die. A family mourns for every one of those corpses. The demonstrators had such hope before the military crackdown. Their celebration in life came through with clarity to this viewer of the great television box. I see images of beautiful white birds flying. To live, what a gift!

Bridget was also one of those beautiful birds. I wonder if she knows what happened and weeps, like a lost child? I wonder if she knows how she's been cheated of her life. I know. *Wanting for Bridge* tries to find Bridget's voice now; it tries to cry out for all those deliberately killed by another. How they weep; their lives have been stolen.

Alongside the recent political murders and massacres in all parts of the world I have watched the brutal social violence in United States cities climb. Bridget's death opened my eyes.

I can not be idealistic about world peace: no country is peaceful, no peoples are peaceful, few individuals are peaceful within themselves. We each kill with different weapons, sometimes by simply looking the other way. Ultimately, I know this will not change, but I desperately and secretly hope it will... and then I feel helpless again.

God, help me mourn for the dead.

Notes on the making of the film

The surreal quality of mixing photos and 3-dimensional computer graphics speaks to me. I think of animation as poetry-dance, a compression of visual phrases that piece together what I want to know, express and/or understand about the world. Animating over photographs, allows me to move through space and time, while burning images into the mind.

All of the backgrounds in *Wanting for Bridge* are photographic images. The bridge photographed for the animation was located on Ohio State University's campus. It has since been repaired. The bridge was wondrous to look at in its crumbled state; it spoke so clearly as a symbol of civilization and became the metaphor for my animation. I had a general idea of what was going to take place at this bridge, but the actual photographs of the bridge both constrained and inspired how I would work.

It was a little bit like having a stack of jumbled images

that I knew possessed some kind of narrative. I had to shuffle the deck, juxtaposing one image and then the next, looking for connections. As I flushed out passages and shots in the animation, I narrowed down the number of photographs The final piece uses about 25 background images. I did not necessarily work in a linear fashion. I finished the sections I knew about first, and let them help me discover what had to happen in another place.

The 3-dimensional computer graphics hand was originally a clay model. I drew a grid over this clay model in order to digitize it as data into the computer using a Polhemus 3Space Digitizer. Although the process is tedious and time consuming (about a month), it is not difficult.

The computer animation of the internal hand movement was extremely tedious, but achieved with some easily adapted motion control software that John C. Donkin had written for another project. The software worked something like 'Gumby' (the green bendable guy), except with 21 simply defined joints. Bending a joint or viewing the hand from various viewpoints could only be done via keyboard or mouse. The motion control program knew nothing about gravity or the way hands move. The motion of the hands looks human hand-like, or bird-like. because I worked hard to make it look that way.

The hands were moved in space via a track-based animation system written by John C. Donkin. The 3-dimensional space is defined using Cartesian coordinates. Objects move in that space by defining their X,Y, and Z positions over time.

The complexity of surfaces and forms in natural light over time can not possibly be recreated using present 3-dimensional computer graphics techniques. The shortcomings in the naturalness of the way my digital hand looks or moves is softened by matting the hands over photographs The mind blends the computer graphics hands into the photo with ease. The result is a quirky kind of surrealism that works somewhere between still and moving images.

When Jeffrey T. Faust and I began work on the sound, we expected to use human voice and sound for the cries in the death scenes, and geese sounds for the flight scenes. In collecting sound samples, Jeff came upon the calls of humped back whales and of distressed elephants. These sounds impressed him as sounding much more mournful and expressive than the human voice experiments we'd done. Using the calls of whales and elephants brought a dynamic to the animation that expressed more about humans as animals, and animals as humans. In fact, the animation does not make clear who is dying–animals or people? Both? All life? It is clear, however, that the dead are mourned over.

Technical Notes

Wanting for Bridge was produced in part at The Ohio Supercomputer Center (OSC) and The Advanced Computing Center for the Arts and Design (ACCAD), The Ohio State University.

Software: Animation software (track based): John C. Donkin OSC/ACCAD.

Rendering software: D. Scott Dyer, OSC.

Motion control software of hands: John C. Donkin OSC/ACCAD.

Image processing software: Jeffrey Light ACCAD.

Procedural animation: Jeffrey T. Faust OSC

Hard ware Sun Sparc Workstations: Animation and calculation. BarneyScan: Slide digitizing. Polhemus 3Space Digitizer: 3-dimensional digitizing of clay model of hands. Abekas Still Frame Store: Recording digital frames to video.

There is very little opportunity for personal or art animation in India. India's most famous animator, Ishu Patel, has made his films at the Canadian NFB, although he was influential in setting up the first, and only facility for teaching traditional animation, at the National Institute of Design in Ahmedabad. The commercial studios make cartoons for children and television. Nina Sabnani, and Benita Desai, who teach at NID (see over) have managed to make their own films, alongside the commissioned public service films built in to the Institute's structure.

Two other promising Indian women animators have both moved to the US to pursue their careers. After a degree in Fine Arts, Chitra Shriram studied animation at NID. She is currently a doctoral student in Computer Graphics at Ohio State University

'As a woman animator, working within the undeniably 'techno-macho' field of computer graphics, I think that *Leela*, my first computer animation, encapsulates my experience in this field in one word: conflict. 'Leela' is Sanskrit for 'the game of the Gods'. In spirit, it is taken to be much like Shakespeare's 'all the world's a stage'. According to popular Indian belief, the world is the playground of the Gods, wherein the eternal conflicts of good and evil are played out. When I encountered the computer for the first time, I could not help seeing it as a magical black box - a theatre in which I played both God and hapless participant. Hence the title. The necessity to bring past experience into what seemed like a completely impersonal work environment created the imagery. The characters are drawn loosely from the Ramayana epic and memories of traditional performances seen by lamp light. The characters symbolise for me the 'system' and the idiosyncratic 'individual' even more than the Gods and demons they refer to.

Maya (Illusion) is my current, much more ambitious project. It combines live-action video with computer generated imagery and animation. In this piece, I am trying to use the surface of the image itself as a dominant expressive element. The integrity of the video image is easily enhanced or mutilated when it is digitised. Much violence can be done to the photo-realistic image that we take for truth in our television society. Here, I am exploring levels of credibility within a narrative by pitting two disparate sources against each other, just as I worked with two different spatial worlds (2-D and 3-D) in *Leela*. My intention is to share my questions about illusion and reality with the audience, not to create a seamless reality which films like *Terminator 2* aim for.'

The thematic of her work is 'the search for the corrrect take on a situation. My traditional animation films, *Khakim Ki Hank* and *Khuror Khol* are based on writing

for children (and use drawing, cut out, pixillation, time lapse). Both present idiosyncratic individuals whose actions cannot easily be deemed brilliant or foolish. Working with the computer, I continue to deal with the theme of conflicting planes of perspective - the conflict between 'system' and 'individual' (leela) and the private world of mind and the external world (maya). Translating the dialectic into formal terms creates new problems with language and technique that I enjoy greatly in any medium. The computer and the technological society it represents is always a little foreign to me. It is therefore, as much a breeding ground of my essential questions as it is the vehicle of my artistic resolutions.'

Simi Nallaseth started in animation via Bombay's commercial studio system. Since commercial animation is very Disney oriented, although she picked up a few tips, she actually taught herself, 'from books and exercises that I did to learn about timing and the fundamentals of motion.' She had 'heard of' McLaren and Caroline Leaf in India, but had no opportunities to see or study other forms of animation, so in 1988 went to study in the US. She took an MFA at New York's School of Visual Arts, where she made *Diabolic Wife,* using computer animation. This satire on male dominance was, she says, 'a reaction to the Indian male dominated society that I come from… it is also somewhat symbolic of every man's desire to dominate his partner. Compelled by his lust for a woman, a devil creates a fragmented wife by juxtaposing varous parts of animals on her, oblivious to all but his own carnal needs. It's more a foray into dynamic storytelling than social commentary.' The film has been well received, but she feels it suffered from distracting technical problems and the frustrations of computer time-sharing. *A House of Cards*, an MTV 30-second commission on social harmony, co-directed with Mike de Seve, was, she feels, more successful. She was able to combine hand-drawn animation with computer images. 'I tried very hard for two months to animate dust blowing off the ground, using TDI software particle systems, but it just didn't have the correct texture and motion. In the end we just took a toothbrush and animated it traditionally and combined it with the rest of the images. As a result, the film has a strange texture and expresses the concept beautifully. It's more conceptual than *Diabolic Wife* and more expressive of my style and ideas.' She's now decided to use computers very sparingly, concerned that questions of technique can override and limit her work as an artist. 'I recently bought a Bolex to experiment with at home and I want to try some crazy mediums like coloured wheat flour and ink swirls in water…' She also works freelance on commercial work in New York.

Nina Sabnani

'As a student I thought of animation as a vehicle for wit, directed mainly at juveniles - dignified, of course, by the animator's technical virtuosity. Fortunately, fate intervened in the form of Roger Noake (at the time a UNDP consultant, seconded to the National Institute of Design) who provoked us all into actually thinking about the possiblities of the medium, instead of assuming that they were given - wrapped and packaged - courtesy Walt Disney.

In a country where dramatic contrasts stare you in the face it isn't hard to find content for making films. What is hard is finding a form that is not a kind of ex-colonial mimicry. I don't find it necessary to forge one distinctive style; I think each film demands its own idiom. Since there are so many wildly disparate things I want to make films about, I need, not one appropriate form, but many. I have on two occasions borrowed styles of representation from painters in India. One was for *Shubh Vivah* (Happy Wedding), an anti-dowry film. The drawing style is that of the women painters from Mithila, Bihar and their paintings are ritualistic. My last film, *A Summer Story*, used the story and drawing style of Professor K.G. Subramanyam who, unlike the women from Mithila, is a formally trained painter.

I began life as a painter with a degree in fine arts, until an acute teacher declared that my talent was for animation. Strange being credited with an aptitude for a craft I wasn't sure I could spell, but at the same time I had heard all those stories about lives being changed by sudden revelations. So I gave animation a go and here I am, one more character in those miraculous stories.

I studied animation for two and a half years at the National Institute of Design, Ahmedabad. Ishu Patel of the National Film Board of Canada inspired us every now and then with his films and persuaded the Institute to take some of us onto the faculty. It's a hard job and there's lots to do, but it's been fun.

An aside: animation and dreaming. Once I realised that animation and dreaming are analogous, I wondered why it had taken me so long to arrive at this conclusion. We respond to both in the same way. We know that they're both 'unreal' and yet we suspend disbelief. Within them time shrinks, stretches or even stops. People can be within two places at the same time, or even dead and alive all at once. Quite often a dream character or an animated figure will look like one person and behave like another. Animation is a domain where we can magic the improbable, the absurd and the utterly impossible into existence. If the 'real' world is to be put into perspective, someone has to dream.

In 1984, I worked on a film *Shubh Vivah* on the issue of dowry with a few women painters from Mithila, Bihar. Painting for these women is an essential part of their social existence. Their stylized, ritual paintings are made around mythological themes and they paint them at festivals, weddings and other similar occasions.

As a radical departure from the normal function of such paintings, a few of these women had made paintings on the issue of dowry. As victims or observers they were revolting against a socially-accepted norm with a language close to them. I saw these paintings at an exhibition and felt an immediate involvement with their attempt. I suggested to them that we work on an animated film using their drawing style in tandem with my experience as an animator. They were bewildered by the idea of animation, but very enthusiastic nonetheless about the project. What I found most interesting was the appropriateness of the form for such a theme. Usually paintings such as theirs are made to form a part of the preliminary instalment of dowry that seals the marriage contract. And here they are used to frame a polemic against this very system.' *Nina Sabnani, 1988.*

Nina Shorina

Nina Shorina is the only woman animator in the former Soviet Union to have created a substantial body of work that ranks her alongside the established (male) names in Soviet animation. Roger Noake, in the essay that follows, demonstrates the recurring and developing themes in her work.

The early films are funny, slightly fantastical stories, whilst her more recent films have become more openly political and probing – although never in a direct, social commentary way. Increasingly experimental in form, and often densely layered in both style and content, they are more difficult, though richly rewarding films, and suggest a transitional phase in her development as an artist. Her films use puppet and model animation, and more recently have incoporated photographs, pixillation, drawing and live-action. Her husband, a highly regarded documentary cameraman, usually shoots her films.

She started in film as an actress, but didn't enjoy the atmosphere of big productions, and the feeling of being, literally, manhandled. She turned to literature and painting, and started publishing her short stories in Soviet avant-garde magazines.

She then studied at the Faculty of Documentary Films at VGIK, the main Soviet film school. She was inspired by Polish documentary and the strain of poetic realism in French films, but felt there were no opportunities under the Soviet system to make the films she wanted to. There wasn't anything like the Polish studio Semafor, (known for its innovative documentaries and animation). She felt Russian documentary studios 'told nothing but lies'.

Animation seemed a way out. Her first films were for children, but even here, she ran up against the system. One film, based on a fairytale, used oriental motifs, and also natural materials... a wipe with sand between scenes introduced each new motif - and drew criticism for 'eclecticism' for mixing styles this way. *Tale of a Tall Man* was criticised for being ideologically unsound. The latter film charts the disruption caused in a small town by the arrival of a very tall man, and his finally frustrated efforts to integrate himself into the community; *About Buka* is a comic look at a little girl's non-conformity. Both are puppet animations for children, although they are as enjoyable for adults, and share a fascinating use of screen space through mixing 3-D with 2-D cutouts. The result is a sense of every frame bursting with life and movement, a wealth of different stories and characters anrachically insisting on their presence, emphasised by an unusual editing style and inventive use of music. *Poodle*, based on a fable by a popular writer, is a fast-moving comic extravaganza about an old lady whose quiet life is disrupted by an anarchic poodle, whose size changes according to each crazy scenario he puts her through.

Things improved when an ex-film magazine editor was appointed Head of Goskino Studios. Although *Door* started as a children's film, under the new regime she reworked it for the adult audiences she had been hitherto denied. An absurdist fable, in which the inhabitants of an apartment block seem unable to use the front door, and have invented a range of crazy forms of entry and exit, it is also a political allegory. When studio colleagues first saw the models (eg the caricatured heroic statues of Soviet workers) - she was told the film would never get made... and without perestroika, it probably wouldn't have been.

Dream is an interrogation of the Russian literary tradition of impotent intellectuals meditating on the state of the nation, dreaming nostalgically of the past, resistant to all attempts to move from lethargy to action. Images of Church and State, of peasant life and superstition, of industrialisation, all fail to move the sleeping figure who longs for sweet entropy.

In *Alter Ego* Shorina contemplates the relationship of art to the everyday, via a self-portrait within a self-portrait. Appearing briefly in Rembrandt's *Night Watch*, she is hauled back to the 'reality' of everyday existence - preparing food, nursing a baby, queuing and shopping for food. The harshness and desperation of food shortages and the stupidity of the bureaucratic machine is mitigated by the possibility of a spiritual existence. Salvation lies in the ability to contemplate oneself and one's life critically. Only when the wrapping is literally removed from the eyes, can life begin.

Hall of Mirrors, or *Funhouse*, is a harsh and quite disturbing film, in which a queue of people pay to be allowed entrance to a dilapidated shed, which contains distorting mirrors, funhouse style, in front of which they act out fantasies of eating, loving and consuming. One figure, however, the artist/witness, sees a true though unflattering reflection of himself. The reflected objects begin to take on life: shoes and disembodied arms attack the man. The people reflected in the mirrors are transformed into their mirror distortions, grossly and grotesquely disfigured. Now their fantasies are propelled into life: eating becomes gluttony, love becomes lust, as the figures claw at and decvour each other in a frenzy. The witness/artist figure breaks the mirror and the grotesques are transformed into stone statues in an idyllic landscape and provided with human and heroic attributes. The skins shed by the transformed grotesques are swept out of the door as another group reach the head of the queue for their turn.

Nina Shorina: the state of narration
by Roger Noake

An aircraft of indeterminate age heads towards the spectator from a fading Aeroflot poster pasted on the crumbling wall of an apartment block. The promise of freedom, of travel, and of the West. Below the poster a half open door invites the tenants to accept or refuse the offer of freedom.

Nina Shorina's later animation films explore this dilemma through a detailed and precise delineation of the shifting boundaries of public and private space in the disintegrating Soviet Union. Her work demonstrates the complexity of defining these frontiers for women in a society where notions of home and of street have always had a multiplicity of meanings, and where state power and the concept of the nation is itself fragmenting.

It is through the conjunction of concepts of freedom, of the individual, and of identity with, literally, a modelling of the space in which these concepts are constrained and coerced, that Shorina elicits meaning.

Door (1986) was the first of Shorina's films to be seen in the West and to gain some critical acclaim. The works of artistic maturity which followed mark out an uncertain path in which mapping the collapse of the boundaries between public and private spheres in Eastern Europe and the development of a personal and original voice are bound together.

Door is the first delineation of this world, a society with public and private clearly separate and apparently correctly aligned. Only the chink in the door suggests otherwise. The film uses puppet animation as had all of Shorina's fil ms to this date. The film's first image is the reflection in a balloon of a boy with a skateboard. The balloon floats away from his grasp. Freedom and innocence are suggested in this reference to Lamorisse's *Le Ballon Rouge,* a film which Shorina has cited as an early inspiration.

The skateboard and the fashion for things western, the child who lacks official space is an insubstantial (because reflected) image. Only reflections of the possible, as ephemeral images, are glimpsed. The first image of established society is that of a large man who floats down from a high window and struts pompously round the corner of the building. The assumption of bulk, the confident movement of arms and legs are of a man going about his business and in doing so of necessity occupying the pavement. A bowler-hatted figure appears next, and approaches the door. But at the last moment he turns away and shins up the drain pipe, clutching his briefcase. As he ascends he raises his hat to a descending wicker basket thereby losing his grip: he begins to fall. This is the first intimation that following the old patterns and established routines may lead to disaster. Society's

response to its impending collapse is shown as seeking to immortalise the heroic dimension, and so the drifting balloon floats up and is caught on the riveting machine of a statue, a Hero of The Soviet Union.

Shorina uses animated cycles to establish this sense of repetition. However rather than focus on the main line of the action for the movement, the traditional approach to animated cycles, she choreographs the characters' movements so as to achieve a decentered but interdependent motion. She establishes a moiré texture which reveals the force fields of social interaction. The world seems firmly in place, the characters go about their daily business accepting that they must leave and enter the building by means other than a front door. They have adapted well.

A wedding party arrives, the movement of their limousine cutting directly across the plane of the action which can be seen through the open car door. The bride-to-be is seen at a window above. Her eager father attempts to load her into a basket to lower her down onto the street but the basket falls without her. The bridegroom, stirred finally to action, tries to open the front door and is joined by one of the drivers of the wedding car, then by a large woman. A gathered crowd struggles with the immovable portal.

The bride, high above this frantic action, falls into the arms of the Soviet Worker Hero. Finally dislodged from his grip by the crowd's hammering at the door below, she is shaken onto the statue of The Soviet Heroine, knocking a basket of food from the statue's arms. Food spills down into the street and rolls amongst card players at a table outside the door: they have given up any interest in entering the building. Shorina seldom uses cuts to clarify the ever more frantic action or to privilege a single event. Instead the proscenium structure is resolutely maintained. All of the activities around the door are of equal

unimportance.

A small bearded man carrying a string bag walks toward the door and drifts through it without any effort or motivation. When he reappears the small boy questions him. The solution to the closed door is to apply some oil to the hinges; the door then opens easily. The boy leaves it wide open but no one seems to notice or show any interest. The fat man strides towards the opening purposefully but then retraces his steps, marching backwards. The boy leads the bowler-hatted man to the door but he takes the handle and shuts the door before shinning up the drainpipe. The bride and groom, now reconciled, descend in a suitcase lowered from a window and are driven away in the car to the resounding crescendo of a Rachmaninov piano concerto. Once again the characters resume the pattern of their lives climbing in and out of the windows, tightrope walking across the rooftops. For one moment the door opens slightly before closing again firmly and finally.

Only the child, the small bearded man and a lone black cat are able to pass through the door. The significance of this passage is emphasised by a bold camera movement across the face of the door moving through 45° which is followed by a shot from inside the hallway showing the reactions of the large man who remains standing outside. This, the first and only time when the spectator's point of view shifts from that of a static position, underlines that it is easier for both characters and spectator to continue perfoming the roles and movements designed for them than to risk change and its disruptive consequences. Some might even prefer to reject utterly the inevitability of being able to move through the door. It is the unimportant, marginalised members of society who are able to make the journey with ease.

Both representation of scale and relative expansiveness of gesture and movement are essential to Shorina's technique and meaning. Grand movements and by implication the way in which these movements are portrayed in film are the antithesis of freedom. Far from being heroic gestures in the face of oppression they serve to implicate the figures/characters in the cause of their own downfall. Their gestures perpetuate catastrophe in proportion to their pomposity and failing machismo.

Shorina's involuntary exile in the world of children's films supplied her with a vocabulary in which relativity of size and permissibility of gesture are essential elements of socialisation. *Door*, for the first time, takes these elements of difference and makes them central to the discussion of identity.

Dream, her next film, is a reflection on the problem of the heroic non-gesture, the traditional Oblomovian position described by Goncharov. It is a portrayal of romantic pessimism, of an intellectual paralysed by dramatic public or private events. Shorina abandons the puppets and narrative form of her previous films. Instead, images are permitted to fade through and out of others in a constant flux. Gesture and movement are suggested by the play of light. Meaning is established through the slipping and sliding of sound and images and by the film's cyclic structure. The opening refrain *In a distant land/Far away/Flow rivers of honey/Their banks are steep/Steep and made of jelly*, acts as a coda for the film in which no single image remains undisrupted or unquestioned, and in which the passage of fragmentary images convey the enveloping atmosphere of impotent nostalgia.

Shorina's abandonment of even the decentred and chaotic choreography of her earlier films in favour of a multilayered and intersecting imagery is significant. The boundaries between the landscape and figure have been eliminated; scale is no longer fixed. The smallest object can take on epic proportions, and the heroic is in itself insignificant.

The film's opening, in which landscape floods with the light from an orthodox church, which then spreads across the face of a sleeping figure, breathing deeply, demonstrates Shorina's approach to structuring the scenes. Image is laid upon image. The form of an old peasant woman slowly replaces the church in the frame. She carries a crown, and spins away across the snows. The face of the slumbering figure, like a death mask, fills the screen and an accordion player fades into the picture. The weight given to each image as it appears and fades is contingent on its relationship to the previous and the following image. But this is the antithesis of classic Eisensteinian montage, in which a third meanng is supposedly created by the juxtaposition of two images. In this case, montage is used to maintain a fluidity of meaning, so that the juxtaposition allows for the existence of both the image and the tone produced by the friction of the images in the same space. Nowhere is this more clearly demonstrated than in this first sequence in which the 'breathing' camera movement in relation to the head of the sleeping figure, the church which is gradually replaced by the peasant sewing, and the landscape itself, set up a resonance of meanings.

The light which spreads from the church is as significant and as solid as the building itself. The dreamer's voice is heard speaking of the impossibility of a good man taking any action in the world. Only scoundrels can achieve anything; it is better to strive to be an insect, he states. All attempts to rouse the slumbering figure fail. The man only exists in his memories. A toy train metamorphoses into a full-size locomotive which travels through the landscape composed of drawings and photographs of historical characters and events, a landscape of memories. The train journey has come to symbolise a linear narrative in film from the time of Porter's *Great Train Robbery*. The voice declaims over the first image of the moving train that 'any consciousness is an illness'. The train moves at a three quarter angle to the film plane. Point of view shifts to that from the carriage windows as scenes

flicker past: crowds in nineteenth-century clothes, a cross, a single bearded figure, crowds of people, in twentieth-century dress.

However, these images do not pass the window in a linear fashion as might be expected. Instead each is repeated in a slightly different position in relation to the viewer. This is not the traditional Russian literary view of history as a linear unfolding of preordained events, a procession towards an inevitable conclusion: it is shifting, stuttering. Memories are disrupted, and the past disrupting.

The driver's cab window is transformed into the spectacles of a watching man, a dark and imposing figure of power and action. The spectacles reflect, in rapid succession, the head and shoulders of a woman, a cityscape, an accordion player, then superimposed and gradually replacing this image is that of a luminous pike wearing a crown. The pike as monarch of fishes is a traditional northern figure of mythology. This is a powerful evocation of ambiguity. The fish/the fish king/ the king/the king fish/the crown /the sovereign/ the state: at no point a static metaphor. In *Door* this ambiguity was achieved by multiple actions in the same field, one action being privileged only at strong narrative points. In *Dream* the metaphor is kept in suspension by the refusal to make any individual figure concrete and specific apart from the dreamer. In the last sequence's final image the old woman tickles the feet of the recumbent figure, whose toes twitch in response and the image fades to black. This blackness or rather lack of image is the only undisrupted static element of the film. Whether or not the Oblomov character will awake becomes irrelevant. It is the dream-state or the state-dream which is under scrutiny.

Once again it is the boundaries of public and private which are being examined. In this film Shorina has used the metaphorical, where meaning occurs by definition at the point of change in order to facilitate this interrogation of these boundaries.

The final sequence shows the eyes of the slumbering figure slowly opening. Saint George and the Dragon, the symbol of Russian resistance to the enemy, and of the Church, are frozen in conflict, and the image fades through the half- glimpsed Russian landscape. Once again the face of the sleeping figure is seen from head on in a coffin/cot, dressed in swaddling clothes - or it could be a shroud. The words of a song, however, offer hope for the future: 'Raise up the coffin lid/Arise, arise, my beloved child.'

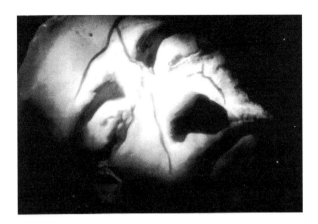

The strong rejection of intellectual and artistic pessimism in *The Dream* was followed by Shorina's most personal work to date, *Alter Ego* (1989). Collage techniques rather than the complex superimpositions and multi-layered planes of *Dream* convey multiplicity of meaning. *Alter Ego* begins with a reference to *Door*. A door opens, beyond it is another open door and just visible the corner of a window. Cut to the profile of a woman, Shorina, her face half hidden by steam from a boiling kettle. The film writes the author and the author's work into its construction.

The techniques which she employs in structuring and staging develop the notion of animation's reflexive nature, the drawing of the drawing, the recreation of movement frame by frame in puppet and pixillated film.

The opening sequence defines the space in which she will operate as that of the frame. It is the frame and the framing which carry meaning, rather than a narrative line. The social reality shown in the live-action footage – people queueing for food, the drunk and the destitute - is used as part of a formal strand in the film's self examination. It is a self-portrait but one which reflects on its own and the spectator's position towards this generic form and its meaning.

She achieves this reflection by recycling Rembrandt's paintings, particularly the self-portraits. The cycle, one of the fundamental processes of industrial animation production, allowing an efficient use of the material through the repetition of movement, is used here and in other films to halt the flow of animation and to reverse its trajectory. Immediately after the film's titles a hand turns the pages of a book of Rembrandt paintings: past one of the late Rembrandt self-portraits to *The Night Watch*: The men gaze out, the camera moves through the crowd and discovers the half hidden woman in the painting. The camera/viewer lingers on this image. A series of mixes follow in which the position of the spectator and the

spectator within the frame shifts constantly. Shorina examines *The Night Watch*, men of the night watch gaze out on Shorina. The image fades once more to the Rembrandt self-portrait. A hand reaches out and turns off a table lamp. The timing of the effect is staggered so that the darkness slowly spreads over the portrait on the page.

Cut to a papier maché figure with a necklace of toilet rolls which unravels and wraps itself around Shorina's head. The idealised alter ego of Rembrandt is replaced by the reality of everyday life. Food, ground to slush in a food grinder, spreads across the open pages of the book, obliterating the Rembrandt portrait still smiling confidently out from the pages of the History of Art.

Her technique once again breaks down boundaries between animate and inanimate (though to radically different effect than the Svankmajer comparisons these sequences have aroused). Pixillated actors mix with puppets, still photographs, and hardly discernible movements in film are fused. The static Rembrandt portraits are given motion and the images of Shorina herself are frozen. The tomatoes/blood and the toilet paper are possessed with more apparent life, certainly more movement than either the Shorina figure or Rembrandt's alter ego. These inanimate objects seem to possess more freedom of movement and chaotic vitality, as if the sleeping protagonist of *Dream* comment that all action leads to 'destruction and chaos' has become manifest in the objects of everyday life.

The bringing together in such sharp contrast of puppets, pixillated figures, photograps and well-known images from art history demonstrates the care with which the filmmaker approaches the delineation of boundaries, and the resonance which she achieves by transgressing them.

Babies, toilets, and blood have been firmly assigned by society to the private sphere, yet here they assume an aggressive life and a freedom of action which is assumed to exist only in a public sphere. Great works of art are integrated into the text in a way which suggests instead a redefinition of what those meanings might be; that it is they which are part of the private world. The meaning of the paintings is presented as no longer for discussion in relation to cultural and art historical realms, but rather in the relationship which they have towards what's taken to be private discourse. In the film's final sequence Shorina, head wrapped in a toilet roll, stands by a window. In a park below, the old Rembrandt sits on a park bench. The camera moves in and the Rembrandt portraits animate in reverse time until the youthful first portrait is reached. The wrapping removes itself from her head and an unwrapped Shorina half turns away from the window, looking back into the film, not out at the spectator, an affirmation of the power of reflection and recreation.

Whereas in *Dream* the sleeping man's memories are distorted by romance and sentimental dwelling over idealised relationships and public roles not played, here the recollection is uncompromisingly self-critical. The gaze of the Rembrandt portraits, the gaze of others, which is delineated and struggled against by the framing devices in the first sequence is turned ruthlessly inwards and at the same time made public.

Shorina's early career, working mainly as an animator, writer and director of material for children, has shown a consistent concern with identity (e.g. *The Tall Man* and *Poodle*) through to the mature recent films. She has moved from overt concern with stories of the displaced and un-socialised finding a place in the world, to an expression of identity in flux through her exploration of the spatial and narrative constituents of film. Her ability as an artist and technician in command of the medium had been established before she her work for adult audiences and yet there is no clinging to a proven technique in the recent films. Each runs its own risk and takes its chance with failure not least on a technical level. However, in the mature work, this concern becomes more than an interest in the outsider or the un-socialised: it takes on a critical dimension. In the films for children, simple notions of identity tend to examine the reconciliation of difference, and at achieving harmony, although they work through a range of positions towards this final resolution. Difference in the early films remains something which has to be overcome either by society, or by the individual finding an appropriate role within society. Difference is permitted.

Increasingly, through the development of a language of juxtaposition and through an approach to narrative and spatial articulation, Shorina has developed a more complex thematic of identity and difference. She has demonstrated that simple notions of narrative resolution and narrative progression are inappropriate to a project which undertakes an examination of the borders of differentiation. This is especially the case when these borders are constantly disputed and redrawn, when they shift and drift, fixed only according to whose history or what perspective is legitimised at that moment. Reading through and beyond style and aesthetics in animation film from what was 'the Soviet bloc' to discover the hidden social or political meaning has been a consistent approach to much contemporary work. This has been particularly so when, as with Shorina, there is a personal history of dissidence or at least of difficulties with the old authorities. It is certainly clear that many animators adopted strategies in the face of oppressive regimes which fully utilised animation's potential to speak publicly through imagery and metaphor. However, it is also clear that a poetic aesthetic was developed by some animators not simply to disguise unpalatable messages, or to create a private language of subversion, but in order to adress those questions or the relationship of the frontiers of author and text, of public and private, of past and memory. In actively pursuing this complex problem through animated film, Shorina, and some of her compatriots, have posed questions for the future understanding of thses works. If we are to hear these voices truly, we must pay attention not only to the novelty of their existence but to the tone of the utterances.

For Roger Noake, see Notes on Contributors.

In the former Eastern bloc

Thesituation of animation in the former USSR and Eastern Europe has been so very different from that in the West, that the concept of 'independent' filmmaking is not very useful. For the last thirty years, the tradition of art animation in these countries has been the envy of many in the West. Even when work has been suppressed it has at least got made, relatively free from economic pressures. Art education and training in film was well developed, seemingly open to talent, and of a very high standard.

However, it is noticeable how very few women animation directors have emerged under this system, though more have developed in the 80s. When talking to animators, male or female, about why this should be, the response has been quite uniform. Animation as art form is an extremely demanding vocation, I have been told, which therefore inevitably excludes most women, given their inherent 'vocation' as wives and mothers. Feminism, as developed in the last three decades, is often seen as an alien and irrelevent Western fashion. Given the difficult living conditions obtaining in most of the countries collectively known as the Eastern bloc, and the fact they have worsened since the 'demise' of Communism, it is hard not to feel some sympathy for women who define independence as marriage to someone with enough money or clout to relieve them of the struggle to manage everyday life.

It is all the more remarkable then, that some women have managed to become animation directors. Nina Shorina has been discussed - although it's worth noting here the credit she gives her husband and family for their support. Yuri Norstein, considered one of the greatest Russian animation filmmakers, is keen to acknowledge the creative collaboration of his wife, Francesca Arbusova, art director on his films.

The former USSR
In what was the Soviet Union, there are around fifty women animation directors, most of whom work in children's films. Of the 102 recent films from the various republics shown at the 1991 'Krok' animation festival in Kiev, 25 were made by women, although again, most of these were childrens' films. As in the West, women working in trace'n'paint and other stages in the production of (other peoples') films tend to outnumber men, particularly in the large-scale studios such as Soyouzmultfilm and Multelefilm (the latter specialising in production for television, mainly films and series for children).

The following comments from women directors at Soyouzmultfilm give some idea of their views. Elena Prorokova considers women 'better adapted to the specifics of animation work, which requires patience, perseverance, and in the final analysis, the necessity to make something out of nothing.' Tatiana Meeteetello feels despite the large number of women working in animation the profession is more geared to a male mentality, whilst Natalia Orlova comments on how difficult it is to get to learn direction. Opportunities for creative self-development often depend on individuals, and personal temperament. She adds that the very effects of the socialist regime have developed womens' capacities in terms of energetic resourcefulness, negotiating between extremes, and skilful handling of people working in groups. 'The patience and organisational skills needed for directing are qualities found to a greater degree in women than men.'

Galina Barinovoy feels the work of a director is subject to constant stress and emotional pressures. Perhaps, she suggests, for that reason women, with their more emotionally susceptible and responsive natures, find themselves in the minority amongst directors in cinema generally and in animation in particular. On the other hand, Mama Miat remarks that 'the professsion of director, like any other, has its specificities. If it doesn't suit someone temperamentally, they quit. If they fit, they stay and make films.'

Elena Gavrilko recounts that before she begins work on a film she becomes oblivious of everyday things and female concerns retreat into the background; she has neither the desire nor strength to deal with household matters, pleasurable or onerous. The filmmaking process is all-consuming. Only 2-3 months after a film is completed can she return to normal living.

She had to fight for her career, first against her father's wish for her to be a doctor, then through the many years making films for children. She was finally able to study scriptwriting and direction, and her first film for adults, *Girlfriend* (1989) was shown quite widely on the festival circuit. A feisty young female fish teaches herself to live on land and strikes up a friendship with a fisherman (hence the 'girlfriend' tag), but is finally drowned at sea. A parable on the perils of stepping out of what is considered one's 'natural' element? The film has a strong graphic design and colour sense, and an idiosyncratic sense of humour. *Parable of the Mouse* (1991) is about the development and incarnation of the female principle, via mythological references and symbols.

Unfortunately, most of the films mentioned below have not been widely seen, and the following accounts are largely reliant on synopses. Natalia Golovanova, after years working on films for children, made *The*

Soldier and the Devil (1990), a visual representation of a soldier's stream of consciousness revealing the psychological damage he has undergone, his consequent anomie, and failure to feel love. The resurgence of state sanctioned religion seems to have encouraged Larissa Kobza's debut film, *Ballad* (1991), which deals with Christian concepts and imagery.

Despite the remarks above about a general mistrust of Western feminism, several films in the 80s which deal with women's experiences. Quite widely seen on the international festival circuit - is Helen Kasavila's *We are Women*. In three parts, each with a different style, the film's first two sections look at representations of women through history, with a wickedly satiric concluding episode on male chauvinism. A housewife has to work around the inertia of her husband - portrayed as a wooden log; a chain-saw finally provides a solution. Rosa Zelma, in *Female Astronomy or Extra-Terrestial Gravity* (1991), explores the roles of women and men, and how masculinity and feminity have been defined in socialist thought.

Frances Kurbanova's *Aquarium* (1983) is a parable in which a housewife changes places with a fish in an aquarium, whilst *One Evening* (1985) is a sombre sketch about a man's visit to a woman aquaintance, and achieves a haunting mood of hidden longing and lack of self-fulfillment. The technique she uses in this film is that of drawing to suggest rotoscoping. Her most recent film *Seance* (1987) is a reflection on war, interweaving historical and contemporary references, and shocked many with its unflinching insistence on the horrors of the Nazi camps and the gas chambers. After studying scriptwriting and animation direction, Elena Prorokova made *Tale of a Foolish Husband* (1986), on male and female stereotyping, then *From 9 to 6* (1987) which charts a day in the life of contemporary urban women.

In the field of experimental animation, there is Lithuanian artist Nyolya Valadkvichite, whose etchings and silkscreen have been exhibited widely. Her films use collage, cutouts, oil paint, superimposition and found material from life and nature (e.g. tree bark, tissues) and reflect a modernist aesthetic, refusing conventional narrative to create a rebus, or puzzle, which has alienated some audiences. More recently, film critic Irina Yevtyeva has turned animator, with the immensely ambitious *The Horse, the Violin and a Little Nervous*, (1992), a challenge to the traditional image of the poet Mayakovsky. After writing a dissertation on animation she was 'desperate to try my hand… We had no technology, not even a rostrum camera, and had to work it all out ourselves' using different levels of sand, stage make-up and a primitive light pencil over stills and live-action footage.

Eastern Europe

In Poland, Eva Bibanska made two interesting films several years ago, *Unfaithful Portrait* and *The End*, but has now abandoned animation, as has, apparently, Zofia Oraczewska, who made over twenty films between 1961 and 1980, characterised by cynical Polish humour. Eva Ziobrowska is a promising young filmmaker, whose films (*Passageways*, *In the Walls*) are interesting for their formal play with the medium, and she is now working on her third film via a state grant.

Vlasta Pospisolova is a veteran of Czech puppet animation, although only after more than twenty years has she been able to direct films of her own. Michaela Pavlatova seems the most promising - and unique for being so - young woman animator in Czechoslovakia. Her films (*Words, Word, Words; Crossword Puzzle*) are sharp and very funny explorations of the ways people can misunderstand one another, even when they think they are communicating, all the more impressive for doing so by purely visual means. Her observational acuity brings to mind the work of American psycho-linguist Deborah Tannen.

The two films Nicole Hewitt, a young Anglo-Croatian, has made in Zagreb at the tiny Luna independent studio explore issues of freedom and identity, particularly in relation to eroticism, and she is clearly a talent to watch.

The Future

The economic difficulties, which in some countries seem likely to lead to economic collapse and chaos, suggest the luxury of animation as art may be dispensed with. In the past, international festival screenings and awards conferred prestige, validation of the system that produced such films - and foreign travel for some of the bureaucrats associated with studios and cultural organisations. Foreign TV sales potential will play a far more important role in future production decisions. Whilst some Western TV channels are keen to support quality animation, acquisition budgets come nowhere near covering production costs. Co-productions provide some opportunities, but are likely to be geared to films of more populist appeal. Some fear that former Communist countries may be used as cheap labour - all the more attractive in comparison to Asia - given their technical proficiency and aesthetic standards. Czechoslovakia seems determined to ensure 'cultural funding, although filmmakers will now have to find matching money to secure grants. Poland still has some a little state money for animation. The volatile situation makes prediction impossible: all the sadder given the time it has taken for women to emerge as filmmakers in their own right.

Australia

Australia has had quite a flourishing commercial animation industry, with major studios such as Yoram Gross and the Americans Hanna-Barbera and Disney all turning out films for children, television series, and animated features, although obviously in the case of the latter two studios, production was for the American television markets. Recent de-regulation has removed quotas for Australian made commercials for television, which could hit independent producers badly; on the other hand, there is increasing interest and offers of work from South East Asia.

It's worth noting that two of the longest established independent commercial studios are run by women, Anne Jolliffe, of Jollification Productions and Maggie Geddes' The Funny Farm. Both got much of their experience and training in London in the 60s. As Jolliffe recounts, when she went to art school, there were no animation courses - hence her move to London to try and learn the craft via the studios, before returning to Australia to set up on her own; and her animation style reflects her training. Both, in a sense, came too early to benefit from the development of funding opportunities for personal filmmaking, although Anne Jolliffe has managed, whilst running a busy studio, to make a couple, including *The Cranky Princess*, selected for the Annecy festival.

Polish-born Antoinette Starciewicz came to Australia when she was a child in the 50s. She studied fine arts, but whilst at college taught herself animation and made a short film, inspired by pop art and its debunking of high art. The film almost cost her the graduation diploma, as 'cartoons' were not considered art, and the film was considered a provocation. At 21 she had her own solo show of paintings, but the idea of making a living doing society portraits didn't appeal. Wanting to study film, she obtained a place at Lodz Film Academy, (withdrawn at the last minute for political reasons). So she came to London and studied animation at the London Film School, and was part of the heady 60s fringe drama and dance scene. *Puttin' on the Ritz*, her graduation film, a stylish tribute to Fred Astaire, made her name. However, she wasn't keen to pursue the resultant stream of commercial offers, and instead made her next film, *High Fidelity,* another retro homage based on an Irving Berlin song, on a tiny British Film Institute grant. Missing the sunshine, she returned to Australia.

She didn't want to work in commercial animation, but was equally unhappy to live on grants: 'It's important to make money...so that you are in touch with an audience, so that your work is accessible'. She prefers the Australian Film Commission's approach, which is to give investment loans: once recouped, the filmmaker receives 75 per cent

of any sales income. *Pussy Pumps Up*, and *Pianoforte* were made this way. Film Australia then gave her given carte blanche to make a four part series on the arts, but she found the institutional environment an unproductive and unhappy one, so only the first film, *Koko Pops*, an inventive historical survey of popular music, was made. She then returned to painting. Since 1987 she has lived in Zurich and London: her films continue to provide income, as do her paintings and commercial graphic work, occasional rock videos, teaching and feature journalism.

Her work, mainly traditional cel animation, is characterised by brilliant colours, a strong identifiable graphic style which draws on art nouveau and déco, and her interest in music and dance. Her current project, a 30 minute film based on the *Lola Montes* story, promises to be a new departure stylistically, and will also use live-action.

The international impact of Australian feature films in the 70s, and again in the 80s was in large part due to government initiatives to develop the industry, particularly via the Australian Film Commission's funding and promotion work, and the development of the Australian Film and Television School. The standard of live-action shorts generally is impressive, particularly for innovative subject matter and technique. A lively Super-8 scene has also encouraged experimentation and a cheap form of development. In animation, Swinburne College of Art has gained a strong reputation. It's notable that in features, women filmmakers in the 80s have been producing some of the most exciting work, e.g. Jane Campion and Joyce Morehouse, and this also seems to be the case with animation.

The development of women filmmakers wasn't accidental: it came about in response to vigorous lobbying by feminist filmmakers. The Creative Development Fund, and the various iniatives it spawned, began to make specific provision for women, (e.g. the Women's Film Fund) discussed in an informative essay by Megan McMurchy (see ß) in relation to the development of feminism and filmmaking in Australia. In the late 80s, individual states began to establish funding agencies too, which has increased the amounts of money available to independent filmmakers, and allowed for development and production monies from these state sources to be combined with federal funding.

Most of the interesting young animators have developed via the institutions mentioned above, usually after graduating from art school. Whilst art and film schools can provide the opportunity for personal filmmaking, the acid test is whether the necessities of making a living allow for such work to continue. Although animation doesn't have specific funding sources, most of the animators mentioned below seem to find work in shorts, features and documentaries whilst making their own animations, often grant-aided by the funding agencies mentioned above; others work in educational production or on films for children. (See also A-Z section for more detailed information.)

Susan Dermody, in an essay in McMurchy's book, reflects interestingly on the development of womens' films generally, and comments in passing on animation in relation to changing currents within feminism… 'two outstanding films which use quite different styles to slip past the guards of ordinary reality and get into the domain of intimate memory and deep and perverse fantasy, respectively - *Ned Wethered* (sketch animation) and *The Lead Dress* (pixillation).'

Working almost entirely alone, and on a tiny budget, Lee Whitmore made *Ned Wethered*, which explores notions of personal and subjective history via recollections of a man she had known as a child, with money from the AFC's Women's Film Fund. She also animates for other people's films, teaches, and freelances as a production designer. Her second, 23 minute film, *On a Full Moon,* about the psychological impact of motherhood is currently in development. She characterises her work as that of 'drawing and telling oblique and minimalist stories, that are personal, that concern me as an adult.'

Wendy Chandler studied at AFTS, and had experimented at art school with Super-8 animation. *Union Street*, an impressive semi-doc on life on a Sydney multi-cultural street, was made on an AFC grant. Backgrounds are a collage of hand-coloured photocopies combined with drawing. The characters are real people photographed against plain backdrops, then printed, photocopied and hand-coloured, and re-photographed against the backgrounds using an animation camera. Another AFTS graduate, who trained as an art director but who made some award-winning animation films as a student, is Sandy Lepore.

Swinburne graduates include Doris Ungar, Anne Shenfield, and Sally Pryor, who looks set to become a leading figure in computer animation. Alongside her commercial work she has made *Waltz Mambo* and a film in which a digitalised Barbie doll is manipulated to comment on female sterotypes. There is also Sarah Watson, who made *Catch of the Day*, a feminist blast at Australian male chauvinism with a strong graphic style.

A woman's working days at a fish market, dealing with a stream of casual sexist comments, are intercut with fantasies of rescuing knights in shining armour, or dreams of freedom at sea. The ending is short, sharp and brutal.

Lucinda Clutterbuck is unusual in that she entered animation via the commercial studios, after studying lithography and etching in France.

Julie Cunningham has combined animation with performance art, and knitting, and for her films has received support from the AFC and the Women's Film Unit at Film Australia. Some of her work has a strong feminist thrust. Her cel-animated *Double X*, subtitled *The Unmentionable Underbelly of His Story*, aims to provoke debate on the role of women and gender differences in culture's development and draws on anthropology, archeology and myth, whilst the earlier *Whatsabody* used cutouts to comment on women and fashion. Maggie Fooke also recieved funding from the AFC, to make *Dream* and *Pleasure Dome*. The latter, a watercolour animation, is an introspective reflection on the nature of landscape that reverberates on many levels beyond its considerable immediate aesthetic appeal. It is a portrait of a crumbling seaside suburb being overtaken by business; a witty reference to Hollywood's fantasy image of the Riviera; a gesture towards the Impressionist painters; Coleridge's Kubla Khan; Australia's relationship to Europe and to the Aborigines.

Some promising young animators draw on Fine Arts backgrounds to experiment with animation. One of the most interesting and impressive filmmakers in this area is Sabrina Schmid. Her formal interests combine with a wonderfully off-beat narrative imagination. She seems to have been destined to pursue animation - aged one, her curiosity was aroused when given an old camera to play with, and this combined with her pleasure in drawing. After taking a Fine Art degree, and making Super-8 animation films she went on to Swinburne to study film. 'I attempt to combine the distinctive qualities of painting and drawing: to juxtapose/contrast loose, painterly and abstracted images with graphic, delineated and more figurative or literal ones. I would like to contribute to the recognition of the animation film genre as one moving beyond cartoons.'

In *Once as if a Balloon* memories of childhood and associated fantasies are evoked and recreated through an innovative combination of animation with a series of still photographs. These stills, taken one day in 1960, represent the filmmaker's own childhood - specifically the experience of being tossed into the air as a one year old - and are reworked and animated from the present adult point of view, reflecting upon the nature of memory, time, and distance. This was followed by *Elephant Theatre*, about a man who has built a tiny theatre he can hold in the palm of his hand, which reveals a world of its own. His dream is that elephants will come to live in it. 'The narrative is loose and the story appears and disappears during the telling. It is an open-ended structure which allows unexpected juxtaposition and detours both visual and verbal.' (Roger Noake).

Her aim in *Middriffini* is 'to achieve a painterly visual style, to tell a strange tale. A humorous fantasy story. A mystery tale. The images follow a red ball, a steam train, an animated photograph, and coloured matchsticks conjured up by the character Nobody-else. A master of disguises, whose breath turns into clouds, he plays flute, piano, and creates Rebecca in whose mind he conjures up

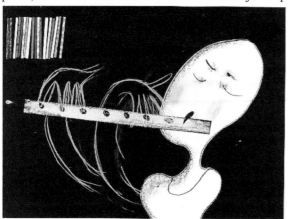

a dream picture, 'Now ladies and gentlemen, we've got a ringside seat into somebody's sleep.' In that nightmarish landscape, the absurd tale of Grosmond unfolds: an archetypal mythical creature, a type of dragon, whose many-coloured teeth can be played like a xylophone, and all of which have individual names and stories to tell. The dragon frolics against the cosmic sky slicing lemons in two, and laments the loss of Middriffini, the cause of his greatest toothache. The identity of the film's mystery character is eventually revealed, while we await a spectacular return. In *Middriffini* I am using voices/ dialogue to create a very closely textured sountrack, where voices often overlap (so therefore does meaning) and I want to explore the possibility of contrasting actions with unexpected sound effects.

Initially torn between her interest in film and art, Kathy Smith took a degree combining fine arts, film and design. Discovering animation, she became hooked - although her first film, *Design Nightmare*, was her last to use cartoon characters (which was the course orientation), as she wanted to combine fine arts with animation. Her first venture was a 45 second film, *A Figure in Front of a Painting,* using paint, charcoal and collage to animate a series of six mixed media paintings. *Ayers Rock Animation,* grew out of a series of postcard sequences. 'I produced the image movement (storyboard) first, then the soundtrack, then timed the film in frames and produced the artwork to match. I always work from beginning to end, and the animation develops in the process. Since I use sections from my drawings, photos and oil paintings in each film, I find that one medium feeds off the other, and in the process of animating one image into the next I am presented with new possibilities.' Re-use and transformation of previous work is a recurrent element of her work, as in *Change of PLACE,* developed from compiling images produced over a four year period, and categorised into 'industrial' and 'landscape', to create an allegorical animation about journey and memory. *Delirium* was inspired by a series of desert deaths due to car failure - or rather, by imagining the progression into a delirious state brought about by the

environment they perished in. 'I was interested in conveying a metaphysical experience via sound and image metamorphosis.' A series of slides zoomed in on sections of a collage of 12 oil-painted panels depicting the car, surrounding desert and bodies. 'From these images I drew the storyboard, and worked out a soundchart and timing. I recorded conversations of people talking about the deaths, then used excerpts mixed with sound effects I'd recorded.' The oil-painted animation film was completed in France and Italy, where she produced another seven large paintings which formed an installation in a Florence gallery. Viewers could alternate between this and the film screening in a room next door.

In 1990 Film Australia invited her to submit a proposal for an experimental animation, and with a supplementary grant from the Visual Arts Board she's developing *Living on the Comet.* 'A recurring metaphorical image links together and instigates a series of four dream sequences about thinking, feeling, sensation and intuition, combining photographs, oil paint, etching and ink.'

Cathy Vasseleu's work is more conceptual and intellectual, and relates more strongly to the Australian tradition of feminist and film-theory inspired political avant-garde established in the late 70s and 80s. Her early Super-8 films experimented with combinations of different techniques. *De Anima* uses cel, model, photo and computer animation, rotoscoping, medical magnetic resonance imaging, animation projected onto bodies for its immensely ambitious thesis: 'To Aristotle the semen was a drop of brain. Today it is frozen and banked. *De Anima* is a heretical framing of ideas about sexual reproduction and the ways that science brings life to life.'

Unlike most of the animators discussed above, Kathy Linsley is a self-taught animator. She studied graphic design and has worked freelance in TV, commercials, museums and music videos for the last ten years. Her film *Secrets of the City* took three years to complete, working in her own time 'in the confines of the director's own bedroom.' The film travels through an unidentified city, searching out the unfulfiled dreams, desires and memories played out in bizarre vignettes set in brilliantly coloured rooms, offset by the relentless monotone of the cityscape. Oil and chalk pastels, paint and coloured pencils on paper and cel are used; motion, including pans and zooms, is achieved through the artwork, filmed with a fixed camera on a tripod.

International Biographical Dictionary

A - Z

Introduction to A -Z

In keeping with the rest of the publication, the A-Z is a compendium of information, comment and description on women animators around the world.

It in no way attempts to be comprehensive, given the limitations of research time and information available. Consistency amongst entries would have excluded many animators, about whom I have only the barest minimum of information - I have preferred to include what little I have in the hope this will elicit further information, or encourage others to follow up. In some cases essays on, or statements by filmmakers are included, to expand upon references in the main body of the book, or when, because of structure and layout restraints, this has seemed the only way to fit them in. There is not much consistency of tone either: as a variety of sources have been used. Long quotations are credited, by initials, which can be checked against the *Key to Abbreviations* below. Where individual filmmakers, or films, are discussed in some detail in the main body of the book, page number references are given, as are indications of whether they are referenced in the Bibliography. In some cases, e.g. the book's geographical survey sections, more information on individual filmmakers can be found. Occasionally, there is some overlap between the sections. By and large, films made for children and commercials are not listed, although some rock videos are since the latter are more likely to have been seen by a wider range of people.

Filmographies are complete, to the best of my knowledge, unless otherwise indicated. Where exact dates are unknown, there is a question mark. Countries cited after a filmmaker's name refer to the country in which they have made most or all of their films, as this corresponds to international filmographical conventions. For the same reason, filmmakers whose films have been made in the former USSR have that abbreviation after their names, although where possible republic of origin, or production studio, is mentioned in the accompanying text.

Since I do not believe in lists for lists' sake, and the number of women who have made only one film then apparently disappeared from sight, is enormous, and listing them does not seem particularly useful. The general rule for inclusion has been filmmakers have made at least two films, although this has been ignored when the film or filmmaker in question has seemed especially worthy of note.

There is, unfortunately, no index. Quite simply, no time left.

Key to abbreviations

AM	Animation Magazine
ß	Bibliography
BFI	British Film Institute
BK	Bob Kalin
Cal Arts	California Institute for the Arts
co-d	co-directed
coll	collaboration on…
CS	Cecile Starr
C4	Channel Four Television
EB	Elaine Burrows
GL	Gillian Lacey
Inc	Incomplete filmography
JC	John Canemaker
JMcG	Jill McGreal
KA	Karen Alexander
l/a	live action
MB	Margery Brown
MFA	Master of Film Arts, US post-graduate degree
MOMA	Museum of Modern Art catalogue notes
NFTS	National Film and Television School
PW	Prescott Wright
RCA	Royal College of Art, London
seq.	sequence
TS	Talia (Thelma) Schenkel
WSCAD	West Surrey College of Art & Design

N.B.
The following are filmmakers who have made more two or more films, but about whom I have been unable to find any more information: they are listed here for the record, and are drawn largely from Bruno Edera's article, see ß.

Austria: Barbel Neubauer, experimental animator. Pre-war Germany: Lore Bierling (silhouette films in the mid-20s). Canada: Viviane Elnecave, 6 films since 1968; Judith Klein, 10 films since 1970; Nicole Robert, 20 or more films since 1973. Holland: Margareet Suzanne Vanderhoeven; Delphine De Pury. Italy: Marinella Pirelli, 3 films since 1969; Japan: Matsue Jinbo, 15 fims between 1958-67, possibly for children. Poland: Zofia Grottowa; Alina Skiba; Janina Hartwig; Lidia Hornicka; Irena Sobierasjska; Jadwiga Kudrzycka: possibly films for children.

US: Cassandra Gerstein-Eckstein, whose *Little Red Riding Hood* (1978) made a great impact for its sexual humour, has made several live-action films and possibly 4 other animation films; Geraldine Freks, 7 films to 1978, then retired from animation although recently went back to work in commercial studios in Los Angeles; Pamela Ramsing; Suzan Rubin;

A - Z

Aaron, Jane   US

See pp. 55-56, and ß. Background in drawing and sculpture. A *Brand New Day* renders in line drawings a morning scene of a woman awakening. *In Plain Sight* is more experimental, intermixing live-action and hand-drawn images, to tell short jokes about our automative society and the passing landscape. The child-like drawings appear inside their own frames, within the movie frame, coloured sparsely and scratchily. The effect is both simple and sophisticated, like daydreams invented by the captive passenger to relieve the boredom of a routine journey. Aaron's technique for this process involves the implantation of animated drawings into real life settings. 'The drawings are actually part of the live action frame and act as comment on the environment. In one section of the film we peer out of a moving car's windshield on which animated drawings of a passing landscape are attached. Sometimes the real and animated landscapes coincide; other times they depict diverse events. In another scene, an animated drawing of clouds is mounted on a post against the real sky. Through these complex visual paradoxes Aaron playfully questions the status of the film illusion.' (MOMA)

A Brand New Day, 1974; Chickens-Cow, 1974; In Plain Sight, 1977; Interior Designs, 1980; Remains to be Seen, 1983; Travelling Light, 1985; Set in Motion, 1987; seq. for Academy Leader Variations, 1986; seq. for Universal Declaration of Human Rights, 1988; This Time Around, 1989.

Andersen, Yvonne   US

For over twenty Yvonne Andersen has been a major force in animation education, particularly with children. In 1963 she founded the Yellow Ball Workshop, many of whose students have continued in animation. She has published several books on how to make animation films and videos, and is currently Associate Professor at Rhode Island School of Design.

Meouw, Meouw, 1969 (co-d Red Grooms); The Laundry, 197?; Appoliniaire 197? (co-d RG); One Hot Dog with Mustard, 197?; Fat Feet, 197? (co-d RG); Trembling Cartoon Band, 1974; I Never Sleep; Amazing Colossal Man; I Saw Their Angry Faces, *1977; We Will Live Forever, 197? (co-d Dominic Falcone)*

Ansorge, Gisele Switzerland

Athough Gisele Ansorge began her career as a chemist, her interest in drawing and etching, plus her meeting with husband-to-be Ernest, led to a lifelong passion for animation. With her husband, she has made films usually with metal particles manipulated with magnets, and sand and powder, and written for radio and television, scripted a live-action feature *D'un Jour a l'autre,* directed by Earnest. Since 1975 they have worked on several TV series.

Pam et Poum, 1957; La Danseuse et Le mendiant/The Dancer and the Beggar; La Lutte contre la Douleur/The Fight against Pain, 1958; La Legende du Pont et du Diable, 1960; Le Poete et La Licorne/The Poet and the Unicorn, 1963; Le Brave Soldat Shwiek; Bonjour Mon Oeil, 1965; Les Sept Nuits de Siberie/Seven Siberian Nights, 1967; Les Corbeaux/The Ravens, 1968; Fantasmatic, 1969; Alunissons; Tempus, 1970; Le Chat Chamelon, 1973; Smile 1,2,3., 1975; Anima, 1978 (solo); Les Enfants de Laine, 1984; Sabbat, 1991 (All co-d Ernest Ansorge).

Aqua, Karen   US

Her style has been described as combining 'a draftswoman's graphic precision, a dancer's sense of movement and musician's sense of rhythm' - perhaps unsurprisingly, as she graduated from Rhode Island School of Design, and has studied African dance for over a decade, and recently took up drumming. Inspired by the 70s climate of experimentation, and crossing of boundaries between the arts - as well as by the work of Caroline & Frank Mouris, Ryan Larkin's films and Norstein. She teaches part-time to allow time for filmmaking on her own terms, her films partly grant financed: 'I live cheaply, I'm resourceful. I don't do cel animation, I work on paper.' Her films are non-narrative, often playing with metamosphosis, lyrical, curvolinear, personal journeys: 'the suggestion of things in a constant state of flux, sometimes subtle, sometimes aggressive, seems to be well suited to be expressed in animation'. *Nine Lives* is a semiotic exploration of cats, memory and landscape; *Yours for the Taking* animates ceramic cups. *Kakania* has been described as her most accessible film to date, 'The urban strife of overcrowding, conflict, crime and poverty is transformed into cooperative living and rejuvenation. Nine figures multiply to fifteen, change into dancing symbols, don animal masks for ritual dances, link arms and begin to move into harmony'. (AM)

Penetralia, 1976; Heavenly Bodies, 1980; Vis-a-vis, 1982; Yours for the Taking, 1984; Nine Lives, 1987; seq. for Amnesty International Human Rights Now, 1988; seq. for Candyjam; 1988; segments for a multi-media work, Shrine to Ritualized Time, 1989; Kakania, 1989.

Arcadias, Laurence   France

Juste une Goutte, 1980; La Main Brune, 1981; Mon Dieu que va dire Marfel?, 1984.

Ashworth, Joan   GB

Joan Ashworth, made *The Web*, a mini-epic, model-animated Gothic comedy based on Mervyn Peake's Gormenghast trilogy, at the NFTS, then went on to found one of the most successful model animation studios today, Three Peach. 'At the Film School I felt I had a rough time because I was female - and short! On the one hand, I got a lot of avuncular advice on old cameras, from older guys who liked to pass on their knowledge, but when it came to using the equipment it was as though men had it by right, whereas I'd have it as a favour.' She feels that model animation might appear more daunting to women because of the technical knowledge demanded, but feels that once this is acquired, it can be very exciting to see how images can be produced, and it is quite easy to direct, although women often make the mistake of trying to be too nice. Before and during her time at the NFTS she had worked freelance, particularly for David Anderson and Gerry Anderson (no relation) on the famous Royal Bank of Scotland ads, plus work on the storyboards for the cel animated *When the Wind Blows,* so had established a reputation for her work. During this period, she was also asked to tutor a student at the RCA, Andy Staveley, in model animation. They both graduated in 1987, and, with producer Martin Grieves, from the NFTS, she set up Three Peach

A - Z

studio, in order to pool resources, space and equipment for model animation being much more expensive than most other animation forms. One of their first jobs was animating the dream sequence for Nick Park's Oscar-nominated *Grand Day Out*. TV credit sequences and commercials have kept them very busy since, and she also recently did the credit sequence for the first *Batman*. At Three Peach she has encouraged younger animators, including Phillip Hunt whose graduation film, *Spotless Dominoes*, and more recently, Sam Fell's, *The Big Cheese* , were made there. She enjoys the creative stimulus of working with other animators, and finds it has taught her some valuable lessons: such as finding she doesn't necesarily have to do it all herself, that sometimes others can do it better, and that it can push her beyond what she thinks of as her limits. Having two small children has also given her a discipline in relation to work, which can offer a way out of the tunnel vision that affects many animators. Although she is keen to make her own films, the capital investment and studio overheads make it difficult to simply take a break, especially with people on staff. She is currently developing *Pearls & Swine*, about a mermaid discovering her fertility, for which she hopes to work with a range of materials, including sand.

The Web, 1987; credit seq. for Batman, 1990. Numerous commercials.

Banker, Gail   US
Sketches for the Elephant Child, 1981; *Handcraft*, 198?

Barbour, Karen   US
Babel, 1981; *Babel*, 1984.

Bardes, Doree   US
Dreams Anon, 1981; *See*, 1982.

Barefoot, Anne   GB
Circus, 1985; *Office*, 1992.

Barrie, Diana   US
Experimental filmmaker who incorporates animation techniques in her hand-coloured silent films; '*Magic Explained* is in the style and spirit of Méliès, with magic wands, fires and lightning, a female magician makes herself disappear but (unlike a male magician) doesn't reappear, conveying the feeling that her magic is real and potent, and that returning to the status quo doesn't appeal to women as much as men. In *My Version of the Fall*, Woman creates Man - an Adam is fated to disappear completely from the picture. Hers is a hand-coloured pardise where nothing remains fixed or permanent - landscape, sky, clothes - change colours constantly. The film itself changes direction at mid-point, running backward to its first image - a hand-painted woman seen in profile, sucking in great clouds of smoke from an ever-lengthening cigarette. *Untitled* is an abstract film combining strict control (scratched-in lines) with chance effects (the action of chemicals on emulsion).' (CS)

My Version of the Fall, 1978; *Untitled*; *Magic Explained*, 1980.

Batchelor, Joy   GB
1914-1991

After art school she worked as designer, in fashion and for Harpers & Queen's. In 1935 she joined an independent animation studio run by Dennis Connolly, then British Animated Films where she met John Halas. They intended to go to Hungary and set up studio there, but lack of funds and the political climate made this impossible. Halas & Batchelor was for very many years one of the most prolific commercial animation studios in the UK. Joy Batchelor's most cherished personal project was her featurette, *Ruddigore*.

The Pocket Cartoon, 1941; *Dustbin Parade*, 1942; *Abu* (series of 4), 1943; *Six Little Jungle Boys*, 1944; *Handling Ships* (feature doc), 1945; *Old Wives Tales*, 1946; *Heave Away My Johnny*, 1947; *Robinson Charley* (series of 7), 1948; *First Line of Defence*, *Fly About the House*, 1949; *As Old As the Hills*; *The Magic Canvas*, 1950; *Poet and Painter* (series of 4); *John Gilpin*; *Catalysis*; *Submarine Control*, 1951; *The Figurehead*, 1952; *The Owl and the Pussycat* (series of 30), 1953; *The Moving Spirit*; *Coastal Navigation*, 1953; *Animal Farm* (feature); *Power to Fly*, 1954; *Speed the Plough*; *Cinerama Holiday* (animation seq. for live-action film), 1955; *History of the Cinema: The World of Little Ig*; *To Your Health*; *The Candlemaker*, 1956; *The Guardsman*; *All Lit Up*, 1957; *The Christmas Visitor*, 1958;

The Energy Picture, 1959; *Dam the Delta*; *Habatales* (series of 3); *Foo Foo* (series of 33); *Snip and Snap* (series of 26); *The History of Inventions*, 1960; *The Colombo Plan*; *For Better Or Worse*; *The Monster of Highgate Ponds* (l/a feature), 1961; *Hamilton the Musical Elephant*, 1962; *Automania 2000*; *Is There Intelligent Life On Earth?* (l/a feature), 1963; *Men in Science*, 1964; *Hoffnung* (series of 3), 1965; *Ruddigore* (feature, JB solo), 1966; *Ellipse & Circle*; *Pole and Polar*, 1969; *The Five* (JB solo), 1970.

Batchvarova, Radka   Bulgaria
The Mouse and the Pencil, 1958; *The Snowman*, 1960; *Long Ears*, 1961; *Deceitful Gosho*, 1963; *Fable*; *The Proud Bulb*, 1964; *The Little Star*, 1965; *A House on Wheels*; *What Shall I Be?*, 1966; *The Balloons*, 1967 (all co-d Zdenka Doicheva); *The Cock and His Money*, 1969; *Bravo*, 1974; *Butterflies*, 1978; *Let There Always Be Kites*, 1980 (solo ?).

Bauman, Suzanne US
Button, Button, 1968; *Joanjo: A Portuguese Tale*, 1970.

Bayerl, Bettina   Germany
Works mainly in cel animation, on her own films as well as commercials, TV credit sequences, etc. She has a strong cartoon style, and satirical approach. *Sexa-pill* is a devastating case-study of the fatal side-effects of the pill. She has also made some live-action shorts.

Moralmord, 1981; *Umwelt/The World Around Us*, 1982; *Die Kehrwoche*, 1983; *...Oder Was is/Or What's Up?*, 1984; *Sexapill*; *Satirika*, 1985; *Michael Jackson*; *Vibration*; *Premiere*, 198?

Beams, Mary   US
See p 70.

Tub Film, 1971; *Seed Reel*; *Solo*; *Going Home Sketchbook*; *Piano Rub*; *Drowning Moon*, 1975; *Rain Seeds*; *Paul Revere is Here*, 1976; *Whale Songs*, 1979; *School in the Sky*, 1980.

Bechtold, Lisze   US
Many of her films play with the transformational potential of animation, and drawing on the styles of early 20th century art such as Picasso, Matisse. In *Moon Breath Beat*,

the friendship of a woman and her cats is disrupted by their natural attraction to birds and the whims of the moon. 'A feminism of a tough-minded allure reminiscent of Monique Wittig's novels...women who are dangerous and exciting rarely apppear in animated films...*Moon Breath Beat*'s heroine is on the prowl, tables turned in the hunt... Seldom has a woman seemed so alive and alluring, so uniquely tough-minded, graceful and independent.' (BK) She has abandoned independent films for the time being and is currently working for studios in Los Angeles.
La Danseuse, 1973; Two Stars, 1976; Dancebridge, 1976; Moon Stars, 1977; Moon Breath Beat, 1980; section of: My Film, My Film, My Film, 1983.

Berkovitch, Leah   Israel
The Best Years of Berka, 1986.

Besen, Ellen   Canada
Born in Chicago, 1953. Studied animation at Sheridan College in Toronto, then worked freelance before founding Caribou Cartoons with other animators. Since 1977 has been at NFB. 'Sea Dream is a modern Grimms' or Andersen fairy tale where all the creepy crawly stuff is kept below the surface... Bruno Bettelheim could unpack this film to his heart's content.' (BK)
To Spring, 1973; Metric-Metrique, 1974; Sea Dream, 1979; Slow Dance World, 1984 (co-d Lonny Baumholz).

Bibanska, Eva   Poland
An Unfaithful Portrait is a clever, sociological statment, using cut-out, and photo-motion film about a woman's search for a good relationship, the fragility and vagaries of romance. She has now abandoned animation.
An Unfaithful Portrait,1980; The End, 1982.

Bielinska, Halina   Poland
Born 1909 in Warsaw. Studied at art college, then worked as journalist, theatrical set designer, children's books illustrator. During the occupation she ran an illegal graphics workshop/studio. In 1946 studied animation in Czechoslovakia. Made her first puppet film in Switzerland with Wlodzimierz Haupe. Scripted many puppet animation films. Since 1961 she has

worked mainly in feature films.
Wawrzyncowy/The Laurel Garden, 1952; Katarynka, 1956 (solo); Zmania Warty/ Changing of the Guard; Albo Rybka/Or Fish, 1958; But/The Shoe, 1959; The Circus Under the Stars,1960; Lucky Tony, 1961; Godzina Pasowes Rozy, 1963 (all co-d Haupe unless otherwise noted).

Bjornberg, Bettina   Finland
Uses cutouts. Mainly makes films for children's television, but has made three films more oriented towards adult audiences.
Candide; Lucifer; Orfeus and Euridice.

Blomquist, Heidi   Canada
Oh Sean, 1982 (collab); Lucretia, 1986.

Bond, Rose   US
Canadian born, lives and works in Portland, Oregon. With a background in drawing and painting, she came to filmmaking in the late 70s, after obtaining an MFA at the School of the Art Institute, Chicago. She works without a camera, painting and drawing on 35mm clear leader under a magnifying glass. Her first films, *Gaia's Dream* and *Nexus* , are impressionistic, semi-abstract films, set to Caribbean music, full of vibrant joy in colour, line and movement. There's an element of conscious reaction against Saturday morning cartoons 'because of their violence. As I've grown older, I also realise I don't like their sexism. The challenge here is to work with a medium that hasn't done women too many favours and with it produce a positive expression of what it is to be a woman.' The next two films are part of a projected trilogy based on Celtic legends and use the same cameraless technique - arguably more demanding when applied to sustained narrative. The project grew out of her research into women's history, and presents strong and powerful female characters whose roles as mothers are acknowledged for their contribution to Celtic culture. *Cerridwen's Gift* is a Welsh story, whilst *Mallacht Macha (Macha's Curse)*, an ancient Irish tale, explores the shift in social allegiance from mother-clan to king-nation, and pits the pregnant goddess Macha in an ill-fated race against the king's horses. 'In the film medium of animation, the animator becomes blatantly responsible for all that appears on the

screen. In one sense, through drawing, the mise-en-scène is unfettered from such tangibles as the lumber in a set construction, the amps for powerlighting, the fabric of costume. Researched realities like the look of a cottage or the clothing of an era, are blended with the aesthetics of palette, line and colour texture. It is cinematic conjuring, a non-realism that carries the recognised. In large part, my work is concerned with transition and linkage. Depth of field allows for greater transitional opportunities - into, onto, through, and across the frame. Drawn small and projected large, the line takes on a boldness, at times pulling the viewer through the piece. Every frame is individually coloured and unique, as if every pixel were refreshed, infusing the work with a vitality and vigour.'
Gaia's Dream, 1982; Nexus, 1984; Cerridwen's Gift, 1987; Mallacht Macha, 1990.

Bonney, Jo   US
Another Great Day mixes photographs, painting, and 3-D objects and plays across realism, surrealism and hyperrealism to convey a day in the life of an everyday housewife. Broadcast media and pulp novels feed her fantasy life whilst reducing the events of the outside world to a chaotic bombardment of news.
Another Great Day, 1980 (co-d Ruth Peyser); Random Positions, 1983 .

Borenstein, Jo   Canada
Born 1950. After studying music and literature, she did post-graduate work in cinema and graphic art at Cal Arts, whilst teaching and running animation workshops. Made her first films independently. In 1974, went to work part time at NFB.
Opus 1, 1972; The Unexpected Answer: Hommage to Rene Magritte, 1973; Revisited; 'Scape, 1974; Garlic; Traveller's Palm (Poets on Film No. 2), 1976; The Magic Hat Box, 1977; The Five Minute Five Billion Year Movie, 1982; The Man Who Stole Dreams, 198?

Bornstein, Marguerita   Brazil
inc. O Rebu; How to Make Your Child a Schizophrenic.

Bottner, Barbara   US
Since she made these films she has re-

A - Z

turned to illustrating children's books. *Made for Each Other; Une Bigue dans une Barque, 1972; Courir en Courant/Later That night, 1976 (co-d H Beckermann).*

Brandt, Maya   GB

Based in Bristol, Brandt uses plasticine, models, mixed media and her own self-styled, 'glitter' animation in short films which aim to be funny and satirical, whilst exploring serious issues, e.g. the zany, subjective view of gynaecological examination in *Inside Job*, or the study of power, sex, greed and consumerism of *What's Cooking?*. *Gladis in the Underground* tells the tale of a young woman's journey through life in a dream-like version of the London Underground. The environment is strange, dark and hostile: Gladis is watched by eyes on posters and pursued by vacuum-cleaner dogs, while disembodied legs parade themselves provocatively, and ballet shoes stand to attention as she passes. *Upmarkette* and *Underworld* are non-narrrative animations set to music, and use imagery more symbolically. She is currently developing a five-part series of ten minute films for television, *The Adventures of Kayto*, about a female alien who interrupts the workings of a well-ordered city, Prudencetown, run by Prudence the Clock, with the help of her computer, Prufax. The drawing style suggests a new graphic depature in her work.
My Funny Valentine, 1979; Upmarkette, 1980; Smile Please, 1981; Inside Job, 1984; Underworld, 1985; What's Cooking?, 1986; Gladis in the Underground, 1987.

Brumberg, Valentia & Zenjeda   USSR

Sisters born one year after the other at the turn of the century (1899/1900), they studied art, and always made films together.
China on Fire,1925 (co-d Ivanov-Vano); The Young Samoyed, 1929 (co-d Olga Kohdataieva); Puss in Boots, 1938; The Story of Tsar Saltan, 1943; The Night Before Christmas, 1951; Flight to the Moon, 1953; Walking Stick for Sale, 1956; The Great Troubles, 1961; Three Fat Men, 1963; The Brave Little Tailor, 1964; An Hour Until the Meeting, 1965; Golden Stepmother, 1966; The Little Time Ma-

chine; I Drew the Man, 1967; Big Misadventures, 1969.

Bute, Mary Ellen   US

See pp. 16-18, and ß. In the early 1930s, Mary Ellen Bute was the first person in the United States to make abstract films and in the early 1950s, the first in the world to use electronically-generated images in film. Her husband, Ted Nemeth, produced and photographed her films.
Rhythm in Light,1934; Synchromy No. 2, 1935; Escape,1937; Spooksport, 1939; Tarantella,1940; Polka Graph, 1947; Colour Rhapsody, 1948; Pastorale, 1950; Abstronic, 1952; Mood Contrasts,1953; Colour Rhapsody, 1958; Passages from Finnegan's Wake (l/a feature), 1965.

Boston, Elizabetha   Bugaria

The Brood Hen and Her Golden Chicks; The Hora Dance; Naica and the Little Fish; Naica and the Stork (short); Naica and the Squirrels (short); Naica Leaves for Bucharest (short), 1955-60; The Kid, 1962; Recollections from Childhood, 1964; Youth Without Old Age, 1968.

Calder, Emma   GB

At art college, one of her first films, *Madame Potato* featured a potato print woman who achieves fame and fortune only to return to the earth which produced her, brought Calder press attention, (and some fabric print work!); *Springfield*, using cel animation, partly inspired by her mother's irritating obsession with hoovering, is a humorous satire on domestic alienation. In 1989 she formed Pearly Oyster Productions with Ged Haney, a college friend and composer for her films. The company works with both cut-out and model animation, for commercials, rock videos and their own films. An off-beat, slightly grotesque sense of humour characterises her work, and continues into her collaboration with Haney: *The Drummer* is a delightfully downbeat, North Country accented variant on a childrens' fairy tale; *The Turds* a 20 second eco tragi-comedy produced for MTV. *1984*, a collaborative venture with other animators used Xeroxed images provided by Edouardo Paolozzi as a starting point for exploring themes from Orwell's dystopic novel. She is currently developing a new project and worked with Haney on his first

solo directorial venture, *Kings of Siam*.
Ilkla Moor Baht Hat, 1981; Madame Potato, 1983; 1984: Music for Modern Americans, 1983 (co-d Susan Young); Springfield, 1986 (solo); Three Feathers; The Drummer; The Turd Family Go on Holiday (MTV eco commercial), 1989 (all co-d Jed Haney).

Chase, Doris   US

An artist and experimental filmmaker who has moved into dance and video, and more recently into live-action drama with feminist themes. *Circles 1* is computer animation of linear graphics; *Rocking Orange* comprises interpretations of the dynamics between Mary Staton's Dance Ensemble and Chase's moving sculpture, recorded on film then reprinted optically and transformed via video synthesiser. *'Improvisation* uses special video equipment to gracefully decompose and recompose dance and movement, colour and design, into a harmonic imagery that combines the abstract and the recognisable. While dancer Kai Takei performs her eccentric thrusts and contractions (sometimes standing, sometimes on all fours), Chase creates and collates changing colours and moving shapes contrapuntally, to a rhythmic drum beat. Bright shades of pink, orange, blue, purple move against contrasting backgrounds, brimming with their own energy and spirit. (CS)
Circles 1 (Kleinsinger),1970; Circles 1 (co-d Subotnik) , Circles/Variations No. 2; Rocking Orange No. 3 Versions, 1974-5; Improvisation, 1977; Dance Ten, 1976-7; Nashville Dance; Jazz Dance, 1979; Dance Frame, 1978.

Chenzira, Ayoka   US

Usually works in live-action. One of the few African-American filmmakers to use animation. *Hairpiece* is a satirical look at the way the fashion and cosmetic industries encourage black women to conform to white standards of beauty, using collage and cutouts.. *Poets on the Dance Floor* is a 20 minute cel and computer animation: the spirit of the African Goddess, Zajota, rises in the halo of the moon. This is the beginning of a story tracing the origins of Afro-American rhythms, dance and music; from Africa to slavery, from the re-birth of Harlem to the Civil Rights Movement.

Hair Piece: A Film for Nappy Headed People, 1984; Poets on the Dance Floor: Zajota and the Boogie Spirit, 1991.

Cholorek, Marian Poland
Night Flights is a comedy about a gigolo who escapes from a tall building in a hang-glider to flee a husband's wrath. (PW)
inc. Bridging the Gap; Dream; Omnibus, Nightflight,197?

Crafts, Lisa   US
Largely self-taught, and has taught animation for several years, as well as programming and gallery exhibitions around animation. Grant and self-financed. Cel, felt tip. *Desire Pie* was admired for its provocative sexual content. *The Ungloved Hand* plays cleverly with sexual stereotyping, a delightfully economic treatment of the power ratio between the sexes. *Glass Gardens* has been described as 'hauntingly surrealistic...a stunning black and white tour of urban decay, combining her own drawings with objects donated by friends...employing a variety of rhythms to weave a visual magic spell. Some images move in an almost static fashion, others move with seamles fluidity.' 'The landscape in *Glass Gardens* represents physical, spiritual and emotional depression, and that the woman in the film is able to overcome it with creativity.' She used the film to overcome her own susceptibility to depression. Currently working as animator on HBO-Swiss TV. Co-produced animation films for children.
Desire Pie, 1976; Ungloved hand; Pituitry, 1979; Glass Gardens, 1982; (featurette) Octopus' Exultation, 1984 ; Shout, 1985.

Cruikshank, Sally   US
See pp. 51-53, and ß.
Ducky, 1971; Fun on Mars, 1971; Chow Fun,1972; Quasi at the Quackadero, 1975; Make Me Psychic, 1978; Quasi's Cabaret, 1979; Face Like a Frog, 1987; Seq. for Animated Self Portraits, 1988.

Cunningham, Julie   Australia
Whatsabody, 1983; Double X, 1986;

Daudelin, Mitsu Canada
After studying politics, worked in engraving and then for a political filmmaking and distribution collective in the early 70s. Her first film was collectively made, based on an oral folktale.
Maricoquette qui n'a chaud ni frette, 1976 (collab); La Chicane; En avant pour la greve generale, 1978; Cogne Dur, 1979 (co-d Estelle Lebel, Rachel St. Pierre); The Lesser Evil, 1980 (collab).

Davis, Strinda   GB
Studied animation at Liverpool Polytechnic. Has taught animation, and led workshops and community resource centres, and the franchised film and video workshop, Open Eye in Liverpool. Has worked since 1990 with Jackdaw Media, in education and production. Her early films explored formal questions around perception and point of view, whilst the later films are largely issue-based, sometimes mixing live action and animation. She has also worked on title sequences for TV.
50 Ways to Look More Beautiful; New Brighton, 1979; Feet; Real Time/Animated Time; Photographic Print, 1980; There Are No Excuses; Making the Grade; For Our Benefit?; It's Outrageous; Namibia Nuclear Reactions, 1987; Life Model, 1991 (collab: Angela Martin).

Desai, Binita   India
After obtaining a degree in fine and applied arts, she studied animation at the National Institute of Design, the only educational institiution in India where animation is taught. She then joined the faculty, and is currently Chair of Communication Design at NID. Teaching duties, liaison between the clients, both state and commercial, and students on projects which are a mandatory part of the course, leave little time to make her own films. *Curiosity Killed* is a variant on the traditional proverb, distinguished by the incorporation of closely observed local customs (the annual kite festival), fluid movements and pleasing range of graphic styles.
Metamorphosis, 1981; Curiosity Killed; Cirrus Skies, 1982; Patang, 1984; Sunday Market, 1984.

Desbiens, Francine   Canada
After working with youth groups, film workshops, she studied and taught applied arts, and began to make animated films.
The Fox and the Crow, 1969 (collab); The Little Men of Cromagnon, 1971; Du Coq a l'Ane, 1973 (co-d Pierre Hebert, Suzanne Gervais); Cherie, Ote toi tes raquettes, 1975.

Dobrowolska, Krystyna Poland
Letni Kozert/Summer Concert, 1969; Two Pierrots; There Was a Gypsy, 197?

Doiceva, Sdenka Bulgaria
Born in Prague in 1922. After studying art in Prague, she moved to Bulgaria in 1955, and became one of the pioneers in Bulgarian animation. She began as a designer, then assistant director to Todor Dinov. In 1958, co-d *The Mouse and the Pencil* with Radka Bacharova. Her films often deal with themes of civic consciousness and duty; many films for children (unlisted).
Futbolnata Topka/The Football, 1962; Dupkata/Il buco, 1966; Dressura/Addrestramento, 1970; Strast/Passions, 1971; Aquarium, 1973; The Little Palombara, 19??.

Dourmashkin, Barbara US
A Ball of String and other Things, 1973; Help, I'm Shrinking, 1974; Petronella, 1978.

Dufour, Nicole   France
La maison Rose/The Pink House, 1972; Souvenirs, 1973; Illusions, 1975; Nuits Blanches/Sleepless Nights, 1979.

Duga, Irra (Irene)   US
Pesca Pisca mixed animation and live action, a sensual film of continuous orgasm, of pulsating colour and image.
Inc. Bust Bag, 1964; Jungle Madness, 1967; Turtle Soup, 1967; Man, 1967; Pesca Pisca, 1968; The Face of Violence; How to Dig a Hole to the Other Side of the World, Beyond the Stars: A Space Story, 1981; The Last Unicorn, 198?

Edell, Nancy   Canada
See ß. Edell's films were seen as rather shocking at the time, full of quite violent sexual imagery: she felt them to have been a therapeutic response to growing up in sexually repressive 50s Canada.
Black Pudding,1969; Charley Company, 1972; Lunch, 1973.

A - Z

Garanina, Irina   USSR
Crane's Plumage, 1978; Poor Lisa, 1979.

Fefer, Sylvie   Canada
Cartoon style; *Personality Software* is a mild but effective feminist satire on new technology and personal identity.
Brushstrokes, 1982; A Short Story, 1985; Personality Software, 1990.

Foldes, Joan   France
Animated Genesis, 1952 (co-d Peter Foldes); A Short Vision, 1956.

Freidman, Yona   France
L'origine des Kabouloukou (Origin of the Kabouloukou); The Adventures of Samba Gana, 1962.

Frischengruber, Lisi   Austria
An experimental animator. ALM , 1987; Sterben/Death, 1989.

Gavrilenko, Elena   USSR
See p.109
Girlfriend, 1989; Parable of the Mouse, 1991.

Georgi, Katia   DDR
Born 1928. Studied applied arts. Began working in animation information films for the DEFA studios, and has made films for children as well as for adults, such as *The River*, mixing rotoscope and optical techniques about a man and a woman separated by the river (which represents the Berlin Wall).
Brave Hans, 1958 ; The Princess and the Pea, 1959 (both co-d Klaus Georgi); The Devil's Valley, 1959; The Pyramid, 1961 (both solo); Cigarette Charlie; Henry and His Chickens, 1962; Cloudiness (each co-d KG); Matches, 1963; Musicians; The Statue In the Park, 1964; Concurrence, 1965 (each solo); Good Day, Mr. H, 1965 (co-d KG); The Thorn, 1967 (solo); Sleeping Beauty,1968; Der Gardinentraum, 1969; The River; Dresden, My Town, 1970 (each co-d KG); A Young Man Called Engels, 1971; Es ist doch unsere Welt/ Then this is our World, 1972; Novelle, 1974; Beauty & the Beast, 1976; The Timid Dragon, 1979; The Fire of Faust; Brave Hans,1980 (each co-d KG & Feodor Khitruk).

Gervais, Suzanne   Canada
Cycle, 1971; Du Coq a L'Ane, 1973 (co-d Pierre Hebert, Francine Desbiens); Climates, 1974; La Plage, 1979: posthumous completion of Clorinda Warny's film, with Lina Gagnon. Premiers jours/First days, 1981.

Goldman, Thalma   GB
Thalma Goldman, of Polish and Russian stock, came to the UK from Israel in the late 60s. Her films were controversial for their frank and disturbing exploration of sexuality and fantasy. In *Stanley* a black cat creeps into the bed of a naked sleeping woman, stimulating a part ecstatic, part nightmarish experience, then slinks away. *Amateur Night* by contrast, shows the performances of four grotesquely distorted comic strippers to a soundtrack of grunts and heckling.

Goldman (now reverted back to her maiden name, Cohen) is an artist who lives her work quite intensely, and in the decade following her first work she describes herself as becoming engulfed by the imaginary worlds created in her films, going through a journey…peeling off layers of the self, exploring concepts of woman as magician, as well as devoting herself to raising a child. Her home is like a theatre set, richly and densely decorated with her imagination's creations, although more recently she has begun to pare down her surroundings, as she is preparing a new film, working from home.
Green Men, Yellow Women, 1973; Self Variations on a Yellow Woman, 1974; Amateur Night, 1975; Night Call, 1977; Stanley, 1979.

Goldscholl, Mildred   US
A husband and wife team, now producing commercials in Chicago, for which they have won several Clio awards.
Night Driving, 1956; Texoprint, 1957; Mag, 1958; Faces and Fortune, 1960; Shaping the World, 1961; Envelope Jive, 1962; Dissent Illusion; From A to Z, 1963; Intergalactic Zoo, 1964; First Impression, 1965; The Great Train Robbery; Pitter Patterns, 1966; Up is Down, 1970; The Beginning, 1972 (All co-d Morton Goldscholl).

Gomez, Andrea   US
Working mainly in water colour paintings, her work draws on Jewish culture and local observation. *Bus Stop* is an impressionistic look at Detroit street life, in exquisite water colour animation; *Nigun*, whose title derives from a Hebrew chant meaning 'rhythm of the world's soul', takes the story of a couple and the birth of their child as meditation on life.
Nigun, 1977; Isaac, 1978; Bus Stop, 1982.

Graber, Sheila   GB
Born 1940, in South Shields, whose culture she has drawn upon for much of her painting. She has contributed enormously to art and animation education in the region. After art college and teacher training she became Head of Creative Studies at a local comprehensive school, where she introduced animation filmmaking across the curriculum, involving students in making films for subject areas as diverse as Home Economics and Geography. She suceeded in getting animation accepted as an exam subject via the Schools Council. She discovered animation via experiments with a Super-8 camera on holiday: 'trying the Single Frame Release - shoot anything that moves - pixillation; then using the S.F.R. shoot anything that doesn't move - and it does: Magic!' Almost entirely self-taught, through trial and error - e.g. problems with focus on models led to the use of cut-outs and painting; she constructed a rostrum from a tea-trolley. *Michelangelo* was inspired by a desire to find ways of making art accesible to her pupils, and was followed by a series on different artists, which led to a Tate Gallery commission for a film to accompany a William Blake exhibition, and another film using Henry Moore sculptures. She works under the camera, usually to pre-recorded soundtracks (a song or piece of music) usually composed by long-time friend and music teacher, Brenda Orwin. As is clear from the filmography, most of her films are produced for educational use, and often draw on local themes. She has also worked on some commercials and TV credit sequences.

In 1980 she resigned her teaching job to work full-time, spurred by a commission from French animation producer Nicole

Jouve, to produce a series based on Kipling's *Just So Stories*. She has continued her education work in other ways, however - often invited abroad to give workshops, and running local workshops for 7-70 year olds. In 1991 she moved into computer animation, via an Apple MacIntosh, used for a video to accompany a Tate Gallery touring exhibition of Turner and other multimedia collaborations with local artists on educational projects e.g. *Making Music the Japanese Way*.

Although the films demonstrate a range of different materials e.g. pastels, paint, cutouts, they are always recognisable in style, which is sometimes seen as primitive. *The Face in Art*, *Expressionism* and *Mondrian* are amongst the most impressive. Sheila Graber might not be considered a personal or art filmmaker in the same way as most of the other animators included here. But her work in education, the countless numbers of people of all ages she has inspired, her trajectory from amateur to professional, her success as a regionally based, one-woman industry (production, distribution on film and video) must be acknowledged.

Zoo; Can-Can; Puff the Magic Dragon; Boy and Microscope, 1972; Monarch of the Sea; The Boy and the Cat; School Cruise Film, 1973; The Boy, the Cats & the Rainbow; A Policeman's Lot is Not a Happy One, 1974; The Twelve Days of Christmas; Michaelangelo; Modern Major General; When I Went to the Bar, 1975; The Boy and the Song; Four Views of Landscape; The Lady of Shallott; Moving On, 1976; The Cat and the Tune; Be A Good Neighbour; Inside Look North; Howway the Lasses; Phil the Fluter's Ball, 1977; William Blake; Mondrian; Marking Time; Christmas Round the World, 1978; Larn Yersel Geordie; Evolution, 1979; Face to Face; Expressionism; The Elephant's Child, 1980; The Cat that Walked by Himself; How the Rhinoceros Got His Skin; The Beginning of the Armadilloes; How the Leopard Got His Spots; The Crab that Played with the Sea; How the Camel Got His Hump; How the Whale Got His Throat; The Singsong of Wild Man Kangaroo; The Butterfly that Stamped, 1981; The Face in Art; Leonardo Da Vinci; Dance Macabre; Henry Moore, 1982; I Guinea Pig; I Fish; I Cat; I Rabbit; I Dog; I Mouse; I Bird; I Frog;

I Pony, 1983; Art Horses, 1985; New Year Round the World; Bio and Bones, My River Tyne, 1986; Body Builders; The Pigeon Cree; Heidi's Horse, 1987; Toys Will be Toys, 1989.

Gratz, Joan   US

In *Mona Lisa Descending the Staircase*, Gratz achieves her painterly, impressionistic style of animation via a mix of clay and mineral oil, for fluid transformation. In *Mona Lisa*, which took two years to make, the history of 20th century painting literally unfolds through a series of reproduction clay paintings which transform and reconfigure into the next impressionist, surrealist or modernist masterpiece in succession.

Joan Gratz was born in Burbank in 1941, daughter of an electrical engineer and a teacher of English. Her early aptitude for painting was tempered by the belief that art was not a respectable occupation so she followed up a degree in painting from UCLA with a professional degree in architecture. But in her last couple of years of study, Gratz experimented with the idea of 'making paintings breathe' through animation and experienced her first thrill of getting a film back from the lab, a pleasure she still enjoys.

After graduating in 1969 Gratz tried out a couple of jobs but soon returned to Oregon where she led a 'pauper's life' in a 9' x 14' room which she shared with her pet parrot. She supported herself in an 'unprofitable cottage industry' making puppets and dabbling in poster graphics. Around this time a couple of unemployed architect friends moved to Portland and were hired by Will Vinton. A year later they phoned Gratz and in 1976 she started work at the up-and-coming Will Vinton Studio.

Working there brought security, comfort and prestige. *Dinosaur*, was followed by the Oscar-nominated *Rip Van Winkle*. *The Little Prince*, with trademark Gratz clay painted effects, came next and in 1982 she designed and animated the award-winning *The Creation*. *Return to Oz* followed in 1985, her first feature experience: she then spent three and a half years working on *The Adventures of Mark Twain*.

But Gratz's experiences of collaboration were not always happy (Vinton took direc-

tor's credit for *The Creation*) so in 1987 she went freelance. She has never looked back. As freelance designer and director, she has also continued with the Vinton Studio, who represent her.

In her other new film, *Pro and Con*, made with Joanna Priestley, Gratz has extended her clay painting techniques to include writing and calligraphy and scratching through black clay on white backgrounds to portray aspects of prison life. Gratz's next project explores how people behave at parties and she will continue to work on commercials, believing that what she can achieve artistically goes beyond the mere selling of a product. (JMcG)

Creation, 1981; Vanz Kant Danz (animator); sequence for Amnesty International Human Rights Now; Candy Jam, 1987 (co-d Joanna Priestley); Mona Lisa Descending a Staircase; Pro and Con, 1992 (co-d Joanna Priestley).

Groschup, Sabine   Austria

Experimental animator. Her work is quite varied stylistically, often using strong primary colours, although: 'influenced by its morbid chracter and the atmosphere of Venice at night, I created the film *Frenzy*. The city appears as a sequence of painted pictures and filmed impressions.'

1220 Komeru Kanfas 7, 1983; Kloppun Konfes; O-Game-O; Muart, 1984; Messer; Geld, 1987; Liebe; Haus, 1988; All das All; Guten Morgen; Madam Mona, 1989: Vahnzinn: aus den Augen, ausserhalb ist der Sinn/Frenzy: Out of Sight, Out of Mind, 1991.

Gross, Aline   Israel

Song Without Words, 1957; We Shall Never Die; And the Earth Was Without Form and Void, 1959.

Guard, Candy   GB

See pp. 88. Her minimally drawn cartoons deal with the everyday problems of women's lives, such as the the terrors of going to the hairdressers, reluctantly trying to lose weight - and her female characters speak out loud those small embarassing thoughts that get audiences shrieking with recognition. A talent for observation and concise scrips characterise her work.

A Little Something; Wishful Thinking; Alternative Fringe, 1988; Fatty Issues,

A - Z

What About Me? 1990; Fantastic Person, 1991.

Hannah, Nancy   GB
Worked in commercial studios, then at Biographic Films. See also entry on Vera Linnecar, with whom she collaborated.
Aquarius, 1963; Quod Libet, 1968; Do Be Careful Boys (collab), 1965; I'm Glad You Asked That Question (collab), 1970; I'm Sorry You've Been Kept Waiting (collab), 1976.

Hayes, Ruth   US
See pp. 64-65. An animator who has developed a living publishing flip books. *Eggs:* A tongue in cheek meditation on the cracking of eggs and out biological origins, whilst *Body Sketches*, an experimental film about drawing suggests the move she'd make into flip books.
Flip books: Eggchase; Bodyscape, 1979; Hot Licks; Running Octopus; Dolphin Cycle, 1980; TV Dinner; Orca Beaching, 1981; Frogs in Heat, 1983; Ron's World, 1984; Gluttony; Five Pelicans Fish, 1985; Animal Husbandry, 1986; The Flip Book of Revelations, 1987; Published by Real Comet Press: Sloth; Birthrite, 1988; Leash Law; Paranoia, 1989; Roses are Red, Violets are Blue, My Cat's in Heat and I'm Thinking of you; The Flip Book of the Dead, 1990.
Eggs, 1977; Body Sketches, 1978; Wanda, 1990; Reign of the Dog; A Revisionist History, 1991; Wanda, 1992.

Healy Deborah   US
Filters and Potions; Little Birds, 1976; Hommage, 1978.

Hewitt, Nicole   Yugoslavia
A young Anglo-Croatian, brought up in both countries, although it was in Zagreb that she made her films, and where she hopes to return. After art school in Britain, she spent six months learning puppet animation in the Barrandow studios in Czechoslovakia. *Herman's Burden* is drawn and cel animated, its distinctive graphic style revealing the influence of Eastern European graphic art traditions, and is about freedom and identity. Her second film, which used model and puppet animation, is the first in an intended triptych, *Notes on Desire and Continuity*, exploring issues of identity in relation to sexuality:

the fear and attraction of loss of self.
Herman's Burden, 1989; Notes on Continuity, 1991.

Heczko, Bozennaz   Canada
A good example of the role the National Film Board of Canada has played in developing animation artists. Born in Poland, Bozenna (known as Zina) was six years old when her family were interned in a labour camp at the outbreak of World War II. After three years they escaped to England, where she was educated, then in 1956 emigrated to Canada. She began work at the NFB as a secretary, but her artistic abilities were soon noticed, and from painting and tracing she went on to work as animator and assistant director, then to make her own films. *A Special Letter* was based on events in her own life, and tells the story of the relationship between a mother and daughter, and memories of the WWII labour camp.
Pictures Out of My Life, 1973; Riverdale Lion, 1977; Laugh Lines: A Profile of Kai Pindal (co-d with Franco Battista), 1979; A Special Letter, 1984; Acid Rain, 198?.

Horvath, Maria   Hungary
After art school, she worked for several years at Panonia Studios, as animator. Made several films for a series on Hungarian folk tales.
Miklos, the Little King, 1980; Az Eiskaka Csodai/Marvels of the Night, 1982; Ajto 8; Ajto 9, 1983.

Houston, Catherine   GB
Known usually by her nickname, 'Spud' Houston got into animation, as she admits 'by accident' after five years of a fine art course at Edinburgh 'which fits you for nothing unless you want to teach'. She was all set to become a dress designer, but it wasn't really to her liking and she felt a certain relief when she was fired for requesting a raise. Her sister pointed out an advertisement for artists at London Films. She got the job, and knowing nothing about animation, was employed to work on *Foxhunt*, which went into production in 1935. She did painting, tracing, and animation, learning as she went along from people hardly more experienced than herself. Neverthelss, the film that emerged is such a recognised masterpiece that Spud

can well say, in retrospect, that 'there's nothing like starting at the top'.
After a brief stint with Henry Elwis, at British Animated Pictures, Spud went to work with Anson Dyer. At Anglia, she was involved in a commercial for Capstan cigarettes, *You're Telling Me*, which Spud recalls, 'was a sort of pre-*Reluctant Dragon*' as it showed something of the studio at work. But not quite as usual: Technicolor built a studio set inside the studio, arranging things according to their own ideas, and made Spud the star turn.
Spud stayed with Dyer until 1942, when she moved to Halas & Batchelor. Her previous experience stood her in good stead. 'I looked at the first dope sheet and it said "frame number 2,154". Well, I just couldn't believe it; not sequences, just frame numbers. So I introduced the Anson Dyer dope sheets, and things went better from then on.' After a spate of Ministry of Information projects, and the inevitable commercials, Spud was seconded to Information Films of India, and went to Bombay to make films as part of the 'Rural Uplift' programme. Back in England, she worked for a while for the Larkins studio and then went with her husband to New Zealand, to spend the next twenty years 'raising the next generation'.
The opportunity to make a film for herself came quite by chance. Some work Spud had done for one of her husband's films was seen by a bookseller friend, who asked her to make a short film to help expand his trade. She chose to work on a version of *Petunia*, by Roger Duvoisin. The project didn't turn out exactly as she hoped – she regarded the final result as an uneasy mix of her own animation and film of the original illustrations.
Back in England again, during the next ten years Spud worked for Bob Godfrey, Beryl Stevens, Halas & Batchelor, Dragon, Bill Melendez, TVC, and others, still finding time to visit New Zealand regularly. It was during one of these trips that she got the inspiration for her next film, *How the Kiwi Lost His Wings*. She heard the story on the radio one day and fell in love with it. She worked on it on and off for five years, finishing it in 1980.
Spud continued to freelance for varous companies until 1984, when she had another stroke of luck. 'I'd been waiting for

something to float down from heaven to me and offer itself as a project, and that's exactly what happened. I was lying on the couch, having my afternoon snooze, and suddenly, I woke up with this voice in my ear…telling these folktales from Zimbabwe.' She bought a copy of the transmission tape of *Children of the Wax* from the BBC, and made the film. (EB/GL) More recently she has been working with Indian animators on a film for children.

What is Life, 1970; Petunia, 1972; How the Kiwi Lost His Wings, 1980; Children of Wax: A Folk Tale from Zimbabwe, 1985.

Huber, Sabine   Germany
Studied at Stutttgart, and a founder member of Studio Filmbilder in Stuttgart. *Turn Around* is characterised by a strong graphic style (pen and ink on paper) and is a statement about the modern world's dysfunctionality.

Top Job, 1988; Turn Around, 1989.

Hubley, Emily   US
As one of John and Faith Hubley's daughters, she was not only brought up amidst animation, also featured, with her sister Georgia, on the soundtrack of such Hubley films as *CockaBoody* and…, inspired by the two young children at play. She had already started making her own films before studying at art college. Also animates most of Faith Hubley's films, and has done inserts for documentaries and sponsored films. Her animation film techniques include bottom lit paper, felt-tip on paper and cel. *Blake Ball* uses the game of baseball as a metaphor to explore the world of poet and painter William Blake. *Deliberating Man* features a man who is manipulated by words, consequently divided into a male and female aspect, misuses the senses and is punished by the false deity creaty by misperception. *Emergence of Eunice* is a powerful evocation of female adolescent alienation, with a spare graphic style that feels like an animation version of New York punk/New Wave. A wry, deadpan narration belies the central characters fears and anxieties: she fears she's pregnant and finds herself in an uncaring home situation which is contrasted with the more considerate world of strangers. Similar in feel is *Delivery Man* in which a young woman discusses her feel-

ings towards surgery, love and death, relating five dreams and experiences involving the doctor who delivered her, her mother who survived surgery and her father who didn't. Both have a hard edge, idiosyncratic humour and are impressively scripted. *Big Brown Eyes* is more light-hearted, a love-chase following two pairs of eyes through a montage of metamorphoses and acrobatics.

Presage, 1976; Liver, 1978; Emergence of Eunice, 1980; Delivery Man; Big Brown Eyes; Let Sleeping Dogs Eat (for Sesame Street), 1982; The Tower (co-d Georgia Hubley), 1984; Deliberating Man, 1985; Blake Ball, 1988.

Hubley, Faith   US
See pp. 19-29, and ß.

The films she has made by herself are characterised by a free-floating style that incorporates her love for the art and iconography of ancient, non-Western and 'primitive' cultures and elaborate her concerns for the ecology, world peace and other global issues. Amazonia, for example, interprets three South American myths; whilst Upside Down, inspired by the medieval Indian poet Kabir, aims to rouse an audience into realisation of the consequences of ignoring the Earth's complex and delicate Eco-system. She presents an alternative vision of continuity with the past and guarded hope for the future, using a viriety of images from 20th century Surrealism to ancient symbols of prehistoric society. She is also an accomplished musician, and has used many leading American jazz musicians on her soundtracks.

The Adventures of an Asterix, 1956; Harlem Wednesday, 1957; Tender Game, 1958; Moonbird, 1959; Children of the Sun, 1960; Of Stars and Men, 1961; The Hole, 1962; The Hat, 1964; Tijuana Brass Double Feature, 1965; Urbanissimo, 1966; The Cruise; Windy Day, 1967; Zuckerkandl; Of Men and Demons, 1968; Eggs, 1970; Dig, 1972; Cockaboody, 1973; Voyage to Next, 1974; People, People, People, 1975; Everybody Rides the Carousel, 1976; A Doonesbury Special, 1977 (all co-d John Hubley).

Women of the World, 1975; Second Chance: Sea, 1976; Whither Weather, 1977; Step by Step, 1978; Sky Dance,

1979; The Big Bang and Other Creation Myths; Enter Life, 1981; Starlore, 1983; Hello, 1984; The Cosmic Eye (feature, incorporating and reworking several earlier films), 1985; Time of the Angels 1987; Yes We Can; Who Am I?, 1989; Amazonia, 1990; Upside Down, 1991; Tall Time Tales, 1992; Cloudland...in production (all solo).

Jackson, Dianne   GB
Dianne Jackson was born in 1944. She worked on George Dunning's feature film *Yellow Submarine* in 1969. She has also made various TV commercials and animated inserts for Stanley Donen's *The Little Prince* (1974). Her first film in her own right was a 26 minute film *The Snowman*, which has become a classic, repeated annually on television. She animated Hilda's dream sequence in Jimmy T Murakami's, *When the Wind Blows*. While working on *Grandpa*, she also prepared a treatment for the forthcoming feature film of Beatrix Potter's work under the working title of *The Adventures of Peter Rabbit.*

The Snowman, 1982; Granpa, 1989.

Jankel, Annabel   GB
Studied animation at WSCAD, although she had originally wanted to work in live-action filmmaking. After working on Geoff Dunbar's *Ubu Roi* daytimes, and evenings with Rocky Morton on *Marx for Beginners*, she joined Morton's Cucumber Studios in 1978. They shared a common frustration with the limitations that then existed in the animation world. They felt it was still entrenched in the 'cartoon' concept of animation that had developed from the 40s, but with neither the finance nor the innovation of the period. Their art college backgrounds led them to draw on Matisse, Mondrian, Malevich and Miro as sources of inspiration, although the films listed below also pay and play homage to animation history. *Pleasure/Genius of Love* is a brilliant tour through 30s American animation, with a particular nod to the Fleischer Bros; *New Frontier's* animation inserts into the live action employs UPA style graphics and references to *Rooty Toot Toot*. Cucumber became one of the most innovative producers of commercials, TV credit sequences and rock videos of the period (including videos for Miles Davis, Tom Tom Club,

Elvis Costello, Debbie Harry, and Nick Heywood). Computer graphics was another area they were keen to develop, compiling the book *Creative Computer Graphics* in 1983. In 1984 they began work on a Channel 4 commission to find a new framework for presenting rock videos, which resulted in the creation of the cult TV *Max Headroom Show*. In 1986 they abandoned animation and commercials to concentrate on live action feature films, and directed a remake of Rudolph Maté's classic B noir *D.O.A.* (Dead on Arrival) in 1987.

Genius of Love, 1982; Pleasure of Love, 1984; Accidents will Happen; New Frontier, 1985. (all co-d RM)

Joritz, Kathy   Germany
'I got into animation at the School of the Art Institute of Chicago – probably the world's most wonderful art-playground. Animation was my bridge from drawing to filmmaking. At the SAIC I made a lot of crazy short films and started scratching on *Negative Man* which I later finished in Germany. Partially as a result of *Negi*'s success I was lucky enough to land several German production grants, enabling me to continue my independent filmwork (animation, documentaries). Subsequent TV contracts from the feminist comedy show *Weiber von Sinnen* also allowed me to try out some other kinds of animation (puppet, mixed-media). I'm very interested in doing commercial animation (music videos, advertisements, spots in feature films…) providing I can stay on the creative side of things and maintain a good deal of freedom. It's also important to me that the commercial work is 'clean' – no sexism, racism, cigarettes or alcohol. I'd love to do some kids' films, and want to keep producing independent zany stuff on my own. I teach college level animation now, and am also interested in teaching little kids at high school level. And I'd like to continue working as a commercial illustrator, which I feel has always had a positive influence on my animation.'

Batman Ann, 1979; Negative Man, 1985; Give Aids the Freeze, 1991; Strip, Santa!, 1992.

Jovanovic, Divna Yugoslavia
Deadline, 1960; Rondo, 1963; It's A Hard Life, 1969; Fetish, 1971; Metamorphosis, 1973.

Kaupinnen, Heini   Finland
There are very few opportunities to make independent animation films in Finland, given the emphasis on produciton for children. Kaupinnen has worked on fellow Finnish animator Marjut Rimminen's films in London, where she also made *Carnage*, a provocative film about men's relationship to women's sexuality. A harsh graphic style mirrors the ferocity of atttack, although there's also a lot of humour.

Carnage, 1990.

Keen, Lesley   GB
Lesley Keen was born in Glasgow in 1953, and studied art at the Glasgow School of Art. From 1975-78 she studied animation at Prague's Brothers-in-Tricks studios, and made *Ondra and the Snowdragon* there, a fairy tale for children. In 1982, with Jam Culik, she founded an independent film company, Persistent Vision. Many of her films have been C4 commissions, and some have been accompanied by documentary films and publications about her work. Support from Scottish funding agencies, along with C4, have enabled her to concentrate on her own films, so there is no pressure to work in commercials. The lack of an established animation industry in Scotland, and the concomitant lack of training opportunities brought problems in attracting and retaining animators for the studio's work. This, coupled with her own interests and abilities, led the company to pursue computerisation, and research association with Cambridge, then Glasgow University, where she has been an Honorary Research Fellow since 1985. This led to the company's development of integrated hard and software, using the Apple MacIntosh, and more recently work in the field of CD-I and interest in virtual reality. Her first film, *Taking a Line For a Walk*, 1983, explored the theories of artist Paul Klee, in collaboration with synthetic music composer Lyell Creswell, and combined cel and computer animation.

Together with Lisze Bechtold and Candy Kugel she particpated in an 'experiment in long-distance filmmaking', in which the three worked individually to a common theme: *My Film, My Film, My Film*. *Orpheus and Euridice* and *Invocation* were both inspired by Greek mythology, and emulate the design of Greek pottery and friezes, and use cel animation. The feature *Ra : The Path of the Sun God* was the fruit of two years' research into Egyptology.

Ondra and the Snowdragon, 1978; Taking a Line for a Walk, 1983; My Film, My Film, My Film; Orpheus and Eurydice, 1984; Running In, 1984; Invocation, 1985; Ra: The Path of the Sun God: A Vision of Ancient Egypt; Burrellesque, 1990.

Kennedy, Sarah   GB
Studed Fine Art at Newcastle Polytechnic, then specialised in animation at the RCA.

As it Happens (cutouts), is a satire on some of the more rebarbative aspects of 70s feminism: the ideological puritanism, and the peer group pressures to conform. *Carol and Mary*, (model and plasticine) is another acerbic comedy, looking at the way women can be competitive with each other, in a very subtle but deadly way. 'It's about two women, sisters, comparing their different lifestyles - one's married, the other's single.'

Honestly, it's the story of my life (cutouts) is a kind of satire on faffing as a fine art, as a student panicks about getting her project done, spending a lot of time worrying, procrastinating, and talking about… the project, which is tell the story of your life.

On the Rail follows two young women on the much reviled package holiday tour to Spain. Like all of her work, it's a look at the gap between fantasy and reality: the unrealistic expectations of holiday romance etc. Its two female protagonists bicker and play not-too-subtle games of one-up (wo)manship. *Family Favourites*, (drawn animation) deals with the nightmare that Christmas family reunions often turn into.

As it Happens ,1986; Carol and Mary, 1987; Honestly, it's the story of my life, 1989; On the Rail,1990; Family Favourites, 1991; First Night, 1991; Any Old Night; Summer Night; Singles Night, 1992.

Kinoshita, Sayoka   Japan
See p. 33. Produces, scripts and animates on films directed by her husband, Renzo. What on Earth is He?, 1971; Made in Japan, 1972; Gross National Product, 1973;

Japonese, 1977; Pica Don, 1978; Frame of Mind, 1988; Flip-Clip; The Morning, 1989; Flip-Clip, 1991.

Kordon, Renate   Austria

Studied art and architecture. Her work is often experimental, characterised by a poetic, lyrical and meditative style, and no dialogue. Has incorporated painted bodies into her films. *Olympus* uses an innovative technique of paper cut-outs on underlit glass. She is also a graphic designer, book illustrator, and makes architectural installations.

Glühbirne, 1976; Augenblicke, 1979; Tageblätter, 1980; Hors d'Oeuvre, 1981; Passepartout, 1983; Olympus, 1984; Buntes Blut/Coloured Blood, 1985; Tonfilm/Sound Film = Clay Film, 1986; Echo; Now For Now, 1988; Raumfahrt/ Space Travel, 1989.

Kravitz, Amy   US

Head of the Animation Department at Rhodes Island School of Design. Works largely in abstraction, using unusual drafting techniques and materials e.g. aluminum powder on black paper, a range of textured papers. *The Trap* was inspired by a quote from a holocaust survivor, Elie Wiesel's book Souls on Fire 'I try to imagine my grandfather in the train that carried him away.' and the film attempts to articulate, by non-narrative means, the difficult and distrubing sensations of that last journey. *River Lethe* explores the metaphoric implications of Greek mythological belief that the dead drank the waters of Lethe to forget their erathly lives. Her current film in progress is *CockaDoodleDoo.*

River Lethe, 1986; The Golden ball: An Armenian Folk Tale (co-d Yvonne Anderson); The Trap, 1988; Literacy MTV (World Problems, World Solutions) 1992.

Krumins, Daine   US

The Divine Miracle; Babobilicons, 198?

Kugel, Candy   US

See p. 34. Works largely in cel; in Snowie and Warm Recption achieves an effect of bright neon on velvety black backgrounds, somewhat reminiscent of Jankel & Morton's *Genius/Pleasure of Love. In-Betweening America* is a three minute

homage to Saul Steinberg, based on his drawings. Hermit Crab wsa made for a children's TV programme. *Fast Food Matador* has a completely different look from earlier films, using paint.

Woman; Who is Me?, 1976; In-Betweening America, 1977 ; Hermit Crab 1978; Audition, 1980; My Film, My Film, My Film (co-d Lisze Bechtold, Lesley Keene), 1983; A Warm Reception in LA, 1987; Snowie and the Seven Dorps: A Passive Aggressive Fable for the 1990's, 1990 (both co-d Vincent Cafarelli); seq. Animated Self Portraits, 1988; Fast Food Matador, 1991 (co-d VF).

Kurbanova, Frances   USSR

See p. 110.

Acquarium, 1983; One Evening, 1985; Seance, 1987.

Lacey, Gillian   GB

See pp. 35-41.

After art school, she found the easiest way into filmmaking was via animation, so submitted an animation project to BFI's Experimental Film Fund, based on an Irish folktale, which Bruce Beresford produced. As a result was offered the job of assistant animator on *Yellow Submarine*, and directed and animated for Halas & Batchelor. A dispute over the content of a film commissioned by the Race Relations Board (Lacey had drawn a scene in which a black man is refused a drink in a pub, which was censored on the grounds it might offend white publicans), led to her withdrawal from the industry. She then taught social studies and ran a community printing press. Founder member of Leeds Animation. Worked on the collective project *Criminal Justice*, about women and law. Arthritis developed through RSI curtailed her animation work, and simultaneously she was commissioned to develop a number of live-action film drama projects, including one for Tony Garnett. Wrote and directed a live-action lesbian comedy short, *Family Turns*, in 1988. Teaches animation; has just co-directed a live-action short, *Capoeira Quickstep*, 1992, and is keen to produce young animation filmmakers.

The Wanderings of Ulick Joyce, 1967; The Condition of Man: Up; If By Chance We Should Meet, 1971; Leeds Animation Collective: Who Needs Nurseries, 1978; Risky

Business, 1980; Pretend You'll Survive, 1981; Give us a Smile, 1983; Council Matters, 1984; Criminal Justice: Murders Most Foul, Someone Must be Trusted (co-d Christine Roche); Family Turns, 1988; Capoeira Quickstep (l/a), 1992.

Lambart, Evelyne Canada

See pp. 30-32.

Maps in Action, 1945; The Impossible Map, 1947; Around is Around, 1951; O Canada, 1952; Begone Dull Care, 1949 (co-d Norman McLaren); Rhythmetic, 1956; A Chairy Tale, 1957; Le Merle, 1958; Short and Suite, 1959; Lines-Horizontal, 1961; Lines-Vertical, 1962; Mosiac, 1965; Fine Feathers, 1968; The Hoarder, 1969; Paradise Lost, 1970; Forest Fire Clips, 1971; The Story of Christmas, 1973; Mr. Frog Went a-Courting, 1974; The Lion and the Mouse, 1976; The Town Mouse and the Country Mouse, 1980.

Lanctot, Micheline Canada

Live-action and animation filmmaker, actress (e.g. *Le Vraie nature de Bernadette,* 1972, *The Apprenticeship of Duddy Cravitz,* 1974, *Blood Relatives,* 1977). In 1980 she wrote and directed her first fiction feature *L'Homme a tout faire.*

Genesys, 1968; Blue Water Sea Food, 1970; Tiki Tiki, 1971; Selfish Giant, 1973; A Token Gesture, 1975; Raggedy Ann and Andy, 1977.

Lassnig, Maria   Austria

Born 1919. A widely exhibited artist in avant garde circles, in Austria, Paris Berlin, and New York, where she lived from 1968-1979. She taught herself animation, and in 1980 founded the Experimental Animation Studio at Vienna's Hochschule für Angewandte Kunst, now run by her former pupil and animation activist Hubert Sielecki. Her films are sometimes self-funded, sometimes grant-aided.

Encounter, 1970; Chairs, 1971; Self-Portrait, 1972; Paare/Couples, 1978; Baroque Statue, 1970-74; Handlesen/Palmistry, 1974; Formen/Shapes, 1976; Kunsterziehung/Art Education, 1976.

Laughlin, Kathleen   US

Currently teaching filmmaking in Minneapolis. Her films explore a wide range of techniques: saturated colour printing

A - Z

in *A Round Feeling* , stop-motion single framing in *Opening/Closing* and *Susan Through Corn*. *Madsong* combines animation and live-action in a young woman's personal cycles of nature. In its artful use of live-action/animation overlap, which echoes the agitated fluctuation of the voices of her mind from fantasy to reality, from 'inside to outside, from backward to forward simultaneously,' *Madsong* is one of the few films about women today that succeeds in being intensely personal and universal at the same time. (TS)
A Round Feeling, 1970; Opening/Closing; The Disappearance of Sue, 1972; Madsong, 1976; Susan Through Corn; Interview, 1974; Some Will Be Apples, 1974-5 (co-d Phyllis MacDougal); Gone By, 1976; Sam E, 1976; Tomato Song, 1979.

Leaf, Caroline   Canada
See pp. 41-47, and ß.
Born in Seattle, US in 1946. She studied at the University of Harvard (Boston) and made her first film *Peter and Wolf*, in 1969, animating sand on a sheet of glass. Her second film *Orfeo* animated paint on glass directly in front of the camera. After she had fully mastered these techniques she made *How Beaver Stole Fire*, an adaptation of an Indian legend, and *The Owl Who Married a Goose*, an Eskimo legend. Two films brought her international fame: *The Street*, inspired by a short story from Mordecai Richler, and Franz Kafka's *The Metamorphosis of Mr Samsa*. In *Interview*, Veronika Soul and Caroline Leaf used different techniques and various materials to describe themselves. In the 1980s she produced a live-action documentary on the singers Kate and Anna McGarrigle, and two other live-action shorts on women's struggle against discrimination at work. *Pies* used animation again to tell a tale about the destructive prejudices harboured by a woman because of misconceptions about a neighbour who keeps a cow. She experimented with actors in costume and drawn sets with *Dog's Tale*, a Mexican legend; *The Fox and the Tiger*, an adaptation of a Chinese tale, and Lear's *The Owl and the Pussycat*, to rather disappointing results.
She made a triumphant return to form with *Two Sisters*, a stunning, though also disturbing film about two sisters living alone, and the power struggles between them. She has recently spent long periods in Ireland, to concentrate on oil painting and develop her gouache style. See ß.
Sand or Peter and Wolf, 1969; Orfeo; How Beaver Stole Fire; Mr. Roger's Neighbourhood, 1972; The Owl Who Marrried a Goose: An Eskimo legend, 1973; The Street, 1974; The Metamorphosis of Mr. Samsa, 1974; Interview, 1979; Kate and Anna McGarrigle; The Right to Refuse, 1981; An Equal Opportunity, 1982; Pies, 1983; The Owl and the Pussycat; A Dog's Tale: A Mexican Parable; The Fox and the Tiger: A Chinese Parable, 1984; Entre Deux Soeurs/Two sisters, 1990; I Met a Man (MTV Art clip), 1991.

Leeds Animation   GB
See p. 35 and ß. A women's collective, founded in 1976 aiming to produce films which would explore issues and stimulate discussion in an entertaining, often witty, and accessible way, and also advocate positive action. Users include arts and community groups, education, trade unions, and special interest groups.
Pretend You'll Survive, an anti-nuclear film, has been widely used in peace campaigns. One of their strongest - and most controversial - films, *Give Us a Smile* expresses the reactions of women to the violence, both physical and ideological, with which they are confronted everyday. 'A strong cocktail of live-action, montage of advertising issues and hand-drawn animation.' *Out to Lunch* graphically demonstrates ways in which men dominate language, monopolise space, and structure women into a subservient role. Issues explored in their films include: anti-nuclear; health and safety in the workplace; participation in local government; the politics of food on a global scale; women and homelessness; the international debt crisis; waste disposal.
Who Needs Nurseries? - We Do!, 1978; Risky Business, 1980; Pretend You'll Survive, 1981; Give Us a Smile, 1983; Council Matters, 1984; Council Matters, 1984; Crops and Robbers, 1986; Home and Dry,1987; Out to Lunch, 1989; A Matter of Interest, 1990; Alice in Wasteland, 1991.

Lepore, Sandy   Australia
Mine, 1987; Australia Story; Crayons, 1988; The Race, 1989.

Lepeuve, Monique France
La Chanson du Jardinier Fou/The Mad Gardener's Song, 1960; Concerto pour Violoncelle, 1962.

Li, Katherine   Canada
Tearing, 1980; La Nuit; Dechirement, 198?; Sabina, 1991.

Lingford, Ruth   GB
Lingford recently graduated from the RCA, after returning to art college as a mature student.
'Working in a medium in which anything is possible holds many terrors. There is a constant compulsion to set oneself boundaries and barriers in order to have a defined space and structure in which to work. These boundaries are dictated in part by notions of good taste and the expected reactions of others. For me it has seemed important consciously to cross these boundaries at times. It is usually clear to me when I am approaching the edge, as I find myself becoming anxious and wanting to work in conditions of exaggerated privacy. The results can be over-personal, unpleasant and, very often, just plain embarrassing, but occasionally there is a magic moment, when I can feel the audience collectively holding it breath and I know I have scored a direct hit. A visceral and perhaps emotional reaction can be achieved by the use of movement, unexpected assumptions, as in the shifting of perspectives or meanings.
The repetitive nature of animation drawing can produce a state in which the internal censor may be lulled into inattention, and small changes may occur in one's drawings which might lead on to something quite unexpected. I like to leave some space in my working method for the rogue voice of the unconscious. My first film, *Tightrope*, was drawn almost completely by this method, literally without knowing what was going to happen next, proceeding by Chinese whispers. My subsequent two films used large elements of unconscious work within a slightly more organised narrative structure, while the film I am working on at the moment is

almost completely pre-planned and storyboarded.

I am more interested in animation as a subtle and effective means of communicating ideas than in its purely aesthetic qualities. For me, content is of primary importance. It is only in the subject matter that I am trying to approach new ground. *Whole Lotta Love,* was built around a Led Zeppelin song, originally released in 1969, but re-released in 1989 into a quite different social and sexual climate. The film attempts to convey the ironically altered message of the song within the context of AIDS, and to explore the dark, barbed aspects of sexuality and desire.

Sea in the Blood, is a rather more introspective film, reflecting my feelings of submersion and passivity as a mother of two young children, and my ambivalence about surfacing. My latest film continues on this theme, and is about a woman haunted by horrific images of her own fertility. I have tried to create images that are difficult to look at, and in this I find feedback from others very useful, as the familiarity with the images that is inevitable during the animation process blunts their emotional impact. I suppose that in this sense, my work has a therapeutic aspect, as it involves confronting, and becoming comfortable with things that I have found extremely anxiety-provoking. Like many animators, I derive some inspiration from my dreams. Animation is the medium of dream-logic, of shifts in time, place and meaning. Many of my ideas come from the moments between sleep and wakefulness. The danger with my style of working is that of verging on the Gothic or psychedelic, and the constantly present spectre of 'bad taste'. It is sometimes hard to own and take responsibility for the more disturbing images in the films. Paradoxically, when trying to tread new ground, it is a great comfort to place myself within a tradition of transgression in the arts.'

Tightrope, 1987; Whole Lotta Love, 1989; Sea in the Blood, 1990; Baggage, 1991; Crumble, 1992.

Linnecar, Vera   GB

One of the few women animation directors working in the UK in the late 60s and through the 70s, after many years working for commercial studios - although she strongly resists categorisation as a 'woman' filmmaker. After art school, she started in animation by accident, working for some years in the 40s on the Halas & Batchelor production line, moving from paint'n'trace to animator. Then moved to Larkins studio, recruited by Peter Sachs, who she credits with creating an atmosphere conducive to self-development, and exciting, revolutionary films, for the corporate sector (or 'sponsored films' as they were then called). She recalls her excitement and awe at being interviewed by David Hilberman (one of the breakaway Disney animators who went to UPA), who had come to the UK in the late 50s to set up commercials company, Pearl & Dean. Only later did she discover he had been extremely nervous about employing women as animation directors! However, once she started she found the working environment stimulating and supportive, with little of the traditional demarcation between workers in the production process. When Hilberman left, she was invited to join Biographic films, in 1960, which comprised of Bob Godfrey, Nancy Hannah and Keith Learner. Biographic was one of the liveliest of London studios in the 60s. There she made many award-winning sponsored films, usually co-directed with Nancy Hanna, with whom she had a close creative realationship, e.g. *Calling All Women*, a cancer campaign film in 1969, and the two of them with Keith Learner, such as *I'm Glad You Asked That Question, I'm Sorry You've Been Kept Waiting.* But the constant financial pressures made making her own films an uphill battle. There was little distribution in cinemas and virtually none on television and she feels that limited time and means affected their quality. There simply were not the funding possibilities open to animators that exist today. And as Biographic grew in size, the early camaraderie and close working relationships lessened. When Biographic's lease ran out in 1900, she retired. Although no longer involved in film, she has returned to her early vocation, and makes sculptures in alabaster, artificial stone, and lead, in an impressive range of styles.

Springtime for Samantha, 1965; The Trendsetter, 1969; 1970; A Cat is a Cat, 1971; 1976; Do I Detect a Change in Your Attitude?, 1980.

Loughlin, Susan   GB

Studied at Liverpool Poly, and is currently at the NFTS. *Grand National*, a powerful evocation of the sounds and move ments of a day at the race-course, is recognisably from the Liverpool school, with its graphic economy, free-flowing lines and edited 'found' soundtrack. She is also keen to work creatively with children.

'My aims have been to capture and evoke emotions from the beauty within simple situations and events, to recapture the first moment of joy and to release those sensations that excited me. Since my mother died in 1986, I have been confused about the differences between life and death. I feel that it is not enough to know that life exists and to celebrate it; now I want to know what it is. *The Occasion* which I started in 1990 is, I feel, a transitional, rights of passage film in which a young girl ventures into a bizarre party world and desperately tries to impress strange, awesome creatures who only make her aware of her inadequacies: only when she gets visibly older and loses her innocence does she realise the superficiality of the situation that once impressed her and gains a sense of her own worth and the strength to redeem herself.

'As part of my research for a planned series for the under fives, I showed slides from all areas of the fine arts to nursery school children. Whilst being a fantastic experience it proved that it is adults, as teachers, parents and TV programme-makers who continually prompt children's own natural responses.

I want to find out what they like, why they like it and then produce an educational series to suit it. I am also preparing an educational series for pre-O Level children to try and inspire them back into the classroom. We have been working closely with teachers and the Department of Education in pinpointing the areas of difficulty.' *Largo, 1985; Playground, 1986; Les Demoiselles, 1987; Grand National, 1989.*

Macaulay, Eunice GB

Born 1923, Lancashire, England. A very varied early career, first as an analytical chemist in the glass industry, followed by service in the navy during the war. She began work at British Gaumont in 1948, as supervisor of the 48-strong Inking and supervisor of the 48-strong Inking and Painting Dept of Gaumont British Animation. After freelance work in film production and graphic design, embroidery design, and draftswoman with telephone companies, she emigrated to New York in 1961 and in 1963 joined the National Film Board of Canada, supervising drawing on others' films. After a stint as production supervisor at Potterton Productions, she returned to the NFB in 1973, as supervisor and colour designer. She also animated, designed backgrounds and co-ordinated each film for the camera. During this period she had a 'hands on' role on every film created in the Studio. She co-directed and animated the Oscar winning *Special Delivery*, with John Weldon, for whom she worked as assistant on *Log Diver's Waltz*. In 1983 she began producing a series *Just for Kids*, based on Canadian childrens' stories, some of which she also scripted. Also contributed as writer to Ishu Patel's *Paradise*, and wrote and produced *Dreams of a Land*. Another series she has launched as producer is *65 Plus*, for and about the growing-old and the elderly.

Special Delivery, 1978 (co-d John Weldon); Log Driver's Waltz, 1979 (asst to JW).

Macskassy, Kati   Hungary

Daughter of the founder of Hungarian animation, Gyula Macskassy, she worked for several years as an artist and animator and editor for the Hungarian animation studio, Pannonia Film. She then studied at the Academy of Theatre and Film Art, and began to mix live-action with animation in her films.

It Could Happen in Budapest; If..., 1970; Gombnyomasra/Push Button, 1973; Nem igaz!/It Cannot be True, 1974; Nekem az elet teccik nagyon/I Think Life's Great Fun, 1978; Children's Rights, 1978; Aunt Lenke, 1980; Our Feasts, 1982; Family Picture, 1983; Another Planet, 1986; The Cricket and the Ant, 1988; Vision, 1988.

Mattuschka, Mara Austria

An experimental painter and artist, some of whose films relate strongly to performance and body art e.g. in which her own body, painted black and white is manipulated via animation techniques.

Has made over twenty films, some grant-aided by arts agencies; *Der Einzug des Rokoko ins Inselreich der Huzzis* is a feature length avant-garde film incorporating animation, made in collaboration with Hans Werner Poschanko and Andy Karner; *Loading Ludwig* also uses animation and features herself as lead performer.

Cerolax 1; Gebet; Vegetarisches Restaurant, 1983; Leibesgeschichten; Moody Blues; Nabelfabel; Cerolax 2; Grsse aus Wien; Kugelkopf; Untergang der Titania; Begegnungen der Vierten Art, 1985; Parasympathica; Pascal Goedel; Rosa Alexander; Schule der Ausschweifung, 1986; Es Hat Mich Sehr Gefreut; Les Miserables; Kaiserschnitt; Mein Kampf; Musikerinnen, 1987.

Mayo, Nina   France

Le Desert Chante, 1957 (co-d Arie Mambouch); Le Cercle, 1958; Le Tapis Volant, 1959; L'Arbre, 1961; Les Six Jours de la Création, 1962.

Maxwell, Stephanie   US

Maxwell studied film (not animation) at San Francisco Art Insitute where she was inspired by Larry Jordan's methodology; her first aniamtion film was inspired by a screening of Len Lye's work and a documentaray about him. Her interst in his work, and writings, has continued, as she has developed her techniques of scratching on film to incorporate other forms. Ga uses paint, scratching and collage directly onto film to create abstract designs and animal motifs, inspired by prehistoric cave paintings; with recorded music from Ghana. *Please Don't Stop* is a study in movement and time, with a number of colourful direct-to-film techniques: airbrush, stencils, chemical reactions and more. Her current project, Where are We Going? is an ambitious attempt to involve the viewer in constructing the film's meaning, incorporating almost subliminally some live-action imagery and text on childhood by Len Lye. She travels frequently between the US and Europe, where she often gives workshops, and curates animation programmes.

Ga 1982; Please Don't Stop, 1988.

Menken, Marie   US

This prominent member of the first generation of underground filmmakers was born in Brooklyn in a Catholic home of Lithuanian parents. She died in Brooklyn in 1970 at the age of 61.

She studied at the New York School of Fine and Industrial Arts and at the Arts Students' League. She worked as an assistant to the Curator of the Guggenheim Foundation (which later became the museum) and helped establish a film library of experimental films. During the war she worked as an artist and technician for the Army Signal Corps, creating special effects for training and war documentary films, building miniatures and dioramas used in the films, and shooting footage. After the war she went to work at *Time* as a copy typist and then as a cable editor from 1946 until 1969.

As a child she had a looped toy projector and she made flip books out of the corners of her textbooks. When she painted, she used a wide variety of materials to introduce texture and unusual lighting effects into her work, including stone chips, stone powders, marble chips, marble dust, ground silicate, sand, cement dust, luminous paints, glass particles, glues and lacquers, string, fibre, glitters, and glass beads.

Her paintings were exhibited in Brooklyn Museum and the Baltimore Museum of Art as well as in New York galleries. At one of her showings, she exhibited luminous paintings. The gallery was blacked out. The pictures had day faces and night faces. They took on another life in the dark and were a sequel in theme to the pictures in the light.

An animator friend, leaving for the Army, left Menken and her spouse, Willard Maas, a pawn ticket for his 16mm camera. Film light became a new avenue of exploration for her. As a painter of some experience, she could frame immediately, with no deliberation of arrangement. In filmmaking she thought of every frame as a picture. Her films are characterised by a unique use of light and motion, and have in common a lyric lightness and a love for jolting visual rhythms. Her diversified background led to a variety of films: portraits, diaries, fantasies, and time-lapse studies.

She did volunteer work for other filmmakers e.g. for Maya Deren she animated the chess sequence in *At Land* and plotted the moving constellations in *Very Eye of Night*.

She also acted in Willard Maas's *Image in the Snow* and *Narcissus*, Dov Lederberg's *Eargogh* and the Warhold-Ronald Tavel *Life of Juanita Castro*, in which it was said of her acting, 'Marie's genius saved the whole proceeding'. She organised Gryphon Films to distribute independently-made films, which led to and influenced Cinema 16 and the cooperatives that now handle most avant-garde film in the United States. In the preface to the second edition of his classic book Visionary Cinema - The American Avant-garde , P. Adams Sitney writes, 'Marie Menken's work deserves a chapter, not the brief passing reference I gave it in *The Lyrical Film*. But five years ago I did not understand how crucial her teasingly simple films were in their dialogue of camera eye and nature - the central theme of this book.'

Stan Brakhage writes that in 1956 Menken's *Visual Variations on Noguchi* was the first film he had ever seen which not only admitted but capitalized on the fact that the camera was hand-held. The influence of Hollywood was such that even the most individual filmmakers would try to make 'smooth' pans, dollies, etc., even though they were for reasons for economy, forced to accomplish this with hand-held equipment. 'As to *Hurry! Hurry!* it was difficult at that time to even consider images which couldn't somehow be related to ordinary visual perception, being as we all, even unconsciously, were influenced by the Old Documentarianism.' (SB) It was not just that Menken used microscopic footage, or even that she superimposed it with flames, but that she employed these images in such a strictly personalised manner, charging them with her own most individual psycho-drama, that *Hurry! Hurry!* occurs on the screen with the authenticity of documentation of her inner spirit in a way far more successfully than the psycho-dramas which Brakhage attempted similarly to document by using actual people reenacting their experiences.

Brakhage says that he got the courage to actually scratch the eyes off the film-base in *Reflections on Black* the same month after he met Willard Maas and Marie Menken and saw their work. He goes on to say, 'McLaren, for instance, could never have so encouraged me because the line, with

him, whether scratched or drawn on film or otherwise, is a means to an end, an ego-centred finality which his work calls forth from the audience. Marie's line, whether painted, scratched, animated or not, is as unpresumptuous as that of a stalk growing, and fascinates for the same reason, because of its unpredictable formality. (It is no wonder McLaren admires her work because a McLaren feeds off the growing process, being incapable of them himself).'

Marie Menken and Willard Maas could be described as the godparents of avant-garde cinema in the United States. Like Frank Stauffacher and Maya Deren, they encouraged and listened to, often fed and housed the new wave of filmmakers who were to be the mainstays of the 'new American cinema' of the 1950s and 1960s. Most important of all was the impact of their films: Willard Mass's *Geography of the Body* (1943), shot by Menken, continues to be a landmark work, the poetry of which, forty-five years later, still fascinates and challenges audiences. Marie Menken's films never became as well-known, but they had an even greater impact on the filmmakers who constituted much of their audience. (MB)

Marie Menken is a lyrical poet, The structure of Menken's filmic sentences, her movements and her rhythms, are those of poetry...Menken sings...She catches the bits and fragments of the world around her and organises them into aesthethic unities which communicate her to us. Her filmic language and her imagery are crisp, clear, wondrous...She retains a visual memory of all that she sees. She recreates moments of observation, of meditation, reflection, wonderment. A rain that she sees, a tender rain, becomes the memory of all rains she ever saw; a garden that she sees becomes a memory of all gardens, all colour, all perfume, all midsummer and sun. We are invited to a communion, we break our wills, we dissolve ourselves into the flow of her images, we experience admittance into the santuary of Menken's soul. We sit in silence and we take part in her seecret thoughts, admirations, ecstasies, and we become more beautiful ourselves. She puts a smile in our hearts...There are poets who are only beginning to sing. You see their clumsy

sentences, vague or muddy imagery, unsure movements. Gropingly, searchingly they move across the screen. Marie Menken's work is evenly finished and mature. There are very few unfinished or unsure lines in her language. (Jonas Mekas, in *Village Voice*, 4.1.62)

Dwightiana, 1959; Visual variations on Noguchi; Hurry! Hurry! Hurry!; Glimpse of the Garden; Eye Music in Red Major; Arabesque for Kenneth Anger; Bagatelle for Willard Mass; Notebook; Mood Mondrian; Andy Warhol; Wrestling; Moonplay; Drips in Strips, 1961; Go Go Go, 1962-4; Sidewalks, 1966; Excursion; Watts with Eggs.

Meske, Ellen   Holland

Born in Los Angeles in 1952 and studied Fine Arts at the University of Southern California. She moved to Holland in 1976. Apart from the films cited below, she has made three series of animated cartoons for Dutch TV, and a series with Monique Renault and Jochgem van Dijk about animation workshops with children.

In nomine Domini; Long Live the Sexual Revolution, 1981 (both co-d Monique Renault).

Millsapps, Jan   US

Is now teaching live action filmmaking in San Francisco.

Family Dream, 1980; Composition 321/ State Highway Pendulum; Folly Beach Journal, 1981; True Romance, 1984.

Moore, Sandy   US

'I am an artist in film, with special interest in experimental animation and special effects. Other concerns of mine include: structure and timing of images (specifically, how a moving image commands attention, outside of narrative modes), film as analogue for mental states and thought processes, and image/sound, image/word relations.'

After a degree and postgraduate studies in film at Yale, she co-founded Videofrontiers, a video and sound facility which provided services to community groups and performing artists, and since then has taught animation, (at one point with Robert Breer), video and filmmaking. Her own art work has been partly financed by grants from arts funding bodies. Her work includes

A - Z

installations, and she has had several one woman and group shows. *Lives of Firecrackers* is probably her most accessible film, in which a bunch of firecrackers amusingly discuss their neuroses, with the aid of Handel's music and Wittgenstein's philosophy, sorting themselves into five personality types ranging from the Erotic to the Paranoid. The films made between 1982-5, are part of an 'aggregate or family of films composed around excerpts from Gertrude Stein's *Tender Buttons*. In this work I am investigating new relationships of drawings to the camera; therefore I have been designing and building special animation camera setups - two multiplane cameras (one room-sized, one a table-top model), a fluid/pivoting animation stand, and a counterweighted camera on a large armature. I have also been re-tooling projectors to extend their capacities beyond the 24 frames per second norms. As these experiments bear fruit, and point my way, I fold them into the multi-partite film project.'

'Sandy Moore was represented with composer Neil Rolnick in the 1985 Whitney Museum of Art Biennial, by her film installation piece *What is the Use*. She constructed a mechanical projector designed like a bicycle that was activated by her pedalling, the frames of her animated film moved through the projector gate and past the beam of light according to the rate at which she pedalled. As in her earlier films such as *Luck in Loose Plaster*, Moore emphasised the handmade quality of her work by means of animated films composed of sequences of imagery either drawn or re-photographed from found footage. Moore's aesthetic is informed by the processes of her medium and by her efforts to understand the world through the study of science. *Reverse Transcriptease* is based on the molecular configuration of the HIV virus. Each frame of the film is composed of an image representing a unit of the DNA compound. The film is the artist's virtuoso representation of science's mathematical transcription of the virus. Moore uses various found images from her own drawings as well as old cartoons to portray a world out of joint, reconstituting itself in flickering images at a vertiginous pace.' John Hanhardt, Whitney Biennial curator.
Lives of Firecrackers, 1979; Luck in Loose Plaster; Gawrsh, I Didn't Know You Were a Lady, 1983; What is the Use, 1985; Reverse Transcriptease, 1991.

Morse, Deanna   US
Graduated from art school, followed by graduate studies in art and technology and film. Deanna Morse's creative trajectory is interesting for the way her teaching work has interacted with her filmmaking and activities in the animation field, as well as her wide range of experience. She is a columnist for *Animation* magazine, has produced for *Sesame Street*, worked for industry, scripted for TV drama. From 1974-8 she worked on the South Carolina Arts Commission's innovative film and education programme, including a teaching stint at the SC School for the Deaf and Blind. She is now teaching computer animation, media production, film theory and history at Grand Valley State University, and is currently developing an interactive computer animation teaching module on basic animation concepts.

Her films are financed by a number of funding agencies, and use a variety of techniques, cut-out, ceramics, markers on card, and computer animation. A recurrent theme, and formal interest, has been memory and home movies, which she manipulates in different ways, including optical printing.

'My early work was a series of visual explorations, followed by a series of films made for children. Then I explored regional themes and memory, based on my life and work as a filmmaker-in-the-schools in the South. My most recent work is around three issues: domesticity and concepts of home, significant visual symbols (including American Sign Language) and the use of computer imagery in our culture.

My newest piece integrates sign language, computer and object animation. For this piece I was able to use a newly developed technology called 'the data glove', a device which replaces a mouse, joystick or keyboard. Wearing the glove, I spoke in American sign language. The computer recorded my gestures as data which then drew a computer modelled hand.'
Déjeuner, Mon Amour (l/a); Colour Field Study, 1970; Marriages (l/a), 1971; 10; Constant Constance, 1972; The Midnight Dance, 1975; Sunny Sunday; Cats at the Door; Flip Film; Ranky Tanky (co-d Jane DeKoven); Jimmy Brown the Newsboy; Starcycle, 1978; Charleston Home Movie, 1980; Help I'm Stranded, 1981; Reality Check, 1981 (co-d Chuck Peterson, Jon Yazell); Hand, 1982; Camera People, 1985; August Afternoons, 1985 (both l/a); The Lumberyard, 1987; Mainstream M, 1988; Artist in the Schools (l/a); Plants, 1989; The A.M. Dream, 1990; Sand Doll (video install., animation and construction); Self Portrait: Artist with Pets, (ditto),1991: Sandpaintings; Lost Ground, 1992.

Mouris, Carolina   US
Collaborated with husband Frank Mouris, co-directed their live action films.
Impasse, 1972; Frank Film, 1973; Screentest; Coney, 1975; LA, LA, Making it in LA, 1979; Tennessee Sampler, 1977.

Neubauer, Vera   GB
See pp. 89-92, and ß.
Genetics; Animation Allegation; Cannon Fodder,1970-2; Pip and Bessie (series of 6 animated shorts), 1973-5; Fate, 1976; Animation for Live Action, 1978; The Decision, 1981; The World of Children, 1984; Mid Air, 1986; The Mummy's Curse, 1987; Passing On, 1989.

Oraczewska, Zofia   Poland
Probably the most prolific female Polish animator, who made over twenty-five films between 1961 and 1980, many of them oriented to adult audiences, and charcerised by mordant humour. *Banquet* has been described as a 'cheek in tongue (sic) satire in which the food eats the guests.' (PW)
inc. The Thirteenth Sheep, 1965; Banquet, 1976; Pictures from the Life of Insects; Flight of the Bumble Bee, 1980.

Page, Marcy   US
Paradisia, a multi-award winning film which deals graphically with female sexuality and desire, is the only personal film yet made by Page, an extremely prolific animator in commercials, TV spots, educational films, feature fim credits and inserts, who also taught animation history and technique for over ten years in San Francisco State University. Since 1990 she has been working on another personal project, whilst

working for the National Film Board of Canada on a range of co-productions. Working in collaboration with celebrated sound and music composer Normand Lepage and provisionally entitled *Waves*, the film uses the Greek story of Thetis and Peli to comment on modern relationships, alternating male and female points of view, and looking at how those are culturally determined.
Paradisia, 1987.

Panushka, Christine   US

Currently Associate Dean at Cal Arts' School of Film and Video, she has worked as a wide-ranging freelance animator, from rock videos to Hanna Barbera. Her personal films have been financed from a variety of funding agencies, and explore mythical and humanist themes. She is also an accomplished and exhibited artist (oils, computer painting, etching and printmaking); designs and illustrates books, and creates original jewellery that displays antique and ethnic works of gemstone and ceramics.

Her films often use simple line drawings, such as *The Sum of Them*, in which 'simply drawn portraits stare at the camera. Some wear clown-like make-up and some wear surreal body adornments. Their images are intercut with words: gait, flank, joint, breath, pulse, cleave, strain, enclose. Sprinkled over the all the images are familiar but subdued sounds - whispering, running water, birds chirping...in the film's penultimate image all the portraits are put together in one composition. The result is a delicate word/image/sound poem composing discrete elements of sensory awareness into an experience of human fulfilment'. 'A completely original work of art. At once sensuous and cerebral, it expresses the complex mystery of womankind with great poetry, compassion and beauty. There is a quiet power to these spare images and soft sounds, a mysterious erotic tension between word and gesture. An elegaic work of masterful restraint and haunting resonance...the film places Ms. Panushka in the front rank of contemporary animation.' Gene Youngblood. *Nighttime Fears* features delicate Edward Lear-like figures moving in a fluid dream simulation of a young girl's fantasy world, 'weaving mythical mon-

sters and dream conjured humans to touch the edges we've always - never wanted to touch'. M. Osoff.
Night's Last Child, 1978; The Birth and Death of Dimetre Poptrovich, 1980; Bioumenos, 1981; The Sum of Them, 1983; Nighttime Fears and Fantasies: A Bedtime Tale for a Young Girl,1986; (collab: Marilyn Osoff) Epilogue; Os Antiquity; Female Auto/Serious Experiences,1992.

Parker, Claire   France

American-born Claire Parker is credited with encouraging and collaborating with husband Alexieff to pursue his development of pin-screen techniques in animation, and they worked together on the films produced this way.
La Nuit sur le Mont Chauve/Night on a Bare Mountain (co-d Alexandre Alexeieff);La Belle au Bois Dormant/Sleeping Beauty (only puppet film), 1934; En Passant, 1942; many commercials; Le Nez/The Nose, 1963; Pictures at an Exhibition, 1972; Trois Themes/Three Moods, 1980.

Parker, Kayla   GB

Experimental animation and video filmmaker, whose work uses a range of techniques (including live-action), and often explores autobiographical themes. After art school, where she went on to specialise in video and performance art, she joined the South Wales Women's Film Group and Chapter Film Workshop (a centre for independent film and video with a strong animation tradition until its closure in the late 80s). In the 80s, has been very active as 'animateur', running courses, workshops in animation, video and filmmaking, particularly with the young and elderly. Based in the southwest, currently in Plymouth, she has produced a fair number of her own films - usually on tiny budgets, with some aid from funding bodies, both national and local, as well as bringing an innovative approach to television commissions. The autobiographically inspired films are *Adult Day Return*, *Lighter Hands* 'in memory of my grandfather's death and his musical cigarette lighter, using frottage, montage, echoes of poetic remembrance, repetitive action, life extinguished.'

'As an artist I've chosen animation because of its unlimited possibilities. Animation to me is about movement and change, the potential for manipulation of image and sound at 24 frames a second. Animation combines all the things I do, writing, drawing, sound composition, and so on. It's also a very physical medium, and has become an integral part of my life. Events that happen, the way I'm feeling, all quite naturally affect my work, so there is a strong autobiographical element. This is more apparent in my own films, but is also present in commissioned pieces - title sequences for instance - for television.
Animation-making is my way of finding meaning, giving sense, to my life and myself as a woman. The ingredients for my work come directly from my notebooks, which are a creative record of ideas, images, dreams, memories. I've kept notebooks in one form or another since childhood, and they are the most constant, continuous element in my life.
The techniques I use in filmmaking originate from my early work in performance art, using notebook material as a basic source, automatic drawing and writing, improvisation, chance and found elements. The final form of the work evolves organically from the creative and technical process of its making.
I am not particularly interested in making humorous, animated comic strips, and I have a fundamental abhorrence of authoritarian structures. I am much more concerned with developing methods of filmmaking which are individual, collaborative, spontaneous. The outreach work I do in the community is an important part of what I do. As a filmmaker, one of the most directly political acts I can make, is to go into a school and enable a group of kids to devise and make their own film. I believe that art, ideas, and the means of production should be accessible to all.
The earliest influences on my work must be, in childhood, the pictures by Cézanne and Van Gogh that my mother cut out of magazines, and stuck onto the kitchen cupboards; also Betty Boop in flickering black and white. As I got older my influences were more literary.
Until recently, I was most familiar with the work of other filmmaker/animators through books. I've been inspired by reading about

A - Z

their ideas - Robert Breer, for example - rather than actually seeing the films.

I've only seen two films by Vera Neubauer - both in a cinema - but the impact of those films remains quite strong, even after several years. Another animator whose work I find interesting is Jane Aaron. Both women make films from a particularly personal standpoint, are innovative, and challenge dominant modes of thinking and perception. This is the kind of work that I feel is closest to my own.

Being an experimental animator based so far from London, on the 'western edge' of Europe, I'm not sure how what I do fits into the British animation scene in general. Most of the interest in my films has come from outside England - Germany, Hungary, Scotland, for example.

However, I keep in regular contact with a number of other women animators in Britain. We're very interested in, and supportive of, each other's work, although we're all pretty spread out across the country and don't meet up very often. I do feel part of this informal network of independent women animators which exists in Britain. I am an artist whose chosen art form is animation. I'm self-taught, I run a business - charge VAT and so on - and my 'product' is experimental animation. I've been self-employed since 1988, and the creative independence I have does mean that it is a struggle, even to make films on low budgets. For instance, I haven't bought a new pair of shoes for two years. My business has to make a profit if I am to survive. Animation is how I earn my living, and the most important thing for me is to continue making films.

Adult Day Return, 1986; The Internal Voice; Out of the Box, 1988; Lighter Hands; Looks Familiar; Gallery, 1989; Nuclear Family; Fanny & Johnny on Acid, 1990; Tongue & Groove; Unknown Woman, 1991; Puirt-a-beul; Cage of Flame; Canntaireachd, 1992.

Pasos en la Niebla   Spain
Collective of women.
Femme attendant dans un hotel/Woman Waiting in a Hotel, 1983; Galeria Noctune, 1984; El Tratado de Odessa, 1985.

Pavlatova, Michaela   Czech
Studied graphics and illustration, and ani-

mation at art school in Prague. All her films deal wittily with (mis)communication between people. They share the same graphic style throughout, though it has become more refined and adventurous. In *Situations From Everyday Life* an elderly couple, discuss via visual expression their thoughts and opinions, each trying to convince the other of their point of view to no avail. *Crossword Puzzle* was originally intended as part of a trilogy: the wife seeks to get her husband's attention, but he is deeply immersed in his favourite hobby, doing crosswords. Her ever more desperate ploys simply provide him with inspiration for his solutions. She earns living through films, book illustrations, and exhibitions of paintings. She wants to alternate films with painting and book illustration work, which are free from hassles of film production.
Etuda z Alba, 1988; Situations From Everyday Life; Krizovika/The Crossword Puzzle, 1989; Reci, Reci, Reci/Words, Words, Words, 1991).

Perlman, Janet   Canada
Comic Strip, 1972; Man of Might; Chicken, 1975; The Bulge (Poets on Film); From the Hazel Bough (Poets on Film), 1977; Lady Fishbourne's Complete Guide to Better Table Matters, 1976; co-d Derek Lamb: Why Me, 1978; Pep Talk, 1979; A Tender Tale of Cinderella Penguin, 1982; seq. Anijam, 1984.

Peters, Maybelle GB
Born and brought up in Ealing, West London, Maybelle is one of the UK's very few Black women animators. From her earliest years she loved to draw and paint and refused to consider doing anything else. She discovered animation through TV programmes like *Mary, Mungo and Midge* and *Vision On*, and decided that was what she wanted to do. After foundation, where she concentrated on painting and sculpture, she did an animation degree at WSCAD. While still at college she made her mark with *A Lesson in History*: text, music, and haunting aerial imaging revise traditional British history, as told in schools, to one of colonial slavery and the strength of Black resistance. Developed out of a college brief then commissioned by BBC Bristol's

David Rose for the *10x10* series. Having to make her first film for broadcast and to a deadline gave Maybelle added confidence for her future work. *Black Skins, White Masks,* her graduation film, was inspired by Fanon's book of the same title. Her latest project, in development is *Mama Lou.* Made in 3-D, using caricatural puppets, a technique she hasn't worked with before, *Mama Lou* (named after the famous 1880s Black American brothel singer) is a tale of myth and superstition told across generations: for two hundred years a group of Black women run a jazz and blues basement club underneath their kitchen. Although her work focuses on her experience as a Black woman in Britain, she sees animation as means of personal expression. She is part of the second wave of independent Black British filmmakers, but her unique choice of animation as medium offers her even greater independence to do what she wants in the way that she wants to do it. As she says 'I hate labels anyway.' (KA)
A Lesson in History, 1990; Black Skins, White Masks, 1991.

Petty, Sara US
Her films tend to play with metamorphosis, and dimensional form, with an art history feel. Teaches animation. *Furies:* has been described as both a study in movement and composition and a projection in imagination of the mysterious consciousness, that is other than human'. On *Preludes in Magical Time* she has said: 'These forms originated in a dream I had in which I swam in an undersea library, pulled out large drawers and found thousands of cloisonne shapes like these. Each fit together with any other, form a relationship, whether harmonious or conflicted, but a relationship nonetheless. When flipped, they showed other, hidden aspects of their relationship.'
Shadrack, 1976; Furies, 1977; Picture Window, 1986; Preludes in Magical Time, 1987; contribution to Pink Concommer.

Peyser, Ruth
Another Great Day, 1980 (co-d Jo Bonney); Random Positions, 1983; One Nation under TV, 1985 (solo).

Philpot, Eloise   US
Offers glimpses of city folk and locales that rarely appear in animated films.
Subway People, 1978.

Pitt, Suzan US
See pp. 57-61; 71-75, and ß.
Bowl Theatre Marble Game, 1969; Cels; Crocus, 1971; A City Trip; Cels, 1972; Jefferson Circus Songs; Whitney Museum commercial, 1973; Asparagus, 1978; Bam Video, 1991.

Pospisolova, Vlasta   Czech
Born 1935. Studied puppetry and set design at Prague School of Applied Arts. She worked as commercial artist, then got the one post advertised to work on Trnka's *Midsummer Night's Dream*, for which she animated the crowd scenes, and Titania's sequence with the glow worms. Worked on other Trnka films. Latal's *Adventures of Robinson Crusoe, The Sailor from York*, and Jiri Barta's *The Pied Piper*, and also on Svankmajer's films. Co-director on classic style puppet film, with Edgar Dutka: Maryshka and the Wolf's Castle. The films she has directed herself are in the tradition of Trnka stle puppet animation, but also have a sharp sense of humour.
Lady Poverty (Pani Bida), 1983. More fairy tales. Mean Barka (Larkoma Barka) from Jan Werich's book of fairy tales. After the Oak Shed Its Leaves/Az opada listi z dubu, 1991.

Praglowski, Susanne   Austria
Experimental animator, working with mixed media, e.g. the yarn-animated *Garn*.
Bett, 1985; Sand, 1987; Fisch; Garn, 1989.

Priestley, Joanna US
See pp. 54; 66- 69; 71-15. Has also designed/animated for music videos, including: Joni Mitchell's *Good Friends* (1985) and Tears for Fears' *Sowing the Seeds of Love* (1988) and segments for Sesame Street.
collab: Lotus Feet,1980; The Rubber Stamp Film, 1983; Voices; Dancing Bullrushes; Jade Leaf, 1985; Times Square, 1986; Candy Jam, 1987 (co-d with Joan Gratz); She-Bop, 1988; All My Relations, 1990; After the Fall, 1991; Hand Held, 1992.

Ramli, Yasmine   GB
Since post-graduate degrees from Croydon College of Art and the RCA, has worked on commercials, TV credit sequences, working in model animation. One of the first recipients of the Arts Council/C4 awards to make the idiosyncratic Naked in which a man embarks on a journey, his destination a woman living in a tower-block on the other side of town. Following him is a mythical window-cleaner whose flying gantry takes us through the city. She is currently animating models of the 'Fat Slags' from Viz magazine.
Thy Kingdom Come, 1989; Naked, 1992.

Reiniger, Lotte   Germany
1919-1979
Silhouette animation existed before 1919, but Reiniger is its preeminent practitioner, transforming a technically and aesthetically bland genre to a recognized art form, albeit a minor one.
Reiniger's professional life was wholeheartedly devoted to silhouette animation, with an occasional retreat to shadow plays or book illustrations when money was not available for films.
Prominent among Lotte Reiniger's talents was her transcendence of the inherent flatness and awkwardness of silhouette animation through her dramatic mise-en-scène and her balletic movements. Her female characters are especially lively and original, displaying wit, sensuousness and self-awareness rarely found in animated cartoons. Few real-life actresses could match the expressiveness with which Reiniger inspired the gestures of her lead-jointed figures as she moved and filmed them fraction by fraction, frame by frame.
For over four decades, Lotte Reiniger shared her professional life with her husband, Carl Koch, who designed her animation studio and, until his death in 1963, served as her producer and camera operator.
Aside from *The Adventures of Prince Achmed*, Reiniger ventured into feature filmmaking only once, in *Running After Luck*, the story of a wandering showman, part animation and part live-acting, which she co-directed with Rochus Gliese. It was a critical and financial failure, perhaps

because of its imperfect sound system. The rest of her films were shorts, mainly one or two reels in length.
Lotte Reiniger worked outside commercial channels, with minimal support. She said she never felt discrimination because she was a woman, but she did admit resenting that great sums were spent on films of little or no imagination while so little was available for the films she wanted to make.
Hans Richter, who know Reiniger in the early Berlin years, later wrote that she 'belonged to the avant-garde as far as independent production and courage were concerned,' but that the spirit of her work seemed Victorian. Jean Renoir placed her even further back in time, as a 'visual expression of Mozart's music.' It is more likely that, like the fables and myths and fairy tales on which many of her films are based, her work transcends time and fashion. (CS)
Der Rattenfänger von Hameln/Pied Piper of Hamelin (title vignettes only - d: Paul Wegener); Das Ornament des verliebten Herzens/The Ornament of the Loving Heart, 1919; Der verlorene Schatten (silhouettes only); Der Amor und das standhafte Liebespaar, 1920; Der Stern von Bethlehem, Der fliegende Koffer, 1921; Aschenputtel; Dornröschen, 1922; Die Geschichte des Prinzen Achmed/The Adventures of Prince Achmed (Die Abenteuer des Prinzen Achmed, Wak-Wak, ein Mächenzauber), 1923-26; Doktor Dolittle und seine Tiere/The Adventures of Dr. Dolittle (3 shorts: Abenteuer: Die Reise nach Afrika; Abenteuer: Die Affenbrücke; Abenteuer: Die Affenkrankheit); Der scheintote Chinese, 1928; Die Jagd nach dem Glück/Running After Luck (silhouette segment within l/a film), 1929-30; Zehn Minuten Mozart, 1930; Harlekin/Harlequin, 1931; Sissi, 1932; Carmen; Don Quichotte (opening silhouettes only - d: Pabst), 1933; Das rollende Rad; Das gestohlene Herz/The Stolen Heart; Der Graf von Carabas, 1934; Papageno; Galathea Kalif Starch ; Der kleine Schornsteinfeger/The Little Chimney Sweep, 1935; Silhouetter; The King's Breakfast, 1936; The Tocher, 1937: La Marseillaise (d: Jean Renoir) (shadowplay within l/a film), 1938; Dream Circus (unfinished); L'Elisir d'Amore (not re-

A - Z

Golden Goose (unfinished), 1944; in Great Britain: Greetings Telegrams; Post Early for Christmas; Radiolizenz; The Daughter; Mary's Birthday, 1949; Aladdin; Magic Horse; Snow White and Rose, 1953; The Three Wishes; The Grasshopper and the Ant; The Frog Prince; The Gallant Little Tailor; The Sleeping Beauty; Caliph Storch, 1954; Hansel and Gretel; Thumbelina; Jack and the Beanstalk , 1955; The Star of Bethlehem, 1956; Helen la Belle, 1957; The Seraglio (interludes for theatrical performances), 1958; The Pied Piper of Hamelin, 1960; The Frog Prince, 1961; Wee Sandy, 1962; Cinderella, 1963; The Lost Son, 1974; Aucassin and Nicolette, 1976; The Rose and the Ring, 1979. Puss-in-Boots, 195?

Renault, Monique Belgium

See pp. 76-78, and ß. Born in France, studied art in Paris, then animation in Prague in 1966 before working in advertising and industrial films with Peter Foldes, and the aaa studio in Paris. In 1976 she went to work in Holland then took Dutch nationality.

El CondoPasa,1971; Psychoderche,1972; A la Votre,1975; Swiss Graffiti,1976 (co-d J Veuve); Salut Marie, 1978; Border Line, 1983; Long Live the Sexual Revolution; In Nomine Domini; Weg Ermee, 1984; Bas les Pattes/Keep Your Hands Off Me, 1985; Teken Film Club,1986; All Men Are Created Equal, 1987; Pas a Deux, 1988 (co-d Gerrit van Dijk).

Rimminen, Marjut   GB

See pp. 37-39. Born 1944, in Finland. After studies in graphic design, she got a government grant to study animation in the UK (as there were no courses in Finland), but was rejected at her preferred colleges. So she began working in commercials in Helsinki, and within 9 months had her own agency, and for the next 5 years was one of the most successful creative and art directors in the industry. A sudden change in holiday plans left her at a loose end one summer, and her brother told her about an animation festival in Bulgaria. She spent the next week watching animation from morning until midnight and came back to Finland determined to make animation films herself. A chance meeting on the street with a friend looking for ideas for a

commercial led to Marjut storyboarding for an animation. Accepted by the agency with enthusiasm, she then had to teach herself to animate to actually make it. The result, an ad for a bubble bath product was banned from TV until it won an award at the Zagreb Festival. (N.B. for filmography buffs: as she was still working for a rival company products, she had to use a pseudonym for this film, *Vivante*). Halas & Batchelor offered her a job some time later, but she stayed only three months, finding it difficult to adjust to their production methods and Disneyfied style. For the next ten years she made a good living making commercials for Finland from her London studio. Commercial work and family life left no time for pursuing personal films. Another chance meeting in the street with Christine Roche, who she'd met at H&B, led to their collaboration on an animated version of Roche's cartoon book, *I'm Not a Feminist, But...*, plus other women animators on the series *Blind Justice*, about women and the law. She again collaborated with Roche on *The Stain*. She continues to enjoy alternating commercial work, which allows continuous play with, and development of, different techniques, with her own projects. With *The Stain*, she used models and puppets for the first time and is keen to explore 3-D further. Her current project is a ten minute film about the home, which will be filmed in a redundant kitchen in her own house.

The Bridge, 1982; Ordnance Survey Maps; 13-19: Pimples, 1984; I'm Not a Feminist, But..., 1985; Some Protection, 1988; The Frog King, 1989; The Stain, 1991.

Ringborn, Antonia   Finland

Began making childrens' films for TV in 1969, like most women in Scandianvian animaton. Uses cutouts, which has become quite a tradition amongst women animators (possibly related to the lack of training opportunities, until very recently, in animation). 'For me, this playing with small pieces of paper (or celluloid) is very exciting. You can improvise, create new details, contacts between the figures, during the shooting. It's not so boring as drawing thousands of cels.' She has just completed her third personal film, *To Walk on a Tightrope*, mixing live-action and animation, about 'being in-between child-

adult, dreaming alone, laughing together.' Her first independent film was about foreigners and refugees coming to Finland. Funded by Finnish Film Foundation, Cultural Ministry and TV.

Inc. Potato Island, 1986; To Walk on a Tightrope, 1991.

Roche, Christine GB

See pp. 37-39. A French-Canadian who has been living in Britain for twenty years, working as an illustrator and feminist cartoonist.

I'm Not a Feminist, But..., 1985 (co-d Marjut Rimminen); Someone Must Be Trusted, 1987 (co-d Gillian Lacey); Criminal Justice (co-d MR); Some Protection, 1988; The Stain, 1991 (co-d Christine Roche).

Rose, Kathy   US

See pp. 62-64, and ß.

'Through their simplified line drawings and bright splashes of colour, they refer to cartoon traditions, while at the same time they explore the self-referential strategies of modern art to fragment illusion and underline the presence of the artist, and the complex relationship between the artist and her creation. With rare candour, Rose charts her own artistic and spiritual journey through these encounters. *The Doodlers* sketches the themes that will be further elaborated in *Pencil Booklings*, through her basic cast of line-drawn characters. From the moment that they are created by the artist's hand wielding a 'magic brush', it is clear that *The Doodlers* have minds of their own; in response to Rose's comment 'It's very pretty', one character disagrees: 'I don't like it.' From this inauspicious beginning, the film moves through all varieties of the mutable relationship between the artist and the art - as experienced and reflected upon by the artist - until, at the end, the artist dives head first into the sheet of paper on her drafting table, metamorphosising into a witch, as the moon circles repeatedly through her fragmented skull.

In *Pencil Booklings* the integration of artist and art is extended still further. Rotoscoping herself, Rose distinguishes the artist from the other characters as belonging to another order of being. Yet later in the film, Rose too becomes a caricatured line-drawn character when one of her characters challenges her to give up the outsider's position (i.e. the naturalistic rotoscoped depiction), by saying 'If you really want to make good cartoons, you have to be in one first.' With these words, doors fly open to nowhere, the 'magic brush' crosses in front of her face, and the rotoscoped Kathy Rose metamorphoses into an infinite recession of concentric eyes, within which her characters appear and disappear. After returning to her realistic self again with a flick of the 'magic brush' the film ends, as once again Rose transforms into a cartoon character, with her characters growing out of all sides of her - like the magical children of her imagination that they are. The constantly shifting spatial parameters of the film, the uncertain boundaries between the artist and her characters, the surreal elasticity of their bodies, and the unpredictable interactions between the frame, the canvas and the screen - all parallel the mutations and flux of the intrapsychic creative processes.

Through focussing on the relationships among the characters and between the artist and the characters, Rose in these personal diaries of creation is sharing her thought processes, courageously exposing the hesitancies and the risks as well as the joys of creation. Through the apparently innocuous surfaces of the film, she shares the painful battles of artistic struggle, battles which take place deep within the imagination and which Rose is one of the few to articulate. (TS)

Portraits, 1971; Movers; Women, 1972; The Mysterians, 1973; Moon Show, 1974; The Mirror People; The Arts Circus, 1974; The Doodlers, 1975; Rubber Cement; Pencil Booklings, 1978; seq. for Anijam, 1985.

Russell, Erica   GB
Born in Auckland, New Zealand, in 1951, her family moved to South Africa in 1953. She was 19 when she came to London. She has had no formal training in art or animation. She started her career with Richard Williams' studio in paint and trace and worked her way up. In 1975 she became assistant to Art Babbit and then progressed to assistant animator to Gerald Scarfe and Paul Vester. Her first big break came when she directed a 60 second Virgin Mega Store commercial which was shown on the BBC's

Arts Review programme. *Feet of Song* was begun in her own time and on her own resources, and given completion money by C4; it is a stunning celebration of African song and dance with stylised graphics which draw on Russian Futurism, with specially composed music by Charlie Hart and Gasper Lawal. Since then she has worked on commercials for German television and on pop promos which have included doing the animation for the instrumental breaks for artists such as Madonna, Elton John and Jean-Michel Jarre. She is currently working on an 8 minute film for C4: ten musicians are composing a piece of world music with a strong African and South American influence - the vocals will be sung by Samba Mapangala, Kenya's top recording artist. She describes the film as a ballet opera.

Sabnani, Nina   India
See p.103. In addition to the films described previously, *All About Nothing* was a new departure, using model animation, with extremely limited resources. A charming and imaginative fantasy about the 'discovery' of the number zero, with some lovely effects such as the light falling through ornamented windows to form circles: hence the number zero.

Drawing! Drawing! Drawing!, 1982; Energy from the Atom, 1983; Shubh-Vivah/Happy Wedding; Gujari/Sunday Market, 1984; Din Pratidin/Day after Day, 1985; A Summer Story, 1987; Shishu-Vikas/Child Development; Maasik-Dharma/Menstruation; Atthara Hi Kyon?/Why 18?; Garbhavastha Aur Prasav/Pregnancy and Labour; Bhadte Kadam/Growing Up, 1988; All About Nothing, 1989-90; One Day in Fatehpuri Sikri, 1990; The Barter, 1991.

Schwartz, Lillian
A pioneer in computer assisted animation at Bell Laboratories in New Jersey, where she wrote and directed several demo/story films using Bell's innovative systems, often working with Ken Knowlton, a computer scientist who has assisted many other artists.

Scwartz's education began immediately after World War II when she studied Chinese brushwork with Tshiro in Japan. Over the following years she studied the fine

arts. She is self-taught with regard to film and computer interfacing, and programming. She began her computer art career as an offshoot of her merger of art and technology, which culminated in the selection of her kinetic sculpture, *Proxima Centauri*, for the 1968 Machine Exhibition. She then expanded her work into the computer area, becoming a consultant at the AT&T Bell Laboratories and for IBM. On her own, and with leading scientists, engineers, physicists, and psychologists, she has developed effective techniques for the use of the computer in film and animation. Besides establishing computer art as a viable field of endeavour, Schwartz additionally contributed to scientific research areas, such as visual and colour perception, and sound. In recent years she has also contributed to debates around art via computer-researching models for paintings -e.g. the discovery that the model for da Vinci's Mona Lisa was in fact himself. Her films have explored abstraction via computers to music; art films about movement; science as a basis for aritstic interpretation.

'Olympiad uses found footage of Olympic runners to set off a complexity of computer generated images in fluctuating colours and variable distortions. The single, double and multiple formation of running men meet, merge, overtake each other, change direction, and grow by bits and pieces – as mysterious as an elaborate cell structure under a microscope.' (CS) 'UFOs proves that computer animation - once a rickety and gimmicky device - is now progressing to the state of an art. The complexity of design and movement, the speed and rhythm, the richness of form and motion, coupled with stroboscopic effects is unsettling. Even more ominously, while design and action are programmed by humans, the 'result' in any particular sequence is neither entirely predictable...being created at a rate faster and in concatenations more complex than eye and mind can follow or initiate'. Amos Vogel.

'Alae begins with footage of sea birds in flight; the film image is then optically scanned and transformed by the computer. The geometric overlay on the live random motion has the effect of creating new depth, a third dimension. Our perception of the birds' forms and movements is heightened by the abstract pattern outlining them'.

'Escher-like images step through the frames to the music of a jazz group in *Kinesis:*' *Pictures From a Gallery* uses picture-processed photos from the artist-filmmaker's family. Faces are abstracted in a divisionistic manner.

'Subtly coloured images combining microphotography and computer generated images with unique editing sequences propel the viewer into a spiral-like endless vortex in *Experiments:*'.

'A single bird in flight is transformed, enhanced and interpreted in *L'Oiseau:* so as to present a unique visual experience. From its original inception in a 128 frame black and white sequence it evolves by programmed reflection, inversion, magnification, colour transformation and time distortion into the final restructured film as art'. *Bagatelles:* 'Abstract images of frame-by-frame animation with subtle growing effects of crystals are enhanced by polarised colours'. *Trois Visage:* 'Study of the mood changes between three heads with slow moving subtle differences. Two heads are made of wood. The third head is of the artist LS'. She has just published *The Computer Artist's Handbook*.

Mathoms; Pixillation, 1970; UFOs; Olympiad, 1971; Enigma (co-d Ken Knowlton); Apotheosis; Gogolplex; Mistakes; Mutations; Affinities (co-d KK), 1972; Papillons; Innocence, 1973; Mayan; Metathesis; Metamorphosis; Mirage, 1974; Kinesis; Alae, 1975; The Artist and the Computer; Pictures from a Gallery; La Spiritata; Fantasies; Experiments, 1976; L'Oiseau; Bagatelles; Vail of Years; Trois Visage, 1977; Newtonian I; Newtonian II; Poet of His People, 1978; Rituel, 1979; The Museum of Modern Art, 1984; Beyond Picasso, 1986.

Selwood, Maureen   US

The delicate lyricism of Maureen Selwood's style is already evident in her first film, *The Box* combines live-action and animation in a lively fantasy of the Astor Place cube sculpture coming to life. *The Six Sillies* made in 35mm cel animation, is rich with the luscious colour and delicate Matisse-like line that evolve in the public service and commercial projects she has done

since then. It's rather like an animated medieval fable. An eccentric flying family have problems finding a suitor for their daughter - but one suitor arrives, falls in loves - and is enabled to fly too. The filmmaker has commented on *Sempre Libera* 'an animated interpretation of the aria from Verdi's opera La Traviata. Although the song expresses freedom and independence, it is being sung by a woman caught between its literal meaning and her own spontaneous feelings.' and the film has been described as a synthesis of Picasso, Matisse, music and motion. With *Odalisque*, she moves away from storytelling into poetry; a series of mythical women undergo the most extraordinary transformations - the kinds of drama-like metamorphosis that Selwood's lyricism brings to life beautifully. (TS) In*This Is Just to Say...*, a sequence ofr a doucmentary, an imagined dialogue between husband and wife over a bowl of fruit suggests the elliptical nuances of William Carlos Willliam's words.

The Box, 1969; The Six Sillies, 1971; Sempre Libera, 1979; Odalisque, 1980; The Rug, 1985; seq. for Animated Self-Portraits, 1989; Beautiful Fit, 1990.

Sharp, Saundra   US

One of the very few African-American filmamkers to use animation her film *Picking Tribes* uses old photographs and water colour animation, the film takes a light look at a daughter of the 40s as she struggles to find an identity between her African American and Native American heritages. She identifies with her gradnfather's Indian ancestry - the 60s when she sheds her feathers for an afro a dashiki. In making the film Sharp draws on her own experiences e.g. for some of the photographs she went back to the newspaper offices in Chicago to seek material that documented the street parades she participated in as a child. Although she works mainly in live-action, documentaries and experimental pieces, she is keen to pusue animation further.

Shenfield, Ann   Australia

La Lune; The Juggler; About Face, 1987; Once I Grew, 1991;

Shorina, Nina   USSR

See pp. 103-108. Russian animator, who began making childrens' films for television, then worked at Soyouzmoultfilm where she produced the following.

About Buka, 1984; Poodle, 1985; Door, 1986; Dream, 1988; Alter Ego, 1989; Hall of Mirrors, 1991.

Shriram, Chitra   India/US

After graduating in fine arts, she studied animation at India's National Institute of Design, and returned some years later to establish an animation studio to train animators. The films made in India use drawing, cut-out, pixillation, time lapse, whilst are computer produced. She is currently a doctoral student in Computer Graphics at Ohio State, and her two-dimensional computer generated artwork has been featured in several exhibitions.

Life; (collab): The Silver Elephant, 1981; Medieval Saints of India; Hakim Ki Hank, 1982; The Barter (collab); Gujjari, 1984; Uncle's Marvel Machine, 1985; The Ducks, 1987; Leela, 198?

Smith, Kathy   Australia

See p.112.

Power & Passion; Designed Nightmare, 1983; A Figure in Front of a Painting, 1984; Ayers Rock Animation; Change of Place, 1985; Delirium, 1987.

Smith, Lynn   US

Born and studied in the US, where she made her first animated film as a student at Harvard, *Office Party* . Working as a freelance animator and illustrator, particularly in education and children's films, she was then commissioned by the Canadian NFB to make anti-smoking films. Two more personal films followed there: *This is Your Museum Speaking* and *The Sound Collector*. Wide range of technique, has also made some computer animated films.

Office Party, 1966; Shout It Out Alphabet Film, 1969; Genesys, 1970; The Wedding Movie, 1970; Before She Paints, 1975; Teacher, Lester Bit Me!, 1974; This is Your Museum Speaking, 1979; The Sound Collector, 1982; seq.for Animated Self-Portraits, 1988; Pearl's Diner, 1991.

Snezkho-Blotskaya, Alexandra   USSR

inc. *The Cat That Walked by Himself; Labyrinth; The Little Hunchbacked Horse*

Snowden, Alison   GB

Alison Snowden and David Fine make up Snowden Fine Productions, based in a complex of studios for artists and craftsmen in south east London. Their partnership, and marriage, dates back to their time as post graduate students at the NFTS. Although both were interested in pursuing live action, they had also experimented with animation. David Fine, a Canadian, had spent some months on placement at the National Film Board, during one of its most productive periods, and had made some model animation films on Super-8 and 16mm on grants from local arts bodies. The first film on which they worked together, the Oscar-nominated *Second Class Mail*, was made at the NFTS, on what was left over from the budget for a live action short.

The film's success led to an offer from the Canadian NFB to make a film for a series on old people, which turned out to be *George and Rosemary*. *In and Out* was made on a Canada Arts Council grant. Their films to date are characterised by fairly traditional cel animation with a gentle but idiosyncratic touch of humour.

Hopes of breaking into live action didn't materialise, and they found little opportunity in Canadian animation, dominated as it is by the NFB in the cultural sector, or the one or two established commercial studios, so returned to the UK, where the animation scene is a lot livelier. They spent almost a year working on model animation for Lily Tomlin on a proposal for a TV series, which didn't pan out. At Marv Newland's request, they made a segment for his outrageous anthology of sexual fantasies, *Pink Concommer*.

As far as their collaboration is concerned, Alison usually designs the characters and look of the film, but they share animation and direction. Although their working methods have become almost instinctive, they would like to explore working with others, and prefer writing and direction to animation. They are currently working on a 10 minute film for C4, working title *Bob's Birthday*, about the male menopause.

Second Class Mail, 1984 (solo); George and Rosemary, 1984; In and Out, 1989;

Test of Time seq. Pink Concommer, 1991 (all co-d David Fine).

Soul, Veronika   Canada/US

How the Hell Are You?, 1972; Tales From the Vienna Woods 1973; Tax: The Outcome of Income 1975; A Said Poem & The Hottest Show on Earth, 1977; New Jersey Nights; The Interview,1979 (co-d Caroline Leaf); Count Down Vignette; Unknown Soldiers, 1991.

Starciewicz, Antoinette GB

See p. 111.

Her work is characterised by a strong identifiable graphic style which draws on the art nouveau inspired styles of the 20s and 30s: brilliant colours and her interest in music and dance. Puttin on the Ritz and High Fidelity were homages to song and dance (Fred Astaire and Irving Berlin respectively) whilst *Pianoforte* is a more narrative film about an ambitious young girl pianist trapped in a decadent nightclub, saved only by the power of love. *Pussy Pumps Up* is a strange tale of male and female narcisissm, with a quite eoritc subtext. Has said she made a conscious choice to pursue art, refusing to see herself as defined by her reproductive role as a woman.

Secret of Madam X, 1971; Puttin' on the Ritz, 1974; High Fidelity, 1976; Pussy Pumps Up, 1979; Koko Pops, 1981; Pianoforte, 1985.

Stavely, Joan   US

See pp. 98-100. Began using computers for animation, image-making and performance art, in 1985.

Broken Heart, 1988; Wanting for Bridge, 1991.

Steeno, Veronique   Belgium

Has been teaching animation as applied art for many years in Belgium, and is extremely active in ASIFA International.

Exortus, 1971; Optica, 1973; Information Sexuelle, 1974; Pukki, 1975; Ludus, 1976; Klein, Klein Kleuterje; Van Pool Tot Evenaar, Het Lied Van Halewyn; The White Dove, 1981; seq. Amnesty International: Universal Declaration of Human Rights.

Swiczinsky, Nana   Austria

Attended Austrian School and Research

Institute for Graphic Art, and currently a student at the Studio for Experimental Animation, Vienna. Uses painting and drawing, fast-moving style e.g. exploring the breaking of a rhythmic structure in *The Unruly Mob.*

A love story; Das ungehobelte Pack/The Unruly Mob,1991.

Thacher, Anita   US

Works in many visual media, including live action, matted frame-by-frame optically printed films.

'*Permanent Wave*, a film collage using the technology of in-camera re-photography. After working for several years in commercials and documentaries, she received a grant to finish *Homage to Magritte*, an optically printed surrealist film. *Sea Travels* further developed her use of film optical techniques. She continues to incorporate her interest in painting and sculpture into her films, video pieces and installations.' (CS)

'Anita Thacher's *Sea Travels* extends the definition of animation in yet another direction from the innovative films of Suzan Pitt and Mary Beams. Like Beams in *Whale Songs*, Thacher begins with live-action filmed material, but rather than trace drawings from the live footage, Thacher uses optical printing techniques to tranform the original material into a complex polyphony of multiple images. *Sea Travels*, a visual incantation to memory and childhood, searches for the links of time through the implausible space of dream and reverie. The opening quotation from Thoreau sets the thematic framework for the film: 'It seems that we only languish during maturity in order to tell the dreams of our childhood, and they vanish from our memory before we are able to learn their language.

'The five sections of the film, *Sighting, The Chase, A Change of Weather, Drawing Companions, Landing*, flow across the boundaries of time, the present calling up the past, the past leaping towards the future, as reverie and memory weave their atemporal web. From the young girl running naked to the sea and the adolescent rolling down the grassy slope to the grown man swimming across the pool followed by the woman and the dog, each image seems almost crystalline in its purity,

A - Z

endowed with the power and simplicity of archetype.

While the images suggest a narrative, albeit a fragmented one, for Thacher the formal construction of the film is of primary importance. She subdivides the screen into multiple images, each echoing the other and linked by the logic of imagination rather than the physical laws of nature or the progressions of causality. At the same time, she explores the spatial and kinetic conventions of cinema, playing ambiguously upon them in witty, unexpected ways. In destroying the security of topographical landmarks - the horizon line, perspective, above distinguished from below - Thacher juggles the laws of physics and the conventions of cinema, as reverie and memory play with time.

Thacher views her work as an exploration of abstraction and perception within a personal context, 'couched in an emotional climate'. In a fusion of 'the so-called masculine and feminine spheres', she combines the scientific, traditionally considered the domain of men, with the emotional, human element, traditionally women's preserve. She sees herself as playing with science, but feels it is important to 'still hang on to who I am as a woman.' With *Sea Travels*, she integrates form and feeling, extending the boundaries of animation and contributing to a synthesis of art and science which supercedes traditional male and female 'provinces' through the search for a human perspective.' (TS)

'Anita Thacher's works project shimmering, magical universes in which our humdrum notions of 'reality' and 'perception' are subverted in the most outrageous, pleasurable manner.' Amos Vogel. 'Thacher's films are haunting surrealistic explorations of the inner landscape of memory and desire.' Ann Sargent Wooster
Permanent Wave, 1967; Back Track, 1969; Mr Story, 1972; Homage to Magritte, 1974; Sea Travels, 1978; The Breakfast Table, 1979; Loose Corner, 1980; Manhattan Doorway, 198?.

Thalmann, Nadia

Currently Professor of Communications and Computer Science at Geneva University, where she researches computer animation, 3-D, computer-generated imagery and computer graphics systems. From 1977-87 she was head of Miralab, a research group comprising inforamtion scientists and designers working in computer animation. Co-authored with Daniel Thalmann Computer Animation, 1985, and Image Synthesis, 1988.
Dreamflight, 1982; Rendez-Vous in Montreal; Eglantine, 1987; Galaxy Sweetheart; Islands Have a Soul, 1989.

Thomas, Gayle   Canada

After studying art and education Thomas, inspired by the work of Norman Mclaren, decided to work in film. Joined NFB in 1970, working in several areas of animation in collaboration with other filmmakers on their projects, as well as on her own: *It's Snow*, *Klaxon*, *The Magic Flute*: the award winning *A Sufi Tale*, strikingly animated in black and white using a scratchboard technique, which gives the effect of woodcut drawings. A childrens' fantasy film The Boy and the Snow Goose; The Phoenix, based on a story by Sylvia Townsend Warner.
It's Snow, 1974; Klaxon, 1977; A Sufi Tale, 1980; The Boy and the. Snow Goose, 1984; The Phoenix, 1991.

Tilby, Wendy Joy Canada

See β. Seen as one of the most promising young Canadian animators. Her student film *Tables of Content*, which recalls Caroline Leaf's techniques, brought international festival recognition. *Strings*, richly rendered in paint on glass, had a more distinctive style, and tells a wonderfully convoluted story of neighbours, in particular a man and woman, getting to know one another via their plumbing problems. In between production assistant on live-action, co-directed with Jill Haras, *It's Raining*.
Tables of Content, 1986; Strings, 1990; It's Raining, 1991.

Tourtelot, Madeleine France

Ancient Footpaths, 1960; Rotate the Body, 1960.

Tyrlova, Hermina Czech

Pioner in puppet animation.
Ferda the Ant, 1941; The Revolt of the Toys, 1947; Lullaby, 1948; The Misfit, 1951; Nine Chicks, 1952; The Taming of the Dragon, 1953; The Naughty Ball; A

Garland of Folk Songs; Goldilocks, 1956; The Swine Herdsman; Lazy Martin, 1957; The Lost Doll; The Little Train; The Knot in the Hankerchief, 1959; A Lesson, 1960; The Lost Letter, 1961; Two Balls of Wool, 1962; The Marble, 1963; The Blue Pinafore, 1965; The Snowman; Boy Or Girl?, 1966; Dog's Heaven; Christmas Tree, 1967; The Star of Bethlehem, 1969; The Glass Whistle; Little Paintings, 1970.

Unger, Doris   Australia

The Sea of Stars; The Closet High-Flyer, 1990; Wanting, 1991.

Vajda, Bela   Hungary

Language Lesson, 1968; Movie, 1969; Egg, 1969; Striptease, 1970; Good Deeds, 1973; Plate Boy, 1973; Moto Perpetuo, 1981; On the Shooting Stage, 198?

Van Goethem, Nicole Belgium

Born in Anvers in 1941. After art school, she worked freelance, as illustrator, poster design and commercial art/marketing campaigns. Worked on the script, design and special effects on Picha's animation feature, *Tarzoon, La honte de la Jungle*; a spell with a British animation studio, then on the storyboard for Picha's second feature, *Le Chainon Manquant (The Missing Link)*, and for other commercial studios in Belgium. *A Greek Tragedy*, a kind of 'secret life of carytids' is a comic allegory of women shedding the burdens imposed upon them by the (male) cultural traditions of Western civilisation. The wonderfully off-the-wall story and perfect comic timing won the film an Oscar. Religious ecstasy takes on a whole new meaning in *Full of Grace*, in which two nuns who find a new way to feel the love of God after a mistaken purchase (vibrators for candles), after a power cut at the convent. Her films use traditional cel animation, and a graphic cartoony style.
A Greek Tragedy, 1983; Vol van Gratie/Full of Grace, 1987.

Vasseleu, Cathy   Australia

Her work is experimental and draws on radical film and communicaitons theory. Comatoes, 1988; At the Breach, 1989 (co-d Jo Tauro); De Anima, 1991 (co-d Beck Main, Amanda Dusting).

Vere, de Alison   GB

See pp. 83-4. Her first two films were great festival successes, for their pathos and humanity as well as their style. Her next two films were more conventional pieces of quality narrative animation, and both were literary adaptations. *Black Dog* had a sharper, more graphic visual style, and brilliant colour palette: a woman's 'journey through the soul' in a dream landscape. It is also a film about sexual realisation with a new tone of acerbic humour. She is currently working on a version of the legend *Psyche and Eros* , 'on one level about the difficulties of growing up a woman, on another about equality.'
Two Faces, 1963; False Friends, 1968; Cafe Bar, 1975; Mr Pascal, 1979; The Angel and the Soldier Boy; Silas Marner, 1984; Black Dog, 1987.

Von Kleist, Solveig   France

Whilst at Art School in Berlin made an animation film at home, then went to Cal Arts to study film graphics. *Criminal Tango* was made there, an extremely accomplished scratched on film narrative of paranoia, drawing on the iconography of film noir with a Cat People-styled woman as femme feline. The film led to a commission from David Bowie to animate for his rock video, *Underground*. Living and working in France since the early 80s, as freelance illustrator, and artist. Her painting - acrylic on paper - is figurative, but she has turned more recently to mixed-media installation, and combining animation with plastic arts. Her favourite artists are Francis Bacon and Giacommetti; favourite filmmaker, Jacques Tati. Currently working on installation with sculpture and animation.
Criminal Tango, 1985; Panta Rhei, 1992

Warny, Clorinda   Canada

The Egg, 1971; Happiness Is; Petit Bonheur, 1972; Premiers jours/Beginnings, 1980 (posthumous co-d Suzanne Gervais, Linda Gagnon).

Watson, Karen   GB

See pp. 96-7.
Daddy's Little Bit of Dresden China, 1987; The Sharpest WItch, 1989.

Watt, Sarah   Australia

Deep Dive, 1990; Catch of the Day, 1991.

Wiertz, Karin   Holland

Together with Jacques Verbeek, has made quite experimental animation. *Keep on Turning* is a dynamic treatment of abstract geometrical art; Take a Cigarette combines drawn animation with photographs. 'Their prediliction for light and shade and three dimensional effects is expressed in *Between the Lights*, a play of light and shadow emphasising the contrast between the human figure and austere monumental architecture.To the sound of obsesive music the human figures in *Easy Action Animated* whirl round in a claustrophobic space. The film's surreal atmosphere is intensified by the use of black and white photographs, some partially hand-tinted. An even greater effect of visual disorientation is achieved in *The Case of the Spiral Staircase*, drawn on cel over photographs taken specially for the film: the effect is disorderly and dreamlike as a woman climbs up an endless and increasingly abstract spiral stairway.'
Fancy Cake, 1971; Reversals; Slippery Slope; Keep on Turning, 1972; Time Takes a Cigarette, 1973; Between the Lights, 1975; Easy Action Animated, 1978; The Case of the Spiral Staircase, 1981.

Woodward, Joanna   GB

See 93-4.
The Poet of Half Past Three, 1984; The Hump-Back Angel, 1985; Two Children Threatened by a Nightingale, 1986; The Brooch Pin and the Sinful Clasp, 1989; The Weatherhouse, 1991.

Young, Susan   GB

Young's brilliant, almost kinetically abstract student film *Carnival* brought her festival honours and many offers of commercial work: ads, TV credit sequences, and rock videos (incl. Fleetwood Mac's *Tango in the Night* and Paul McCartney's *Once Upon a Long Ago*). After college she set up in partnership with fellow graduate Jonathan Hodgson, then with Mike Smith's Felix Films and recently she established Mojo Working, to produce commercials and rock videos whilst insisting on quality and integrity. Her latest rock video, to a Jimi Hendrix track *Fire* looks set to cause some controversy for its unusual and explicit depiciotn of male sexuality.
Studied at Liverpool Polytechnic 'where I became aware of the vast scope of animation. My tutor, Ray Fields, encouraged loose spontaneous drawing. *Thin Blue Lines* is an observation and expression of the Toxteth riots, which took place round my house. It's a non-narrative documentary, but highly charged with my own feelings – which is a combination that animation by its own nature can achieve, being part intense observation, and part individual expression. My own personal visual style is centred on a passion for rich, fluid movement which I developed in *Carnival*. I became engrossed in capturing the spirit of dance through a rhythmic combination of broad masses of colour and a flowing calligraphic line. Carnivals have logic inside their apparent chaos , and that's how I approached the film, arriving at abstraction via the discipline of accurate movement. I rarely use conventional animation materials, such as cel and cel paint, or techniques like overlays, multiple exposures, etc. – preferring the simplicity and directness of working on paper with brushes and pastels. I avoid the traditional methods of characterisation; the personality of my figures comes from their movement and rhythm. One exception to this is a cutout film, *Tempting Fate* in which the characters are important. They are nude and unglamorous. I made the film in opposition to the conventional treatment of women in animation (i.e. one-dimensional) but it's also a personal expression of frustration: do you do what you feel is right for you, or what others wish…while society waits greedily to pass judgement?
Getting the right balance between personal and commercial work is difficult. I like to know that at any given point, I can stop for a time to make another personal film. The animation factory set-up is fundamentally wrong for my work, and seems to encourage a hamster-on-a-wheel approach: the faster you run – the more jobs – the more people to employ – the wheel turns faster, and you can't get off.
Thin Blue Lines, 1982; Trafalgar Square, 1983; Tempting fate, 1984; Carnival, 1985; The Doomsday Clock, 1987 (co-d Jonathan Hodgson).

Ziobrowska, Eva Poland

Passageway, 1990; In the Walls, 1990.

Bibliography

GENERAL

John CANEMAKER: Britain's Independent Animators in
PRINT Nov/Dec 1980
Bruno EDERA: L'Animation au fémin in
LA REVUE DU CINEMA December 1983
Maureen FURNISS: The Current State of American
Independent Animation and a Prediciton for its Future.
Unpublished thesis for San Diego University, 1987.
George GRIFFIN ed: FRAMES - A Selection of Drawings
and Statements by Independent American Animators New
York G Griffin 1978
Barbara Halpern MARTINEAU: Innovators in Animation
in BRANCHING OUT v5 n2 1978
Interviews with NFB animators Ellen Besen, Caroline Leaf,
Lynn Smith, Joyce Borenstein & Veronica Soul; expanded
upon for essay Women and Cartoon Animation, or Why
Women Don't Make Cartoons or Do They? in THE
AMERICAN ANIMATED CARTOON: A Criticial
Anthology eds. Gerald and Danny Peary E.P. Dutton, New
York 1980
Megan McMURPHY and Jennifer Stout (Ed.) SIGN OF
INDEPENDENCE: TEN YEARS OF THE CREATIVE
DEVELOPMENT FUND Sydney, 1990
Thelma (now Talia) SCHENKEL: American Women
Animation Artists of the Seventies and the Third
Renaissance of the Cinema of Animation Paper presented at
a Conference on Women in the Arts Pittsburgh University
1980
Cecile STARR: Contemporary Women Animators:
Struggles and Breakthroughs in
SIGHTLINES Summer/Fall 1989
Cecile STARR and Robert Russett: EXPERIMENTAL
ANIMATION: AN ILLUSTRATED ANTHOLOGY (Van
Nostrand Reinhold, New York, 1976)

Jane AARON
John CANEMAKER: Jane Aaron - Paper Pictures
HOW v3 n5 Jul/Aug 1988
Judith TROJAN: Jane Aaron - In Plain Sight
SIGHTLINES vl9 n2 Winter 1985/86

Karen ACQUA
A. Sullivan LEAH: Karen Aqua and the Fine Art of
Endurance
ANIMATION MAGAZINE Winter/Spring 1990

Halina BIELINSKA
IMAGE ET SON nl70/171 Feb/Mar 1964

Mary Ellen Chaplin BUTE
AMERICAN FILM INSTITUTE REPORT v5 n2 Summer
1974 interview
FIELD OF VISION nl3 Spring 1985
FILM COMMENT v8 n4 Nov/Dec 1972
Jonas MEKAS: The Most Representative American Poets
FILM CULTURE vl n3 May/June 1955

Lillian SCHIFF: The Education of Mary Ellen Bute
FILM LIBRARY QUARTERLY v17 n24 1984
VISION vol n2 Summer 1962 filmography and interview

Doris CHASE
Rob EDELMAN: Who's Who in Filmmaking: Doris Chase
SIGHTLINES Summer 1986

Sally CRUIKSHANK
John CANEMAKER: Sally Cruikshank: Ruthless
Animation v3 n1 Nov/Dec 1986
B Ruby RICH: Cartoons with Character
CHICAGO READER 4.3.79
FILM CULTURE n46 Autumn 1967 pp44-45
TAKE ONE v3 n2 Nov/Dec 1971

Nancy EDELL
Brian Clancey: Of Black Pudding and Pink Ladies
CINEMA CANADA v3 n25 Feb 1976 pp38-39

Faith Culhane and John HUBLEY
Mike BARRIER: John and Faith Hubley: Traditional
animation transformed in MILLIMETER Feb 1977
John CANEMAKER - The Happy Accidents of John and
Faith Hubley PRINT Sept/Oct 1981
T SCHENKEL: Exploring the cinema of figurative
animation: a special consideration of the work of John and
Faith Hubley and Jan Lenica Unpublished PHD dissertation
New York University, 1977
Belinda STARKIE - An essay on the art of Faith Hubley
ANIMATRIX n5 1989 (UCLA)

Evelyn LAMBART
ASIFA CANADA vol 15 no3 January 1988. Collection of
interviews with, and articles about Lambart.

Caroline LEAF
ASIFA CANADA BULLETIN v19 n2 January 1992
Special issue on Caroline Leaf
John CANEMAKER: Redefining Animation: Caroline
Leaf, Dennis Pies, Will Vinton in PRINT Mar/Apr 1979
John CANEMAKER, Moderator: A Conversation with
Caroline Leaf in STORYTELLING IN ANIMATION -
THE ART OF THE ANIMATED IMAGE
Maurice ELIA: Caroline Leaf interview
SEQUENCES n91 January 1978
Irene KOTLARZ: Entry in THE WOMEN'S GUIDE TO
INTERNATIONAL FILM, ed. Annette Kuhn with
Susannah Radstone.
Jacqueline LEVITIN: Caroline Leaf et le cinéma
d'animation FEMMES ET CINEMA QUEBECOISE
ed. Louise CARRIERE (Boreal Express, 1983)
Grant MUNRO: Sand, Beads & Plasticine: Interview with
Caroline Leaf and Veronika Soul in
WIDE ANGLE v3 n2 1979
T SCHENKEL: Talking with Caroline Leaf

FILM LIBRARY QUARTERLY v10 n182 1977
T SCHENKEL: Storytelling as Remembering - Picturing
the Past in Caroline Leaf's *The Street* in STORYTELLING
IN ANIMATION - THE ART OF THE ANIMATED
IMAGEProceedings of the Ninth World Congress of
Jewish Studies
T SCHENKEL: A Child's Perception of Death and its
Ritual- Caroline Leaf's Film Adaptation of Mordecai
Richler's 'The Street'
Denyse THERIEN: Interview on *Entre Deux Soeurs*.
PERFORATIONS v16 n2 April 1991 NFB. Also very
useful article by Pierre Hebert: Scratching on Film: A
Technical Description.

LEEDS ANIMATION
Reviews: Crops & Robbers
MONTHLY FILM BULLETIN Nov 1986
Penny FLORENCE: WOMEN'S REVIEW December
1985: Review of several films.
Entry in THE WOMEN'S COMPANION TO
INTERNATIONAL FILM, op cit.
Antonia LANT: Women's Independent Cinema: the Case of
Leeds Animation Workshop in BRITISH CINEMA &
THATCHERISM: FIRES WERE STARTED Ed. Lester
Friedman University College London Press, London, 1992

Deanna MORSE
Maureen GAFFNEY and Gerry LAYBOURNE: What to do
when the lights go on Oryz Press, 1981
Ellen MEYER: Independent Outlook
SIGHTLINES Summer 1990.
Robert RUSSETT and Cecile STARR: Experimental
Animation Da Capo Press, 1988
Chris STRAAYER: Women in the Director's Chair
Susan LEONARD and Gail MUNDE, At the Movies with
Bad Dog: Using Nontraditional Film and video with
children, American Film and Video Association, 1989

Vera NEUBAUER
Claire BARWELL: Interview and article in UNDERCUT
n6 Winter 1982/83

Suzan PITT
Robert BECKER: Suzan Pitt
in Andy Warhol's Interview
Robert W. BUTLER: Suzan Pitt's Asparagus
in HELICON NINE, A JOURNAL OF WOMEN'S ART
AND LETTERS
John CANEMAKER: Asparagus: Rich and Cool
FUNNYWORLD n21 Fall 1979
TAKE ONE v7 n8
Joan 'D' COPJEC: Asparagus in
MILLENIUM FILM JOURNAL
Judith MAYNE discussion of Asparagus
in Chapter 6, Revising the Primitive in

The Woman at the Keyhole: Feminism and Women's
Cinema Indiana University Press
Deborah PERLBE: Review of Asparagus in
ARTFORUM April 1981
Shooting the Wild Asparagus (unsigned)
THE REAL PAPER Feb 24, 1979
B Ruby RICH : Cartoons with Character
CHICAGO READER 4.3.1979
Bob STEWART: HEAVY METAL June 1980
AmosVOGEL: Independents: Stalking "Asparagus"

Lotte REINIGER
H BECKERMAN: Animated Women:
FILMMAKERS NEWSLETTER Summer 1974
Leo BONNEVILLE: Lotte Reiniger et les ombre chinoises
SEQUENCES n81 July 1975
She Made First Cartoon Feature
FILMS AND FILMING Dec 1955
Lotte REINIGER: Scissors Make Films
SIGHT AND SOUND v5 n17 Spring 1936
Lotte Reiniger at 80: In the Picture
SIGHT AND SOUND v48 n3 Summer 1979
Cecile STARR: Lotte Reiniger's Fabulous Film Career
SIGHTLINES v13 n4 Summer 1980
Eric WHITE: Walking Shadows London 1931

Monique RENAULT
Experiences d'animation: Entretien avec Sarah Mallinson et
Monique Renault in PAROLES...ELLES TOURNENT
Edition des Femmes, Paris, 1976
Liz McQUISTON: Monique Renault in Women in Design:
A Contemporary View Trefoil Publications, London 1988

Kathy ROSE
FILM LIBRARY QUARTERLY v15 n4 1982
Kathy Rose: Evolution of a Style. An interview in
WIDE ANGLE v2 n3 1978

Sabrina SCHMID
Sabrina SCHMID: Making Elephant Theatre
CANTRILLS FILMNOTES Nos 51/52 December 1986

Wendy TILBY
Wendy Tilby talks about Strings
PERFORATIONS v16 n2 April 1991, NFB

Notes on Contributors

ALFIO BASTIANCICH is active in animation as a programmer, via Treviso Animation Festival and TV programmes for RAI; as historian and scholar, whose publications include *L'Opera di Norman McLaren, Lotte Reiniger, Immagine per Immaginne - Cinema d'animazione al National Film Board of Canada, and Bruno Bozzetto;* as organiser of ASIFA Italia, and edited *Animafilm.* He also teaches History and Language of Animated Film, at Rome's Centro Sperimentale di Cinematografia. With Caterina D'Amico, co-curated *Teaching Animation,* an International Symposium, held in Urbino, September 1992.

JOHN CANEMAKER is an internationally known animator, filmmaker, author, teacher, and lecturer. He has written over 100 articles in animation history, techniques and artists for periodicals, such as *Film Comment, Time, Horizon, Variety, How, Print, Sightlines, Film News,* and *Millimeter.* He has written 4 books on animation: *Felix, The Twisted Tale of the World's Most Famous Cat; Winsor McCay: His Life and Art; Treasures of Disney Animation Art; and The Animated Raggedy Ann & Andy.* His award-winning animations and documentaries include *Confessions of a Stardreamer, Bottom's Dream, The Wizard's Son, Remembering Winsor McCay, Otto Messmer and Felix the Cat;* also made *The Creative Spirit, John Lennon Sketchbook, Aids Dance-a-Thon.* Has produced, designed and directed animation films for major clients including Warners Bros., HBO, PBS, and CBS. Former Visiting Lecturer at Yale, he is now Associate Professor and Head of Animation Programme at New York University Tisch School of the Arts.

LORENZO CODELLI is an Italian film critic and historian, and regular contributor to the French film magazine, *Positif.*

SHARON COUZIN studied painting and sculpture at the University of Michigan. In 1975 she won a Silver Medal at Cannes Amateur Festival and began making independent experimental films. In 1978 she began teaching at the School of the Art Institute of Chicago's Filmmaking Department, where she has been Chairperson for the past 8 years, and teaches Film History and 4-D. Her intellectual pursuits attempt to reconcile feminism with a more poetic, lyric sensibility which heretofore has not been a part of the larger conceptual feminist framework.

PATRICK MCGILLIGAN's books on film include *Robert Altman: Jumping Off the Cliff,* the *Backstory* series of interviews with Hollywood screenwriters, and the recently published *George Cukor: A Double Life.*

ROGER NOAKE is Course Leader on the Animation degree course at West Surrey College of Art & Design, Farnham, Surrey. He has written numerous articles and published the book *Animation,* dealing with techniques and concepts. He has taught in Japan and in India, with the United Nations Development Programme, based at the National Institute of Design in Ahmedabad.

LINDA PARISER came to Britain from the US, after 4 years working in film and video festivals at the American Film Institute. After graduating in Film Studies from the University of Warwick, she worked as a film programme adviser on the London Film Festival and in Regional Exhibition at the British Film Institute, before moving to Cardiff's Chapter Arts Centre as Cinema Director.

JAYNE PILLING is Head of Exhibition Services in the British Film Institute's Exhibition & Distribution Division. She has been active in promoting a wide range of animation via programming for cinemas, art galleries and festivals in the UK and abroad; in distribution, and more recently as Series Editor for the BFI/Connoisseur Video's Animation Collection. Publications on animation include *Ladislas Starewicz,* and *That's Not All Folks: A Primer in Cartoonal Knowledge.*

KAREN ROSENBERG is a film and literary critic and teaches at the Institute for European Studies in Vienna. Her articles and reviews have appeared in books and periodicals in the US, Japan, and Western Europe, and she is contributing editor to *The Independent.*

TALIA (formerly THELMA) SCHENKEL, PhD, has written and programmed extensively on American independent animation. She teaches Film Studies at Baruch College City, University of New York, and has taught Animation History and Theory at Yale University and at the University of the Arts in Philadelphia. See ß.

LESLEY FELPERON SHARMAN is an American postgraduate student researching a PhD on Children and Animation at the University of Canterbury, and teaches part-time at Goldsmith's College, London. She has written on film and animation for various publications including *Screen* and *Sight and Sound.*